Queen Victoria's Granddaughters
1860-1918

by

Christina Croft

Contents

Acknowledgements
A note about appellations
Prologue
The Granddaughters in Birth Order

Part I
"Like the Rabbits in Windsor Park"
The Royal Families

Chapter 1   The advice of a mother of nine children
Chapter 2   The Prussian influence
Chapter 3   A constant increase
Chapter 4   Frail puny babies
Chapter 5   Poor dear Lenchen
Chapter 6   After all they are English
Chapter 7   Grandmama will try to be a mother to you.
Chapter 8   My beloved Leopold

Part II
"A Very Doubtful Happiness"
Happy and Unhappy Marriages

Chapter 9   Nature has made her so
Chapter 10 Great matches do not make great happiness
Chapter 11 A Jubilee baby
Chapter 12 If you love him set him free
Chapter 13 Happiness is not to be hers
Chapter 14 My Benjamin
Chapter 15 It really is not wise to leave these girls *dans la vague*
Chapter 16 All I can repeat is that I am perfectly happy
Chapter 17 Tell my granddaughter to come home to me
Chapter 18 A mere child & quite inexperienced
Chapter 19 Who can guess what his tastes may be?
Chapter 20 She is like my own child

Part III
"The Last Link Is Broken"
Changes and Conflicts

Chapter 21 One must be tolerant
Chapter 22 We were all so hoping for a boy
Chapter 23 The sun has gone out of our lives
Chapter 24 We shall never see her anymore
Chapter 25 Poor girl she is utterly miserable now
Chapter 26 Revolution is banging on the door
Chapter 27 A sensible girl full of good intentions
Chapter 28 The terrible illness of the English family
Chapter 29 A saintly heroine & a lascivious satyr

Part IV
"Marching To Their Death"
War and Tragedy

Chapter 30 The Bulgarians have gone off their heads
Chapter 31 This is the end of everything
Chapter 33 Hessian witches and German spies
Chapter 34 Poor Nicky! Poor Russia!
Chapter 35 Have I not English blood in my veins?
Chapter 36 I would rather die in Russia
Chapter 37 Victors & vanquished
Epilogue   After Atlantis

Appendix I – *Thoughts on the death of Prince Albert*
Appendix II – *Queen Victoria's Excessive Mourning*
Appendix III – *Queen Victoria & Alfred, Lord Tennyson*
Appendix IV – *Queen Victoria's Favourite Authors*
Appendix V – *The Murder of Archduke Franz Ferdinand*

Recommended Reading
Index & References

Acknowledgements

I would like to thank the following for assisting in finding copyright holders and granting permission to include the quotations in this book:
Artellus Ltd;
The estate of James Pope-Hennessy;
Michaela Reid;
Professor Sarah McNair Vosmeimer; Hanover College, Indiana, http://history.hanover.edu/project.php ;
Wendy Reid Crisp 989 Milton, #3D, Ferndale, California, U.S.A. 95536;
Francis Barnard,
http://www.barnardf.demon.co.uk
Michael Nelson;
Tom's Place   www.tkinter.org;
The Folio Society;
Pearson Education;
Richard Birch Associates;
Greg Newby, www.gutenberg.org;
HarperCollins;
Random House UK;
The Russian Orthodox Church outside Russia, Diocese of Great Britain and Ireland,
http://orthodoxengland.org.uk/hp.php
Pan Macmillan;
The Leopard Magazine;
Mark Burstein and the Lewis Carroll Society of North America, http://www.roydavids.com
English Heritage
The curators of Osborne House
The curator of Leeds University Library, Russian Collection

A note about appellations

Throughout this book, after much consideration, I decided to use the familiar names used between members of Queen Victoria's family. My reason for so doing is quite simply that, with so many characters who share the same name, it would be confusing to the reader to discern to which Victoria or Marie etc. the text was referring.

The book was written as a labour of love and no disrespect is intended towards any of the characters.

Prologue

On 6th July 1868, when told of the birth of her seventh granddaughter, Queen Victoria remarked that the news was 'a very uninteresting thing for it seems to me to go on like the rabbits in Windsor Park.' Her apathy was understandable – this was her fourteenth grandchild, and, though she had given birth to nine children, she had never been fond of babies, viewing them as 'frog-like and rather disgusting...particularly when undressed.' The early years of her marriage had, she claimed, been ruined by frequent pregnancies; and large families were unnecessary for wealthy people since the children would grow up with nothing worthwhile to do.

Nevertheless, her initial reaction to the birth of Princess Victoria of Wales belied the genuine concern that Queen Victoria felt for each of her twenty-two granddaughters. 'As a rule,' she wrote, 'I like girls best,' and she devoted a great deal of time to their wellbeing and happiness, showering them with an affection she had seldom shown her own children.

Though at times she found them too big, too noisy, too boisterous or too ill-mannered, she was ever on hand to offer support and to welcome them into her homes. No matter how pressing affairs of state, she never missed their birthdays and was always available when they were in need. When one was in labour, the Queen was at her side, holding her hand and mopping her brow; when one's marriage failed or another's love was unrequited, the Queen held her as she wept. She felt deeply for their troubles, sympathised with their sorrows and worried about their futures. Even when they exasperated her by ignoring her advice, she was quick to forgive them. She missed them when they were far away and took offence if they did not accept her invitations to Osborne, Balmoral, or Windsor. The truth was that, almost in spite of herself, she loved them deeply: 'They are like my own children;' she wrote to the Earl of Fife, 'their happiness is very near my own heart.'[1]

The twenty-two princesses were raised in eight separate family groups: the Hohenzollerns (or Prussians), the Waleses, the Hessians, the Edinburghs, the Christians, the Connaughts, the Albanys and the Battenbergs – and their lives and personalities were as varied as their names. Some lived and died in virtual obscurity, others played a major role in world events. Some were pale and sickly, others robust and energetic; some strikingly beautiful, others tragically plain. Several met with appalling violence and tragedy, while others enjoyed the carefree lives of wealthy Victorian women. They grew up as far apart as England, Germany, Malta, and India, sometimes amid great wealth, other times struggling to maintain royal standards. Twenty-seven years passed between the birth of the first and the birth of the last but they shared the common bond of being shaped by their English grandmother, whose influence was apparent even in their names. The Queen often expressed the hope that all her grandchildren would be called after her or their grandfather, Prince Albert, resulting in seven Victorias, while the majority of the rest had Victoria or Alberta somewhere in their litany of names.

---

* To lessen the confusion, within the family they were generally known by nicknames (e.g. Ducky, Ena, and Patsy), or diminutives (Thora, Toria, Vicky).

By 1914, through a series of dynastic marriages, the Queen's granddaughters included the Empress of Russia, the Queens of Spain, Greece and Norway, and the Crown Princesses of Roumania and Sweden. As their brothers and cousins occupied the thrones of Germany, Britain and Denmark, Prince Albert's dream of a peaceful Europe created through bonds of kinship seemed a real possibility.

"All our cousins," wrote Princess Marie Louise of Schleswig-Holstein, "were more like brothers and sisters than mere blood relations."[2]

Yet in little more than a decade after Queen Victoria's death, the Prince Consort's dream would lie shattered in the carnage of the First World War. Royal cousins and even siblings would find themselves on opposing sides; two of them would die horrifically at the hands of revolutionaries and several others would be ousted from their thrones. They had lived through the halcyon days of the European monarchies but their lives, like the lives of millions of their peoples, would be changed forever by the catastrophe played out on the battlefields of France.

Through all the upheavals, tragedies and conflicts one person had bound them together and, even when wars had divided their nations, to the end of their lives, they would look back and remember 'dearest grandmama' with love.

The Granddaughters in Birth Order

Charlotte of Prussia, Princess Bernhard of Saxe-Meiningen (1860-1919). Daughter of Vicky

Victoria of Hesse-and-by-Rhine, Princess Louis Battenberg, Marchioness of Milford Haven (1863-1950). Daughter of Alice

Ella, Elizabeth of Hesse-and-By-Rhine, Grand Duchess Serge/Elizaveta Feodorovna (1864-1918). Daughter of Alice

Moretta, Victoria Moretta of Prussia, Princess Adolph of Schaumburg-Lippe (1866-1929). Daughter of Vicky

Irène of Hesse-and-By-Rhine, Princess Henry of Prussia (1866-1953). Daughter of Alice

Louise of Wales, Duchess of Fife (1867-1931). Daughter of Bertie

Toria, Princess Victoria of Wales (1868-1935). Daughter of Bertie

Maud of Wales, Queen of Norway (1869-1938). Daughter of Bertie

Sophie of Prussia, Queen of the Hellenes (1870-1932). Daughter of Vicky

Thora, Princess Helena Victoria of Schleswig-Holstein (1870-1948). Daughter of Lenchen

Alix of Hesse-and-By-Rhine, Tsarina Alexandra Feodorovna (1872-1918). Daughter of Alice

Mossy, Margaret of Prussia, Landgravine of Hesse-Kassel (1872-1954). Daughter of Vicky

Marie Louise of Schleswig-Holstein, Princess Aribert of Anhalt (1872-1957). Daughter of Lenchen

May, Princess Marie of Hesse-and-By-Rhine (1874-1878). Daughter of Alice

Missy, Marie of Edinburgh, Queen of Roumania. (1875-1938) Daughter of Affie

Ducky, Victoria Melita of Edinburgh, Grand Duchess of Hesse, Grand Duchess Kyril/Victoria Feodorovna (1876-1936). Daughter of Affie

Sandra, Alexandra of Edinburgh, Princess Ernest of Hohenlohe-Langenburg (1878-1932). Daughter of Affie

Daisy - Margaret of Connaught, Crown Princess of Sweden (1882-1920). Daughter of Arthur

Alice of Albany, Countess of Athlone (1883-1981). Daughter of Leopold

Baby Bee, Beatrice of Edinburgh, Infanta of Bourbon-Lyons (1886-1975). Daughter of Affie

Patsy, Victoria Patricia of Connaught, Lady Alexander Ramsay (1886-1974). Daughter of Arthur

Ena, Victoria Eugenia Battenberg, Queen of Spain (1887-1969). Daughter of Beatrice

Part I
"Like the Rabbits in Windsor Park"

The Royal Families

Chapter 1 - The Advice of a Mother of Nine Children

Hessians
Alice: Queen Victoria's second daughter
Louis: Alice's husband, heir to the Grand Duchy of Hesse-Darmstadt
Victoria: Eldest daughter of Alice and Louis
Ella (Elizabeth): Second daughter of Alice and Louis
Irène: Third daughter of Alice and Louis
Ernie (Ernst Ludwig): Eldest son of Alice and Louis

Hohenzollerns (Prussians)
Vicky (Victoria): Queen Victoria's eldest daughter; Crown Princess of Prussia.
Fritz (Frederick): Vicky's husband, Crown Prince of Prussia.

A swish of black skirts broke the silence as a short, round figure bustled along the corridors of Osborne House, huffing in indignation. Queen Victoria was definitely not amused. She sat down at her desk, her back as straight as a rod, and taking a pen in her podgy red hands, hastily scratched at the paper.

It was ridiculous and hurtful – she poured out her pain and exasperation – that her own daughters should disregard the advice of a mother of nine children, who surely knew better than anyone the correct behaviour for women of their station!

Determined that the letter's recipient should feel suitably shamed and repentant, her hand flew over the paper but, even before she had reached the end of the page, she might well have suspected that her increasingly wayward daughter would probably ignore the reprimand.

Princess Alice

It was not the first time that Princess Alice had offended her mother. Before she left home, she had been a dutiful daughter and in the weeks following Prince Albert's death, Queen Victoria could not have coped without her*. As the Queen withdrew into her own inconsolable grief, Alice was left to attend to her mother's duties, without a thought for her own distress at the loss of a father she loved. In fact, she had proved such a devoted and diligent child that, had Albert himself not already made preparations for her wedding, the Queen would have been content to keep her at home forever.

In the two years since her marriage to Louis, heir to the Grand Duchy of Hesse-Darmstadt, however, Alice's behaviour had become increasingly out-of-hand. It was one thing to show an interest in Florence Nightingale's theories of nursing, quite another to develop so unseemly a fascination with anatomy. Alice thought nothing of discussing unsuitable matters with all and sundry and so indelicate was her conversation that the Queen was reluctant to allow her younger daughters to visit Darmstadt for fear of what they may hear.

And now this!

It had been traumatic enough for Queen Victoria to hand over her innocent child to a husband but the speed with which Alice became pregnant had been even harder to bear. At the time of her wedding in July 1862, Alice had expressed such a horror of having children that the Queen was sure she would prefer to remain childless but

---

* See Appendix II

exactly nine months later she had returned to Windsor to give birth to a daughter. For the Queen, who remained at her side throughout the eight-hour labour, the experience was more harrowing than if she were going through it herself and she promptly berated Louis for inflicting such torture on her child. Though placated by the news that the baby would be named Victoria Alberta, the Queen made it clear that she hoped it would be a long time before the ordeal was repeated.

Alice ignored the advice and in less than a year she was again in *an unfortunate condition*. This time she spared her mother's nerves by staying in Germany for the birth of a second daughter, Elizabeth (Ella), but the Queen barely had time to breathe a sigh of relief when the appalling news arrived from Darmstadt: Alice had dispensed with wet nurses to breast-feed her baby herself!

Queen Victoria could hardly contain her revulsion. That her own daughter should indulge in such an *animal* and time-consuming practice, which was demeaning for any woman but for a princess unheard of and unnecessary, was beyond her comprehension. And still more devastating was the discovery that Alice's elder sister, Vicky, was to blame!

The podgy red hand flew over the page. Alice might offer the excuses that she had adopted the practice for the good of her health and because no pressing social duties demanded her attention, but the same could not be said for her elder sister.

Princess Victoria Adelaide Mary Louise (Vicky), her late father's favourite child, had seldom, if ever, stepped out of line before. Intellectually brilliant, artistically gifted, she had even conveniently fallen in love with her parents' first choice of marriage partner: Crown Prince Frederick (Fritz) of Prussia. Through the ups and downs of life in Berlin (and in spite of Fritz's

16

unfailing love there were more downs than ups) she had maintained a frequent, almost daily, correspondence with her mother and struggled against insurmountable odds to live up to her parents' expectations. Until now!

Not only had Vicky defied the Queens of both Britain and Prussia to breast-feed her own fourth baby, but had also positively encouraged Alice to do the same! Queen Victoria put down her pen and seething with disgust sent word to the Royal Dairy that a cow should be named 'Alice.'

In the quaint German Grand Duchy of Hesse-Darmstadt, twenty-one-year-old Princess Alice received the reprimand with equanimity. She was used to raising eyebrows in Hesse as well as in England. It had taken the Hessians some time to accustom themselves to the sight of their future Grand Duchess wandering in and out of the homes of the poor or carrying out the most menial tasks in their hospitals. In aristocratic circles too, there were those who were quick to criticise the number of controversial characters she invited to her home to discuss her unorthodox views of feminism, politics, philosophy and religion. Even her husband found aspects of her character unfathomable and, much as she loved him, after two and a half years of marriage Alice doubted that he would ever be able to understand her fully.

When it came to raising her children, unconventional Alice was equally determined to go her own way. Unlike many princesses of the day, she was not content to abandon them to the care of nannies in remote nurseries but intended to take personal responsibility for their welfare, education and upbringing. Aristocrats might gape askance and the Queen might rant and rave, but when infant mortality rates were so high, breast-feeding was the surest means

17

of protecting her daughter from dysentery, and on this, as on so many matters, she refused to be swayed.

Moreover, as Alice constantly reminded her mother, life in Hesse was very different from the comfort of the English court. The Queen could afford to employ numerous retainers to wait on her every need, but Alice, denied that luxury, had to keep her staff to the minimum.

By royal standards, she and Louis had never been wealthy. At the time of their wedding there were many in England who looked down on the paltry Grand Duchy, ruled by a mere Serene Highness, considering it unworthy of a daughter of the British queen. Alice, very much in love with her dashing young husband and undoubtedly eager to escape from her mother's excessive mourning, paid little attention to the criticism. She had not objected to living first with her parents-in-law at Bessungen, nor afterwards in the damp old Schloss in Darmstadt until her mother sent sufficient contributions for the building of the New Palace in the town.

Now, with children of her own, even unworldly Alice was beginning to feel the strain of raising a royal family on a less than princely income. Much of her £30,000 dowry had been spent on the building of the New Palace, and her £5,000 annuity barely covered her expenditure or the numerous charitable institutions she had established. Irksome as it was to Queen Victoria, Alice's frequent requests for more money were anything but selfish. Since childhood, her father had instilled in her the belief that those in privileged positions had a duty to help the less fortunate and from the moment she arrived in Darmstadt she had, at great cost to herself

---

* Alice's husband, Louis was styled His Grand Ducal Highness but raised to a 'Royal Highness' in England by Queen Victoria at the time of his marriage. The title was effective in Britain but not in Hesse.

both physically and financially, made a commitment to improving the lot of her husband's people.

> "I earnestly devote myself to the duties of my new life," she had written to the Queen, "striving to act always as dear papa would wish."[3]

Inspired by Florence Nightingale and the housing reformer, Octavia Hill, she embarked upon numerous schemes for updating the medical services, founding hospitals and a 'mental asylum', establishing groups of district nurses, and instigating housing programmes and co-operatives of women workers. Though her projects were gradually winning the hearts of the Hessians, they were proving very expensive and, within eighteen months of Ella's birth, Alice, pregnant for a third time, faced an even greater strain on her resources. In June 1866, the little Grand Duchy was about to become embroiled in the Austro-Prussian War.

The Hessians had neither the desire nor the means to take on the might of Prussia but, fearing that they would lose their independence to Bismarck's rising Prussian Empire, saw no alternative but to side with Austria. For Alice the prospect of a costly war was made all the more difficult by the fact that her elder and closest sister, the Crown Princess of Prussia, was now, in effect, her enemy.

Still more disturbing, at a time when the spread of disease was an inevitable side-effect of war, she feared for the safety of her children from whom she could hardly bear to be parted. Nonetheless, she hastily dispatched Victoria and Ella to their grandmother in England, confident that:

> "In your dear hands they will be so safe; and if we can give you a little pleasure in sending them, it would be a real consolation in parting from them, which we both feel very much."[4]

Within a fortnight of the children's departure, Alice, almost nine-months pregnant, faced a second wrench as she watched her husband set out for battle at the head of his ill-equipped cavalry on their fourth wedding anniversary, 1st July 1866:

"The parting now was so hard!" she told the Queen, "and he feels it dreadfully. I can scarcely manage to write."[5]

In spite of the sweltering heat and her advanced pregnancy, Alice immediately set to work organising hospitals to receive the wounded while assuring Louis that she would join him at the front as soon as her baby was born.

In the event, the plans proved unnecessary. After only seven weeks the triumphant Prussians marched into Hesse and, as the sound of their boots echoed on the palace walls, Alice gave birth to a third daughter, Irène, named after the goddess of peace.

By the terms of the peace treaty, Hesse fared better than many of its neighbours. The Grand Duchy, renamed Hesse-and-by-Rhine, was permitted to retain its independence but a large area of Hessian land was appropriated by Prussia and the reparation payments virtually bankrupted the Grand Ducal family.

"We are almost ruined and must devote all our energies to the reconstruction of our suffering country,"[6] Alice sighed to her mother with further requests for financial assistance – assistance that the volatile Queen was not always willing to give.

Regardless of the pecuniary difficulties, Alice's first experience of war gave even greater impetus to her philanthropic schemes. As cholera and smallpox spread through Darmstadt, she applied herself more fervently to improving the medical services. Wandering incognito through the slums of the poor, she tirelessly sought out new schemes to improve their lot. Often unrecognised by her patients, she personally tended the sick in their own homes and, on a larger scale, established a committee of trained nurses who would be ready to tend the wounded in any future conflict.

Her commitment to the reconstruction of the Grand Duchy, however, did not distract her from her responsibilities to her own children. All three little girls grew quickly; Victoria flourished, breast-fed Ella soon became quite chubby and strong, while Irène thrived on donkey milk.

More enlightened than the majority of German princesses who saw the purpose of their daughters' education as creating future wives, Alice firmly believed that 'marriage for the sake of marriage is the worst mistake for a woman,' and was determined to prepare her children to live independent lives.

"I strive to bring them up totally free from pride of position, which is <u>nothing</u> save what their personal worth can make it. I feel…how important it is for princes and princesses to know that they are nothing better or above others, save through their own merit; and that they have only the double duty of living for others and of being an example - good and modest. This I hope my children will grow up to do."[7]

Naturally, Alice's daughters had to master all the accomplishments expected of 19th century princesses: riding, painting, music and the art of making polite conversation with strangers. An accomplished musician who had once accompanied Brahms on the piano, Alice inspired in them an appreciation of music, and many leading performers of the day were invited to the New Palace to introduce them to opera and literature. She was equally eager to provide them with a far broader curriculum of academic and practical subjects. According to Alice's plan, the girls followed a strict regimen of study in a purposely created schoolroom within the New Palace. Their lessons began early in the morning and continued throughout the day, broken only for physical exercise and meals. From their earliest years they were fluent in two languages, speaking German to their father, and English to their mother, and tutors were employed to instruct them in religion and French. Though later their grandmother would complain that they sought any excuse to escape from their lessons, Victoria in particular proved a remarkably enthusiastic and gifted pupil, whose 'facility in learning is wonderful,' as Alice told her mother, 'and her lessons are her delight. Her English history and reading she has learned from me. I give her a lesson daily...'[8] Victoria's aptitude for languages and love of learning would continue throughout her life.

Though the academic curriculum was wide-ranging, Alice also ensured that her daughters developed practical skills. She taught them cookery, book-keeping and household management, and even at the age of three Ella displayed a 'wonderful talent for sewing'. From their father they learned to tend the gardens and grow flowers and vegetables.

"All my children are great lovers of nature," Alice told the Queen, "and I develop this as much as I can...I bring up my children simply and with as few wants as I can, and above all teach them to help themselves and others so as to become independent."[9]

To outsiders they were princesses but within their own home they cleaned their rooms, made their own beds, laid fires and black-leaded the grates as their mother insisted that they must not expect servants to carry out duties which they could easily perform for themselves.

Above all, Alice was determined to instil in the children her own unstinting sense of duty. From their earliest childhood they participated in fund-raising schemes for her charitable institutions, sewing clothes for the poor and donating many of their toys to the less fortunate children of Hesse. They accompanied their mother on her regular visits to hospitals and the homes of the sick, where they assisted in rolling bandages and talking freely with patients of all classes. 'It is good to teach them early to be generous and kind to the poor,'[10] Alice wrote, and her efforts would prove far-reaching. Witnessing her mother's willingness to carry out the most menial chores, inspired Ella with 'a longing to help those who suffer,' – a longing which, many years later, would come to fruition in a most remarkable manner.

Notwithstanding the long hours in the school room and the time devoted to the poor, life was not all duty and study for the little Hessian princesses. They had inherited their mother's quick sense of humour and delighted in each other's company, playing tennis, riding through the parklands, caring for their pets and boating on the lake. As the eldest, Victoria soon gained dominance over her younger sisters but, while Ella was happy to let Victoria take the lead, she could be as intransigent as her mother when it came to matters of principle. Princess Alice confessed to Queen Victoria that at times she found Ella less biddable and more difficult to manage than her elder sister, but her stubbornness was balanced by a deeply spiritual nature that made her 'the personification of unselfishness, always ready to do anything in order to give pleasure to others.'[11]

While the sisters were devoted to one another and to their parents, the birth of a brother, Ernst Ludwig (Ernie), in 1868 brought them additional joy. Visitors to the New Palace were touched by the tranquillity of the bright, airy rooms decorated in the English style, and the obvious devotion of the close-knit family whose happy boisterousness was commented on by everyone who met them.

"On the same floor as the nurseries," wrote Baroness Buxhoeveden, "were [Princess Alice's] rooms, and there the little Princesses brought their toys and played while their mother wrote or read...Sometimes all the old boxes containing their mother's early wardrobe were brought out for dressing up. The children strutted down the long corridors in crinolines, and played at being great ladies, or characters from fairy tales, dressed in bright stuffs and Indian shawls, which their grandmother, Queen Victoria, could not have imagined being put to such a use...The children were full of fun and mischief."[12]

There were regular dinners with their father's eccentric uncle, the Grand Duke of Hesse, and visits from their numerous royal relations including their father's sickly aunt, Tsarina Marie Feodorovna of Russia. Although money was scarce, holidays were plentiful. There were trips to the seaside in Belgium, and annual holidays in England, staying, when Alice was in favour with the Queen, at one of their grandmother's palaces or in a hotel in Eastbourne, where the girls played on the sand while their mother toured the poorest fishermen's cottages. There were visits to romantic Heiligenberg, the summer residence of their father's Battenberg relations, and occasional trips to Potsdam, near Berlin, the home of Aunt Vicky and their Prussian Hohenzollern cousins.

In spite of the delight that Alice took in her children and the evident happiness that filled the New Palace, the princess's frequent confinements and her work for the Grand Duchy were gradually taking their toll on her health. Since contracting scarlet fever in childhood, she had never been physically strong, and the stress of the Austro-Prussian War had left her so frail that Queen Victoria feared for her psychological state – or, as she put it, 'her nerves'.

By the late 1860s, Alice's nervous problems, exacerbated by exhaustion, often led her into bouts of depression. Watching her boyish and well-meaning husband enjoying the company of their children and finding contentment in their childish pursuits, highlighted her awareness that, for all his good intentions, Louis was totally incapable of understanding her spiritual and emotional needs. While he willingly supported her charities and welcomed reformers into their home, there was another more enigmatic aspect to her character which he could never quite reach. A talented artist and accomplished musician, Alice longed for someone with whom she could share her aesthetic feelings but deep conversation bored Louis; he fell asleep during musical evenings; and his inability to empathise with her spiritual doubts left her lonely and unfulfilled.

In the summer of 1869, the aging and controversial Swabian theologian, David Strauss, arrived in Darmstadt. His contentious work *La Vie de Jesus,* in which he disputed too literal an interpretation of the scriptures, had horrified the established Church. Alice, however, intrigued by reports of his unorthodox opinions, eagerly invited him to the New Palace. Unused to the company of royalty, Strauss accepted the invitation with some trepidation and yet, from his first encounter with the princess, he was amazed not only by her friendly manner but also by her 'rare intellectual qualities.' Regardless of the disapproval of the Hessian aristocracy, their meetings became more frequent and with each conversation Alice fell deeper under the philosopher's spell, delighted that at last she seemed to have found the soul mate that her husband could never be. Yet Strauss's cynical opinions did little to alleviate Alice's spiritual doubts as, according to the French Ambassador, Maurice Paléologue:

"... [He] at once obtained a great influence over her. But the romance of their minds and hearts was still wrapped in a deep mystery, though it is impossible to doubt that he shook her faith to the depths and that she passed through a terrible crisis."[13]

In the midst of her terrible crisis, during which the superficial Prussian Queen Augusta, branded her an atheist, Alice sought the support of the one person who might best empathise with her doubts: her elder sister, Vicky.

The Austro-Prussian War had not damaged the relationship between the sisters, and in the summer of 1869 the Hessians enjoyed a visit to Potsdam where the sisters planned a second holiday later that year. That autumn their husbands were to travel together to Egypt for the opening of the Suez Canal, and in their absence the princesses seized the opportunity of embarking on a trip of their own.

In early winter, Alice and Vicky arrived with their children in the French resort of Cannes where, as the young cousins played together, their mothers shared memories of a childhood in England, their various experiences of marriage and the effect that their now very different lives were having on their children.

Chapter 2 – The Prussian Influence

Hessians
Alice: Queen Victoria's second daughter
Louis: Alice's husband, heir to the Grand Duchy of Hesse
    Children of Alice & Louis:
    Victoria
    Ella
    Irène
    Ernie

Hohenzollerns (Prussians)
Vicky (Victoria): Queen Victoria's eldest daughter; Crown Princess of Prussia.
Fritz (Frederick): Vicky's husband, Crown Prince of Prussia
    Children of Vicky & Fritz:
    Willy (Wilhelm/William)
    Charlotte
    Henry
    Sigi (Sigismund)
    Moretta (Victoria Moretta)
    Waldemar

A cool winter wind blew in from the Mediterranean as Queen Victoria's two eldest daughters strolled along the sea front in Cannes. To all outward appearances, Vicky, the elder and cleverer of the two, had made the better match. Prussia was so much wealthier and more powerful than the impoverished Grand Duchy of Hesse-and-by-Rhine, and she could not have found a more devoted husband than Fritz, with whom she was still in love after eleven years of marriage. Yet, as she watched the children playing croquet, running on the sand, swishing through rock pools and collecting botanical specimens, the Crown Princess could not help but wonder who had the happier lot.

Princess Victoria (Vicky)

Short in stature and, by the age of twenty-nine, already developing her mother's matronly figure, Vicky had always considered her sister far prettier than she was, and the sight of Alice's girls running beside her own clumsy daughter, Charlotte, gave rise to a rueful envy. Although Victoria of Hesse was quite a tomboy with a tendency to talk too much, both she and her younger sister, Ella, looked so much healthier than their painfully thin Prussian cousin, who suffered continuously from nose and throat complaints and appeared far younger than her nine years.

Only two years earlier, Vicky had written hopefully to Queen Victoria that Charlotte 'is very good looking and much admired' but seeing her now beside her Hessian cousins, the optimism seemed premature. Confident yet unassuming in their hand-me-down clothes, Alice's daughters appeared elegant and charming compared with the nervous and graceless Charlotte, whose hair was so thin it had to be cropped short like a boy's and who was such a nail-biter that Vicky had resorted to strapping her hands to her sides and making her wear gloves all day. When Queen Victoria played down the difference, remarking that Alice's third daughter, Irène, was plain, Vicky replied frankly that her own son, Henry, was 'ugly,' though conceding that he could not help being ugly and could be very amusing.

More disappointing for Vicky than her children's appearance, was their behaviour. With true Hohenzollern pride, her eldest son, ten-year-old Willy, strutted about giving orders and reminding his cousins of the recent Prussian victory over Hesse. Even in his more placid moments he changed his mind on the spur of the moment, abandoning one game to start another. While his younger sister and brother, Charlotte and Henry, were happy to follow his lead, Alice's boisterous but impeccably mannered daughters yielded to his whims, perhaps making allowance for his pomposity out of pity for his atrophied left arm. Though every attempt had been made to conceal the deformity – specifically-designed suits with raised pockets and shortened sleeves – it served as a constant reminder to his mother that she had failed in her first duty to produce a flawless heir.

The trauma of her his birth still haunted the Crown Princess. After thirty-six hours of a tortuous labour, during which the doctors gave up hope of saving either mother or child, the baby was found to be in the breach position and was forcibly removed by forceps. In the process, the nerves in his shoulder were badly damaged and consequently his arm failed to develop. For a boy in Willy's position as heir to the Prussian throne the deformity was more than a handicap; it was a humiliation. Already Vicky had heard cruel muttering that a 'one-armed man' should never be king and she had watched helplessly as he endured various brutal and unsuccessful attempts to correct the abnormality. The painful treatments were exhausting, frequently leaving him too tired to study or attend his lessons. Consequently, his academic development was slow. He had difficulty writing and appeared, quite erroneously, to be intellectually inferior to other boys of his age.

"The poor arm is no better, and Willy begins to feel being behind much smaller boys in every exercise of the body. He cannot run fast because he has no balance, nor ride, nor climb, nor cut his food etc. I wonder he is good tempered about it."[14]

Through sheer strength of will, after suffering numerous falls, he eventually learned to ride one-handed and became a competent horseman but even by the age of ten he had difficulty using a knife and fork and the resultant shame left him with a hatred of any sign of weakness and a need to exert his own superiority.

If the trauma of his birth explained Willy's erratic behaviour, there was no apparent excuse for his equally tempestuous sister. Charlotte's moods swung from total apathy to sudden tantrums and rages and her sense of her own importance led her to treat her social inferiors with disdain. She had deeply offended Queen Victoria, who insisted that all her servants should be treated with respect, by refusing to shake hands with her favourite ghillie, John Brown. The Queen wrote a strongly worded letter to Vicky expressing her disapproval of such behaviour but the Crown Princess could only respond by protesting that she was not to blame. She was well aware of her elder children's arrogance but what could she do when their Hohenzollern grandparents spoiled them terribly and infused them with such Prussian pride?

Grey clouds gathered over the sea and the princesses assembled their children to return to the Grand Hotel. Archdeacon Dealtry of Madras had arrived to speak English with the elder Prussian boys and, as Willy and Henry prepared for their lesson, Vicky set up her easel to paint a portrait of the Archdeacon's daughter, carried in the arms of an Indian servant.

Art was virtually the only one of Vicky's many talents that had not been stifled since her marriage. Eleven years earlier, she had arrived in Berlin filled with high hopes for the future. Germany at the time comprised a number of independent kingdoms and grand duchies of which Prussia was the most dominant. For years, ideas had been mooted about a confederation of the various states and when Vicky married the liberal-minded Fritz, she believed that together they could realise her father's vision of a peaceful and unified Germany governed along the lines of the British constitution. It did not take long to discover that few members of the Prussian court shared her dream.

Fritz's father, first Regent then King, believed in an absolute monarchy and, when he appointed the formidable Otto Von Bismarck as Chancellor, all hopes of a more democratic society were dispelled. From the start, it was Bismarck's intention to create a powerful German Empire rivalling its European neighbours in military supremacy and prestige. Within five years of Vicky's wedding, he had annexed the disputed Danish duchies of Schleswig and Holstein before embarking upon the war with Austria, dragging other states – including Alice's Hesse-Darmstadt – into the conflict.

In spite of the Prussian victory, the war had been even more disastrous for Vicky than it had been for Alice. In her anxiety about Fritz's impending departure for battle, she gave birth to a premature baby, whom, to her mother's satisfaction, she named Victoria Moretta. Vicky scarcely had time to recover from her confinement when tragedy struck the family. No sooner had Fritz left for the front when his son, two-year-old son, Sigismund, developed a fever.

The same age as his cousin, Ella, little 'Sigi' had a special place in his mother's heart as the first of her children to be breast-fed. He seemed such a healthy child – 'so pretty and merry and so wonderfully strong, with such a fine colour, always laughing and so lively,'[15] – that his illness was all the more shocking. To make matters worse, most of the court doctors had left with the army and by the time that meningitis was diagnosed, the child was beyond hope. His death in mid-June plunged the Crown Princess into the depths of despair.

> "What I suffer none can know, few knew how I loved," she wrote to Queen Victoria. "It was my own happy secret, the long cry of agony which rises from the inmost depth of my soul, reaches Heaven alone."[16]

With Fritz far away and no one on hand to comfort her, Vicky's grief took a rather macabre turn. Sealing the room in which Sigi had died, she placed an effigy of a baby in his cot and visited it regularly to the horror and disgust of the court.

The decisive Prussian triumph at Könnigratz did little to raise her spirits. She half-heartedly rejoiced in the honours that victory accorded her husband but military success brought small solace when she considered the plight of her sister in Darmstadt. Moreover, she could only watch in despair as Bismarck, claiming most of the credit for the Prussian triumph, urged the king to continue his belligerent ambitions further afield.

> "I rejoice as a Prussian at the heroic conduct of our troops but my joy is damped with the fear that they have shed their blood in vain. With such a man and such principles at the head of our Government how can I look forward to satisfactory results for Germany, or for us?"[17]

In a militaristic climate, there was little room for a liberal-minded and very English princess, whose insistence on clinging to her native customs and tactless comparisons of Britain and Germany did nothing to endear her to the court. Like Alice, she had shown initiative and imagination in her philanthropic activities. She had established homes and training schools for the unemployed, and organised schemes to provide them with temporary work. She had sponsored evening classes, arranged educational programmes in health and hygiene, founded schools of nursing, and an institute to train young women in a variety of trades; but her efforts were largely unnoticed or simply ignored. The Press drew attention only to her Englishness and her outspoken opposition to Bismarck until she became so unpopular that many Berliners were happy to believe that outlandish stories that the Chancellor fabricated about her.

If she hoped for support from Fritz's parents, she was quickly disillusioned. As far as Fritz's father was concerned, women had no business meddling in politics, and a Crown Princess's sole purpose was to provide the country with heirs.

Unfortunately, Vicky did little help her own cause. Like Alice, she was prone to bouts of depression and illness, exacerbated by frequent pregnancies and the stifling of her many talents. Moreover, according to one of her English nieces, there was:

"...a curious trait in her character – she was never really satisfied with the moment itself. When she was in Berlin, everything in England was perfect: when she was in England, everything German was equally perfect."[18]

Even in Cannes, as Alice wrote to Queen Victoria of the 'heavenly blue sea' and the beauty of the sunsets and countryside, Vicky complained of the expense of the place and the dullness of its architecture.

Her elder children, too, left her dissatisfied. It was frustrating for a woman of Vicky's intellect to discover that her children were not great scholars. Impulsive Willy was hindered by his arm; Henry was lazy; and Charlotte was, in her mother's eyes, 'backward' and 'dull.'

Brilliant herself, the standards she set for her children were so far above their ability that Queen

Victoria herself felt it necessary to intervene, urging Vicky not to press them so hard and to make allowance for their slowness in learning.

In response, Vicky wrote effusively that, in spite of his ugliness, Henry was 'a great darling', and Willy was 'very intelligent and good-looking' but often a compliment was followed by a hint of disappointment:

> "I am sure you would be pleased with William if you were to see him. He has Bertie's pleasant, amiable ways and can be very winning. He is not possessed of brilliant abilities, nor of any strength of character or talents, but he is a dear boy, and I hope and trust will grow up a useful man."[19]

In the midst of their mother's criticism, Willy, Charlotte and Henry ran to their grandparents for praise. The Prussian Queen Augusta made no secret of her contempt for her English daughter-in-law and actively encouraged Willy's rising hostility towards her. The King, meanwhile, regaled his grandson with tales of past Prussian victories, filling his head with dreams of ruling a mighty empire surpassing that of his British grandmother. The giant Bismarck, ever willing to flatter the impressionable boy while privately viewing him with contempt, appeared to personify that dream and beside the Iron Chancellor the Crown Prince and Crown Princess seemed weak, unpatriotic and unworthy of respect or imitation. Proud of his Hohenzollern ancestry, Willy alternatively adored and despised his English mother, and Vicky could only take refuge in Fritz's abiding love and the determination to keep her younger children free from the 'Prussian influence.'

By the time of Moretta's birth in 1866, Vicky, frustrated in her aspirations and increasingly isolated from Berlin society, had no option but to confine her many talents to her charitable works, the decoration of her home and the upbringing of her family. 'Every moment she could spare…she spent with us,' Moretta recalled, and consequently she was able to develop a deeper bond with her younger children than had been possible with their elder siblings.

Despite extreme shyness among strangers and an irrational fear of old ladies, Moretta, endeared herself to everyone by her cheerful affection and lack of precociousness; and Vicky wrote to the Queen with some relish that the little girl almost always spoke English and used very few German words. Before Moretta was eighteen months old, a fourth son, Waldemar, was born and he too, under Vicky's care was so 'dear' and 'honest' that he soon became her favourite child.

The holiday in Cannes brought a brief respite to Vicky and Alice. Spending the time quietly together, they seized the rare opportunity of sharing memories of their idyllic childhood and confiding in one another their present troubles. Until then, Vicky had always believed that Alice's life was so much easier and less complicated than her own, but now she began to understand that Alice, too, had her own share of difficulties.

The winter moved on and the return of Louis and Fritz on the 19th December brought a happy reunion of both families in time for Christmas. Yet, while the children listened intrigued to their fathers' accounts of adventures in distant lands, both Alice and Vicky had reason to anticipate their return to Germany with some trepidation. With a heavy heart, Alice set out with her children to the 'stifling' atmosphere of Darmstadt, while for Vicky there came a brief respite as she and Fritz broke their journey in Paris. Entertained by the charismatic Emperor Napoleon III, and delighting in the Parisian culture, neither Vicky nor Fritz could have suspected that within seven months the Prussian Crown

Prince would be leading his troops towards the French capital in the midst of a bitter war.

Chapter 3 – A Constant Increase

Hohenzollerns (Prussians)
Vicky (Victoria): Queen Victoria's eldest daughter; Crown Princess of Prussia
Fritz (Frederick): Vicky's husband, Crown Prince of Prussia
   Children of Vicky & Fritz:
   Willy (Wilhelm, William)
   Charlotte
   Henry
   Moretta (Victoria Moretta)
   Waldemar
   Sophie
   Mossy (Margaret)
Hessians
Alice: Queen Victoria's second daughter.
Louis: Alice's husband, heir to the Grand Duchy of Hesse-and-by-Rhine.
   Children of Alice & Louis:
   Victoria
   Ella
   Irène
   Ernie
   Frittie (Friedrich)
   Alix
   May

Queen Victoria, who considered all things relating to pregnancy and childbirth distasteful, frequently expressed astonishment at her eldest daughter's alleged 'baby-worship.' While conceding that children could occasionally bring comfort to their parents, she claimed that the anxiety they wrought far outweighed the pleasure they gave and was therefore incapable of understanding Vicky's delight in their 'constant increase.'

But the constant increase continued apace. Seven months after leaving Paris, Vicky gave birth to her seventh child, Sophie – an ugly name in Queen Victoria's frank opinion. Five days later, 19th July 1870, France declared war on Prussia and, for a second time in four years, Vicky had barely recovered from her confinement when she was faced the prospect her husband's imminent departure for battle.

War against France was something for which Bismarck had long been planning and preparing; not only would it provide the Prussians with the opportunity of seizing the French territories of Alsace and Lorraine, but also it would draw together the German states, leading ultimately to unification. All that was needed was an excuse for war, and in the summer of 1870 the perfect situation arose as a result of the Prussian nomination of a candidate for the vacant Spanish throne.

Four years previously, a revolution in Spain had brought an end to the reign of the unhappily-married and allegedly promiscuous Queen Isabella. The unpopular queen abdicated in favour of her son, Alfonso, but the Spanish, dissatisfied with the dynasty, were considering alternative candidates from other ruling Houses. Several European princes had been suggested, but when the Prussians nominated Prince Leopold of Hohenzollern-Sigmaringen, the French were appalled. Wary already of Bismarck's designs along the Franco-German border, Napoleon III could not countenance the prospect of a Hohenzollern ruling Spain, and sent a minister to the Prussian King at the spa town of

Ems, insisting that Prince Leopold's name be withdrawn.

On Bismarck's advice, the King accepted the demands but when the French went further, insisting on both an apology for having suggested Leopold in the first place and a guarantee that no other Hohenzollern candidate would ever be put forwards, they played straight into Bismarck's hands. The Chancellor edited the so-called 'Ems Dispatch' and arranged for it to be published and circulated throughout Europe in the full knowledge that the insult would spur the French into making a declaration of war. The scheme proved successful. The whole of Germany responded to France's perceived aggression with self-righteous indignation and for the first time a sense of unity pervaded the country.

Among the uniformed guests who gathered in Potsdam for Sophie's christening on Monday 25th July 1870, were the rulers of several South German states who had joined the Prussian alliance. The disputes of 1866 were forgotten as Prussians and Hessians united against a common enemy. Even the Crown Princess was caught up in the atmosphere of patriotism and, in spite of her aversion to bloodshed, she had no doubt that the French had provoked the conflict, and the Germans had no option but to fight.

The morning after Sophie's christening, before Vicky was awake, Fritz slipped quietly from their rooms and left at the head of his army.

In Darmstadt, too, there were echoes of 1866, as Alice, six months pregnant for a fifth time, watched Louis depart with the troops, knowing that he, as commander of a small division, would be far more exposed to enemy bullets than her brother-in-law, the Crown Prince of Prussia. At least she found comfort in the knowledge that this time she and Vicky were on the same side and could work together in making preparations for the care of the wounded.

No sooner had Fritz departed than Vicky set to work in Berlin and Homburg, applying Florence Nightingale's theories of nursing to provide light and airy wards for the casualties. In Hesse, Alice established four base hospitals to which she paid daily visits, often taking her elder daughters with her to assist in rolling bandages and talking with the injured soldiers.

So devoted was Alice to her duties that she barely had time to sleep but, rather than winning the admiration of the Hessians, her concern for the French prisoners-of-war earned her only 'a heap of criticism' and, in a foreshadowing of events which would later overtake her daughters, roused suspicion that both she and Vicky were secretly working for the enemy.

British neutrality angered the Prussians and it was widely observed in Berlin that, while the London newspapers claimed to support the Prussian cause, Queen Victoria's government had made little attempt to dissuade the French from taking up arms. It was even suggested that the British were secretly backing the enemy – a suspicion which seemed to be confirmed when it was discovered that French ships were supplied with British coal, and French shells were manufactured in Birmingham.

As a result of this discovery, the English were, as Vicky told her mother, even 'more hated than the French' and the brunt of German anger was aimed at the English princesses. While Vicky was pleading with Queen Victoria to send British soldiers to support the Germans, Bismarck seized his opportunity to further denigrate the Crown Princess by accusing both Vicky and Alice of passing military secrets to their mother who was in turn passing the information to the enemy.

Undeterred by the criticism and the acute lack of supplies, Alice continued her work in such appalling conditions that by the eighth month of her pregnancy, her health began to fail.

"I had a violent inflammation of eyes and throat with two days strong fever and strong neuralgia,"[20] she told the Queen in mid-September, and still more worrying was prospect of her imminent confinement in a town filled with disease and 'without even a married lady in the house' to assist her. In the event, the baby, Frittie, was born prematurely on October 7th 1870, but, in spite of Alice's anxieties, the 'fat, pink' little boy with pretty features, thrived. Disregarding her exhaustion and myriad of ailments, his mother returned almost immediately to her duties until December when she was finally able to enjoy a brief respite as she took her children to visit the Crown Princess in Berlin.

"It is a great comfort to be with dear Vicky," she wrote to Queen Victoria. "We spend the evenings alone together, talking or writing out letters."[21]

Tactfully, she omitted to mention that part of the 'great comfort' of being with Vicky was that her sister was helping her by sharing the breast-feeding of little Frittie.

In the course of the conflict the German states were united and, when at last the victorious armies returned home in March 1871, Fritz's father was elevated from King of Prussia to German Kaiser and Emperor. Though deeply affected by the horror of war, Fritz had proved a gallant and competent leader and his triumphal entry into Berlin was greeted with great applause. To the delight of the crowds he and Vicky appeared in the palace window where the Crown Prince held his little daughter, Sophie, in his arms.

In Hesse there were similar scenes of celebration. Louis' gallantry had earned him the Order *Pour la Mérite* and the streets were decorated with triumphant lights and banners:

> "Our house will also be illuminated," Alice explained to her mother, "and I take the two eldest girls [Victoria and Ella] out with me to see it all. It is a thing for them never to forget, this great and glorious though too horrid war."[22]

In that moment of triumph neither Victoria nor Ella could have known that one day they would suffer the effects of a far more terrible conflict.

The ensuing peace brought a return to a calmer existence for the Crown Princess of the newly unified Germany. In April 1872, she gave birth to her eighth and last child, named Margaret after one of her godmothers, the Queen of Italy. For once Queen Victoria thoroughly approved of the name but within her family the princess was known as 'Mossy' on account of her downy hair. Her christening in Berlin was a far less militaristic affair than Sophie's had been and the guest list of artists, writers and academics, demonstrated that the Crown Princess was no longer prepared to endure the militaristic Prussian influence that had so blighted her early years in Berlin.

Now, with more time to consider the needs of her family, Vicky realised that much of her elder children's arrogance was due to the flattery they received at court. More than ever she saw the need to take them away from Berlin at every opportunity and was delighted when she found an old country estate, the Bornstaedt, to which she and Fritz could escape with the children for a few months every summer. There, as the family enjoyed a simple life, renovating the house and working on the land, the elder children, free of Bismarck's influence, became more amenable. The return to Potsdam, however, inevitably brought with it the old tensions and it was increasingly obvious that, while the Crown Princess undoubtedly loved all her children, a clear and natural division had already emerged within the family.

The three eldest – Willy, Charlotte and Henry – continued to disappoint and frustrate their mother. Willy was 'quite good looking' but there was no improvement in his arm, and his shyness often created the impression of aloofness; Charlotte's thin hair, frail physique and poor health were a constant worry; and Henry, who had not 'grown prettier,' she continued to describe as 'ugly.'

For the younger children, however, Vicky had nothing but praise. Waldemar, she said, was so much cleverer than his brothers and so handsome and manly; Moretta clung to her with affection; Sophie was pretty; and Mossy was gifted, good, charming and tender-hearted. The bonds between Vicky and her younger daughters would never be broken.

In Darmstadt, too, the constant increase continued. In June 1872, two months after Mossy's birth, Alice gave birth to a fourth daughter whom she named Alix because, as she explained to Queen Victoria, the German pronunciation 'murdered Alice.'

Doted upon by her elder sisters, little 'merry little' Alix soon earned the nickname 'Sunny' for her ready smile and cheerful disposition but, within a year of her birth, tragedy struck the Hessian household marking the first in a series of misfortunes that would cloud her entire life.

In January 1873, three-year-old Frittie had a slight cut on his ear which continued to bleed profusely for several days. It soon became apparent to Alice that her little boy was suffering from the hereditary condition haemophilia, which had already afflicted her own younger brother Leopold˙. After some days the wound began to heal and Alice naively hoped that in time he would outgrow the condition.

In the spring, for the good of her health, she travelled to Italy leaving her children in the care of their paternal grandmother who had been given strict instructions about their meals, bedtimes, and hours of study. The much-needed holiday was refreshing and invigorating for Alice but she missed her children terribly and was delighted by the reunion at the beginning of May. A few weeks later, the family enjoyed a long walk and picnic in the countryside beyond Darmstadt prior to Louis' departure to review the troops in another part of the Grand Duchy. The next morning, Alice sat in bed working through her letters while Frittie and Ernie played beside her. Their game became increasingly boisterous and, when Ernie ran out to wave from an opposite room, Frittie climbed onto a chair to wave back to him. Suddenly, he leaned forwards, the chair slipped and he fell through the open window. Alice flew from the room and found him lying dazed but miraculously uninjured on the stone below. Her

---

˙ See Chapter 8

relief was short-lived. That evening, he suffered a brain haemorrhage and died before morning.

The death of her little brother was Alix's first introduction to the hereditary 'bleeding disease' that would so blight her own life and bring such disaster to Russia˙. Her mother never came to terms with the

Princess Alice & Her Children

loss. 'To my grave,' she wrote to Queen Victoria, 'I shall carry this sorrow with me.'[23]

With Frittie's death, Alice appeared to abandon her spiritual seeking in favour of a return to the comfort of her childhood faith, while, at the same time, she developed a heightened awareness of her own mortality and wrote prophetically to her mother:

"I feel more than ever that one should put nothing off; and children grow up so quickly and leave one, and I would long that mine should take nothing but the recollection of love and happiness from their home with them into the world's fight, knowing that they have always a safe harbour and open arms to comfort and encourage them when they are in trouble."[24]

Though Queen Victoria commissioned a statue of Frittie, which remains at Frogmore House on the Windsor estate, and invited the family to England for their annual holiday, her response to Alice's grief was cold and unsympathetic in the extreme. The loss of a child, she suggested, was nothing to the loss of a husband. Her heartless reaction was, no doubt, a reprisal for Alice's criticism of her own excessive

---

˙ See Chapter 28

mourning for beloved Albert and reflected the mounting irritation that the Queen felt towards her daughter in Darmstadt.

By the following year, when Alice gave birth to her last child, May, (an 'enchanting little thing' with sparkling eyes) Queen Victoria's patience with Alice was reaching its limit. She could not deny that Alice had selflessly nursed her father through his last illness and had given her unwavering support through the early months of her bereavement but now her 'excessive demands' for more money, her lack of quietness and her constant 'interference' in matters that did not concern her were more than her mother could bear.

"She has done herself such harm," the Queen complained to Vicky. "She has become so sharp and bitter, and no one wishes to have her in their house."[25]

Though Queen Victoria was reluctant to admit it, the root cause of her annoyance was far more personal: Alice not only had the audacity to disapprove of her favourite highland servant the ubiquitous John Brown, but worse, she had dared to criticise the Queen herself.

Rumours of the Queen's inordinate dependence on the rough-spoken ghillie were already circulating through the country. Republican papers even suggested that the Queen had secretly married Brown and some went so far as to imply that she had borne him a child. That the Queen was a little in love with him, there was no doubt. His devotion to her was absolute; nothing was too much trouble for him and she repaid him with complete confidence, making allowance for his drunkenness and allowing him, as Alice complained, to speak freely in her presence while her children were confined to discussing only those subjects which appealed to their mother.

It was not simply the Queen's infatuation with the ghillie that irked her family so much as the imperious and disrespectful manner with which he treated other members of her household. If he deemed the Queen too tired to receive them, Brown thought nothing of denying her own children access to her rooms.

Alice was not the only member of the family to object to his constant presence; her brothers Bertie, Alfred and Leopold, could not stand the man; Vicky had gone so far as to suggest that all the Queen's children should sign a petition demanding his removal from court; but outspoken Alice was most vociferous in her objections. Her complaints struck a raw nerve but now she went further and dared to voice openly what everyone else only whispered: the Queen had become so self-absorbed that she was neglecting her duties as Sovereign.

Since the death of Prince Albert in 1861, the Widow of Windsor had settled into a semi-reclusive existence, cut off from her people and refusing to appear in public 'alone.' In the early years of her widowhood, the country had sympathised with her grief but as the mourning continued unabated for over a decade, pity was rapidly turning into frustration. In the face of an absentee monarch, the republican movement was gaining ground to the extent that in 1864 a sign had even been hung on the gates of Buckingham Palace:

"These commanding premises to be let or sold, in consequence of the occupant's declining business."

The Queen ignored the protests and neither ministers nor princes could edge her out of her self-indulgent isolation when Alice boldly declared it was time for the mourning to stop.

Alice had overstepped the mark, and the princess, who exhausted herself in serving the poor, was accused of having airs and graces, of having 'too high an opinion of herself,' and of upsetting her mother's staff by her arrogance.

That year, in a fit of pique, the Queen threatened to refuse the Hessians the annual invitation to England and only Vicky's tactful intervention persuaded her to grudgingly change her mind on condition that Alice should refrain from complaining and must accommodate her mother's wishes. The change of heart undoubtedly came as a great relief to Alice's daughters for whom the holidays in Windsor, Osborne or Balmoral were among the brightest and most exciting events of their childhood.

Chapter 4 - Frail Puny Babies

Waleses
Bertie: Albert Edward, Prince of Wales
Alexandra: 'Aunt Alix' Princess of Wales
    Children of Bertie & Alexandra:
    Eddy (Albert Victor)
    George
    Louise
    Toria (Victoria)
    Maud

Hessians
Alice: Queen Victoria's second daughter
Louis: Alice's husband
    Children of Alice & Louis:
    Victoria
    Ella
    Irène
    Ernie
    Alix
    May

Hohenzollerns (Prussians)
Vicky (Victoria): Queen Victoria's eldest daughter;
Crown Princess of Prussia
Fritz (Frederick): Vicky's husband, Crown Prince of
Prussia
    Children of Vicky & Fritz:
    Willy (Wilhelm, William)
    Charlotte
    Henry
    Moretta (Victoria Moretta)
    Waldemar
    Sophie
    Mossy (Margaret)

The turrets of Windsor rising through the clouds, beckoned like a fairy-tale castle to the German cousins for whom few childhood pleasures were more thrilling than their regular visits to England. The sight of the 'pretty little English houses,' and their gardens, and above all, the pleasure of meeting 'dearest grandmama' again made the long journey and Irène's sea-sickness suddenly seem worthwhile. Whatever her disputes with their parents, Queen Victoria was a kindly and tolerant grandmother who went out of her way to make their holidays a pleasure.

> "There are none of us," Alice wrote to her mother, "who would not gladly have our children live under the same roof where we passed such a happy childhood, with such a loving grandmama to take care of them."[26]

Their boisterousness might irritate her nerves, and she could sigh that it was no wonder Alice appeared constantly exhausted with so many big children to care for, but the Queen was far more lenient with her grandchildren than she had ever been with their parents.

To four-year-old Sophie of Prussia, her tiny grandmother appeared like a 'very very pretty little girl,' while to the young Alix of Hesse she was '…a combination of a very august person and of a Santa Claus.'[27] Even when far away in Germany, their grandmother was seldom far from their thoughts. They celebrated her birthday with parties during which they sang the British national anthem, and they received constant assurances of her affection with short letters and gifts for their birthdays and Christmas, which never failed to delight them:

> "They showed [the presents that the Queen had sent] to everyone," Alice gratefully wrote to

the Queen one Christmas, "shouting, 'This is from my dear English Grandmama;' and Ella, who is always sentimental added: 'She is so very good my Grandmama.' Irene could not be parted from the doll you gave her, nor Victoria from hers."[28]

Visits to England brought even greater excitement.

"...Her voice was shy when she talked to us," wrote one of her granddaughters, "even her smile was shy, for strange as it may seem, Queen Victoria had something shy about her till the last days of her life. She had tiny, even, white teeth and just a wee foreign accent when she spoke; and she filled us with awe."[29]

As the Queen worked on her papers, the children played around her feet and on one occasion little Waldemar of Prussia released a live crocodile under her desk. They charged along the corridors of Windsor Castle, darting through rooms filled with priceless treasures in noisy games of hide and seek. Outside in the acres of woods and parklands, they rode on ponies or visited the farm and collection of exotic animals including an ostrich and a kangaroo.

Animals were an important feature in the lives of the Queen and her granddaughters, as dogs, cats, birds and other creatures were constant companions in their homes. Letters between members of the family are speckled with happy and sometimes tragic references to their pets: the Queen's collie, Noble, and her puppies; the gift of a lamb for Alice's birthday; Vicky's missing cats; a finch killed by an owl in Darmstadt; and Beatrice's little dog who was killed by a carriage on the Isle of Wight. Among the numerous portraits of the Queen and her children at Osborne House, there are paintings and statues of beloved pets which were viewed as part of the family. Queen Victoria and Prince Albert had commissioned several prominent artists and sculptors – Edwin Henry Landseer, John Francis, and the silversmiths, Garrard's – to portray his beloved greyhound, Eos, in oil, marble and silver. The wildlife artist, Joseph Wolf, was commissioned to paint the Queen's favourite bullfinch; Friedrich Keyl painted several of her collies; and the Queen, herself a talented artist, made several sketches of her children with their animals. Animals were so close to her heart that she openly supported the anti-vivisection league and permitted 'Royal' to be added to the name of the recently-founded Society for the Prevention of Cruelty to Animals.

Circus troupes and theatre companies were invited for the children's entertainment and the Queen took particular pleasure in watching amateur theatricals performed by members of her family and household.

Sometimes the visits coincided with the Queen's annual migration between her homes. At Balmoral, the Scottish castle despised by courtiers for its remoteness and by the household for its gloom, the children enjoyed pony rides amid spectacular scenery. At the beautiful Italianate Osborne House on the Isle of Wight, they played on the private beach, learned to swim, cooked and picnicked in the quaint Swiss Cottage, imported by Prince Albert for the practical education of his own children, or charged around the miniature Victoria Fort and Albert barracks, raising the standards of Prussia, Hesse and England.

Although inevitably, Grandmama plied them with questions and grilled them about their behaviour, education and development, she was equally quick to offer praise: Willy's manners had improved; Charlotte's German was faultless; Moretta's handwriting was neat; Victoria was clever; Ella was wonderfully pretty; and Irène was good tempered and affectionate.

In stark contrast to the militaristic atmosphere of Potsdam or the homely New Palace in Darmstadt, there was something strangely exotic about the British Court. Though Queen Victoria clung to her seclusion from society, she surrounded herself with fascinating personalities, from the turbaned Indian secretaries and tartan-clad ghillies to a whole host of relatives of various ages and characters. Aunts and uncles from all over Europe wandered in and out of the palaces: Aunt Beatrice, only two years older than her eldest niece, was always a willing playmate, as was young Uncle Leopold, who refused to allow haemophilia to prevent him from living life to the full. Beautiful, artistic, though occasionally acerbic, Aunt Louise often came accompanied by her handsome Scottish husband, the Marquis of Lorne. There was intriguing Aunt Marie, a Russian Grand Duchess, and the German Uncle Christian who entertained visitors by displaying his collection of false eyes.

For the sake of her nerves Queen Victoria might insist that her grandchildren be brought to her room in twos but young cousins of all ages abounded in her palaces. The gentle and unassuming Christians lived on the Windsor estate; the histrionic Edinburghs arrived from time to time; and there was always the possibility of a visit to the timid Waleses at Marlborough House or Sandringham in Norfolk.

Uncle Bertie, the Prince of Wales, was a congenial host, with, according to one of his nieces, a 'charm that... endeared him to all who had the privilege of knowing him.'[30] His Danish wife, Alexandra, radiated beauty and charisma and, as the laughter of partygoers echoed through their London mansion from evening until the early hours, the German children realised, even from the remote nurseries, that this was a world far removed from the cloistered court of their grandmother. They might well have noticed, too, the frown of disapproval on their grandmother's face whenever Uncle Bertie was mentioned.

Of all her nine children, none had caused the Queen as much consternation as her eldest son and heir. Compared throughout his childhood to his elder and more brilliant sister, Vicky, Bertie could not have been a greater disappointment to his parents. His lack of enthusiasm for study, his inability to learn, and even his appearance distressed his mother to the extent that she feared that he had inherited the wayward characteristics of her degenerate Hanoverian uncles.

The Queen was haunted by the memory of those terrible uncles who, a generation earlier, had brought the royal family into such disrepute. Since her accession both she and Prince Albert had worked hard to restore the reputation of the monarchy, presenting the nation with an ideal of marital fidelity and domestic harmony that was beyond reproach. No one, least of all their eldest son, could be permitted to tarnish that image and from his earliest years Bertie's parents aimed to mould him into their ideal of the perfect prince. To prevent the taint of any outside influence, he was isolated from boys of his own age and provided instead with strict tutors and even stricter regimes of study. The scheme was not a success. Bertie, criticised on all sides, struggled in the schoolroom while his natural gifts of diplomacy and congeniality were stifled and ignored. When his frustration exploded in rage, he was beaten.

Unsurprisingly, the young prince leaped at the first chance of freedom. Escaping from the 'minders' sent to protect him (or rather his morals) during his student days at Cambridge, he sought the kind of friends who were the antithesis of his parents and who encouraged his budding interest in drinking, gambling and fine cigars. During the university vacation in the summer of 1861, while he was attached to a regiment of guards stationed at the Curragh near Dublin, his companions managed to smuggle a pretty actress into his rooms. That night, the delighted prince embarked upon a womanising career that would continue for the rest of his life.

When word of his escapade reached Windsor, the pious Prince Consort was appalled. Although already exhausted and probably suffering from the illness that finally killed him, he set out at once to Cambridge. On a wet November afternoon, father and son walked for hours in the rain, Prince Albert expressing his disappointment in Bertie's foolishness and warning him that such scandals could pose a threat to the monarchy. Bertie was duly repentant but by the time his father returned to Windsor, his health was already failing.

The Queen refused to believe that her angelic husband was dying, and when the end came, less than a month after his visit to Cambridge, she was convinced his death was due to the shock of Bertie's misdemeanour. For months she could hardly bear to look at her son 'without a shudder' and found it

---

* At the time, the Prince Consort was reported to have died of typhoid. Please see Appendix I for an alternative view.

virtually impossible to forgive him no matter how hard she tried. Nevertheless, he was 'My dear Angel's own child – our Firstborn' and would one day be king, so to deliver him from further temptation, he urgently needed a wife.

Even before Prince Albert's death, Vicky had been entrusted with the difficult task of finding a suitable bride for her brother. Detailed with the necessary qualities – good health, good looks, an unsullied background and preferably a German – she had scoured the pages of the Almanac de Gotha, the bible of royal matchmakers, and made lists of all the available young princesses she had met in European courts. The Queen read her detailed reports with interest and, having rejected various others on the grounds of bad teeth, a frail constitution, or adherence to the wrong religion, she noted that one princess stood out above all: Alexandra, the attractive seventeen-year-old daughter of Crown Prince Christian of Denmark.

Intrigued by Vicky's effusive descriptions, the Queen decided that the princess was worth 'looking over' and arranged a meeting on neutral ground: the Laeken Palace in Brussels. From the first encounter, Queen Victoria was enchanted and wrote enthusiastically to Vicky assuring her that, though Alexandra suffered from a

The Prince & Princess of Wales (Bertie & Alexandra)

slight deafness, her recommendation was perfect – what a pity that she wasn't German! By the time that Bertie was introduced to her, his mother and sister had effectively decided that Alexandra was to be his bride. The wedding took place in March 1863 – an occasion marred only by the behaviour of four-year-old Willy of Prussia, who squealed throughout the service and bit and kicked his young uncles Arthur and Leopold when they tried to restrain him.

Ten months later, Alexandra did her duty by providing the country with an heir, Prince Albert Victor (Eddy) – 'a perfect bijou,' in the Queen's opinion. The following year a second son, George, was born but the lure of a beautiful wife and the responsibilities of fatherhood did little to quell Bertie's love of the high life. Unable to win the Queen's confidence and consequently denied any serious role in constitutional affairs, he passed his time in an endless round of parties, race going and shooting with the 'Marlborough House Set' of fast living, wealthy and fashionable cronies who shared his taste for eating, drinking, gambling and womanising.

Reports of the goings on at Marlborough House irritated and worried the Queen. While she could not deny that the beautiful Alexandra had undoubtedly won the hearts of her people, she had turned out to be – in the Queen's opinion – a naïve and rather empty-headed young woman whose persistent unpunctuality drove Bertie to such despair that he eventually ordered all the clocks in Sandringham House to be set half-an-hour fast.

Still worse, Alexandra shared her husband's love of entertaining to the extent that the Queen felt obliged to warn her that such late nights and frivolous behaviour would not only damage the reputation of the royal family but also ruin her health and that of her 'frail puny' babies who lacked the robust constitutions of their German cousins.

Bertie and Alexandra paid little heed to the warnings and, in the winter of 1866-7, the Queen's predictions proved accurate. During the course of her third pregnancy, the princess contracted rheumatic fever and lay for several days in a critical condition. While the country anxiously awaited news, Bertie ignored the telegrams urging him to return to London, choosing to remain instead at the Windsor races. Even when he did eventually arrive at Marlborough House and made the token gesture of moving his desk to his wife's bedside, he continued to entertain his rowdy friends while she lay on her sickbed upstairs.

On 20th February 1867, after a tortuous labour unrelieved by chloroform, Alexandra gave birth to a daughter, Louise (whom the Queen believed *should* have been named Victoria). Three months later the baby was christened by the Archbishop of Canterbury at Marlborough House where her godparents included three of her aunts: Alice, Lenchen and Beatrice.

Though the Princess of Wales gradually regained her strength, the illness had accentuated her deafness and left her with a permanent limp*. Throughout her protracted convalescence, Bertie embarked on numerous affairs so openly that even the Queen was to comment that her daughter-in-law's lot was not an easy one. As rumours of his neglect became known, his reputation plummeted, reaching its nadir when he was cited in the infamous Mordaunt case.

While suffering from post-natal depression, Lady Harriet Mordaunt, a close friend of the prince, confessed to her husband that her child's father

---

* Such was her popularity and beauty that it became fashionable for upper class women to imitate 'the Alexandra limp.'

could have been one of several highly placed men including the Prince of Wales. Her outraged husband immediately began divorce proceedings and Bertie was summoned to court. Though, thanks to his mother's intervention, he acquitted himself well, Lady Mordaunt was declared insane and the prince's standing in the eyes of the public seemed irreparably damaged. Hissed in the theatre and jeered in the street, he was very much in danger of doing precisely what his mother had feared: destroying the image of the monarchy. Yet, neither public outcry nor family criticism could curtail his pleasure seeking.

By a strange freak of fortune it took a near-disaster to restore his tarnished reputation. In the winter of 1871 he contracted typhoid and for several days his condition appeared to be fatal. His sister, Alice, who been staying at Balmoral with the Queen, was soon at his bedside playing the same role as she had played during her father's fatal illness a decade earlier. On the 14th December – the tenth anniversary of the Prince Consort's death – Bertie was believed to be dying when quite unexpectedly in the evening he began to rally.

The country rejoiced at his recovery and the Queen forced herself out of her seclusion to attend a thanksgiving service at St. Paul's Cathedral after which she appeared in public on the balcony of Buckingham Palace for the first time since her widowhood. When the Queen returned home, satisfied that the monarchy was secure, she felt certain that Bertie's brush with death would lead him to adopt a less frivolous lifestyle. It was a vain hope. With so few responsibilities to occupy his time, it was not long before he returned to his old routine of gambling, shooting and womanising.

Alexandra endured Bertie's infidelities with a dignified silence, and bore him two more daughters: Victoria (Toria) on July 6th 1868, and Maud a year later. A third son, Alexander, was born at Sandringham in 1871 but died within hours of his birth.

If her husband failed to give Alexandra the attention she craved, she was determined to receive it from her children. Jealously overprotective, she virtually smothered them with affection. No aspect of their lives escaped the notice of 'Motherdear', leaving Queen Victoria to complain that she spoiled them terribly. For all her glamorous lifestyle, she was in constant attendance in the nursery, bathing the babies and tucking them into bed each evening before donning her jewels and ball gowns to entrance her guests at dinner.

To the young German princesses, dazzled by the glamour of the Marlborough House Set, it must have come as a surprise to find their Wales cousins so insipid. Of the three girls, only Maud, whose love of the outdoor life and manner of speaking in schoolboy slang earned her the nickname *Harry*, showed any of the spirit common to her cousins. The 'frail puny babies' grew into frail puny children, constantly prone to colds, toothache, abscesses, sciatica and a myriad of other real or imaginary ailments. So fearful was Louise for her health that she took her physician on holiday with her, while 'precious' Toria collapsed at the slightest provocation.

"The children are very dear and pretty," observed Alice, "but my boy is as tall as little Louise, and of course much bigger."[31]

Even when they were well, they were hardly the most scintillating companions for their highly-educated cousins. Unlike her sisters-in-law, the Princess of Wales saw little need to tax her daughters with learning, and Bertie's recollection of his own miserable years in the schoolroom made him loath to inflict the same torture on his children. Maud was an able linguist and Louise a talented musician, but their education was so haphazard that Queen Victoria despaired of their ignorance and lack of serious interest in anything.

Occasionally the girls accompanied their mother to hospitals and the homes of their Sandringham tenants but for the most part life beyond the narrow confines of their nursery remained a mystery to them. They lived and played in their own sheltered world, innocently delighting in each other's company to the extent that Queen Victoria complained that Alexandra was 'unfortunately most unreasonable and injudicious about her children.'[32] On one point, however, Alexandra satisfied the Queen: she insisted on raising her children with an absence of arrogance or pride.

Unfortunately, the 'absence of all pride' was coupled with a complete lack of confidence. With the exception of Maud, who had inherited her mother's fine features, they were not viewed as pretty girls and, overshadowed by their charismatic parents, they found few occasions to shine. Unused to the company of strangers, their diffidence left them tongue-tied in social gatherings and warranted the cruel if apt epithets 'the whispering Waleses' and 'their Royal Shynesses.'

> "They always, if I can so express it," wrote their cousin Marie of Edinburgh, "spoke in a minor key *en sourdine*. It gave a special quality to all talks with them, and gave me a

strange sensation, as though life would have been very wonderful and everything very beautiful, if it had not been so sad."[33]

Even as they grew into their late teens, Alexandra was determined to keep them as little children, making them emotionally and intellectually far younger than their years. Princess May of Teck, who would eventually marry their brother, George, was astonished to attend a birthday party for nineteen-year-old Louise only to discover that it was to be a children's tea party. Their 'sweet and prettily arranged' rooms, cluttered with ornaments, shells and souvenirs, resembled nurseries and they continued to refer to each other by childish nicknames: Toots, Gawks and Snipey. They found their greatest enjoyment in games and giddy pranks, which doubtlessly bored the more serious Hessians and were treated with contempt by the Hohenzollerns.

The Germans' opinion, however, was of no consequence to the Danish Princess of Wales. Since Bismarck's seizure of Schleswig-Holstein from Denmark, she made no secret of her dislike of all things German and more especially Prussian. For Vicky, whom she liked, Alexandra made an exception but her prejudice was never more in evidence than when it came to the wedding of Bertie's younger sister, Lenchen.

Chapter 5 – Poor Dear Lenchen

Christians
Lenchen: Helena Victoria; Queen Victoria's third daughter
Christian of Schleswig-Holstein: Lenchen's husband.
>Children of Lenchen & Christian:
>Christle (Christian Victor)
>Albert
>Thora (Victoria Helena)
>Marie Louise

Princess Helena Victoria, known in the family as Lenchen, trudged through the corridors of Windsor Castle, doing her utmost to fulfil the Queen's requests in the manner appropriate to her station. It was not a role that she relished. As a child, having neither the vivacity nor intellectual brilliance of her elder sisters, she had preferred to play with her brothers in the model fort at Osborne than to master the usual accomplishments of a young princess. Her father, with an understanding ahead of his time, appreciated her skills as a horsewoman and her love of the outdoor life and, rather than stifling her natural talents, encouraged her to develop her gifts however unconventional they appeared. It did not matter to him that she lacked the grace of Vicky and Alice. He recognised her musical, linguistic and artistic abilities and praised her equestrian skill; and few things in life gave Lenchen greater joy than winning her father's approbation.

Now, as she moved awkwardly along the corridors of Windsor, Lenchen was only too aware that Prince Albert's untimely demise had brought those halcyon days to a premature and permanent end.

Only seven months after the Prince Consort's death, Lenchen faced a further wrench when her sister Alice departed for Darmstadt, leaving her to take over her duties as their mother's chief support and confidante. Forced into a role

Princess Helena (Lenchen)

to which she was ill-suited, Lenchen had seen her talents smothered in the morbid atmosphere of the court and there were times when she had to confess that she wished she had been born a boy.

In 1865 the future appeared bleak for Queen Victoria's third daughter. Her only hope of escape from the gloom of perpetual mourning was marriage but finding a suitable husband was proving no easy quest. The Queen, considering her easier to please than her elder sisters, had become so reliant on Lenchen that she was unwilling to part with her. There were younger sisters, who might eventually replace her, but Louise was so volatile and Beatrice so young that for now there seemed little hope of escape. The Queen was not totally opposed to the idea of Lenchen marrying but, having already lost two daughters to foreign courts, she insisted that any prospective suitor must be willing to settle in England. Since a commoner was out of the question for a daughter of the monarch and few foreign

* Later, Lenchen's younger sister, Louise, did in fact marry a subject – the

princes would accept the Queen's stipulations, the prospects were unpromising.

To make matters worse, Lenchen herself believed that she had few personal charms to attract an appropriate *parti*. A plain girl, in her mother's opinion, with a tendency to put on weight too easily, Queen Victoria left her with few illusions about her desirability:

> "Poor dear Lenchen," she had written to Vicky, "though most useful and active and clever and amiable, does not improve in looks and has great difficulties with her figure and her want of calm quiet graceful manners."[34]

Vicky remained optimistic. In spite of the Queen's disparaging remarks, her sister, she believed, had a good deal to offer a husband. Though she may not have been the most beautiful of princesses, her amber eyes were accentuated by her masses of wavy brown hair and, apart from the fact that she was the daughter of the Queen of England, her docile nature and kindly manner gave her all the attributes of an ideal Victorian wife.

Clutching her Almanac de Gotha, Vicky scoured the German principalities and eventually a suitor was unearthed in the person of an old friend of Vicky and Fritz: Prince Christian of Schleswig-Holstein.

At first sight, Christian had little to offer the twenty-year-old princess. Fifteen years her senior, balding, with poor teeth and a propensity to stoutness, his family, the Dukes of Augustenburg, had lost their lands during Prussia's annexation of Schleswig-Holstein. To the Queen, however, his impoverishment proved advantageous: landless

---

Marquis of Lorne – and though she had Queen Victoria's full support, the marriage was the subject of much controversy at the time.

himself, he would be more than willing to settle in a house that she would provide in England. Lenchen was whisked off to Germany for a meeting and was delighted by what she found. What Christian lacked in youth and good-looks he made up for in kindness and good manners; he shared her love of horses, and was, as his daughter later recalled:

"...a very remarkable person...a splendid shot, a very keen horseman, and had a profound knowledge of forestry. In addition to all these outdoor interests he loved poetry and literature...He had inherited from his mother a love of flowers and gardening."[35]

What was more, since he readily accepted the Queen's offer of a home in England, Lenchen would face none of the traumas of leaving the familiar world to become a stranger in a foreign court as her elder sisters had done.

From their first meeting, Queen Victor liked Christian enough to make allowance for his habit of chain-smoking cigars and, though she sighed, 'if only he looked a little younger,' she shared Vicky's view that, with a few adjustments to his teeth and manners, he would make an ideal son-in-law.

The future suddenly appeared brighter for Lenchen, and when Christian proposed she gladly accepted him. The Queen was content; Lenchen was happy; Vicky was satisfied with her part in bringing them together; and none of them was prepared for the furore that the engagement was about to raise.

The outraged Princess of Wales complained that, since Christian had fought against the Danes in the seizure of Schleswig-Holstein, she could not accept him into the family. Bertie, the Prince of Wales, supported his wife and stated categorically that if the wedding took place they would not attend.

From Darmstadt too, Alice opposed the match. Her sister, she believed, was being rushed into marriage with an unattractive and older man simply so that her mother could keep her in service forever. The Queen responded by writing to her relatives across Europe that Alice had ideas above her station, and when the press caught a whiff of the dispute, all kinds of improbable stories appeared in the papers. Christian, it was reported, was a madman and a bigamist who had already fathered several children whom the princess was about to adopt.

In the end, it was left to much-maligned Alice to restore the peace. When a flustered Lenchen assured her that she truly wished to marry her not-so-handsome prince, Alice relented,

"I am so glad she is happy," she wrote to the Queen, "and I hope every blessing will rest on them both that one can possibly desire."[36]

Though her third pregnancy and Austro-Prussian War prevented her from travelling to England for the wedding, Alice was delighted to hear that the Queen had provided her two elder daughters with new frocks for the occasion and even succeeded in persuading Bertie to attend the ceremony, which took place at Windsor Castle in July 1866.

The newly-weds settled into Frogmore House on the Windsor estate where life was peaceful but dull. As Alice had predicted, Lenchen remained on call to the Queen's slightest whim, following her progress through Balmoral each spring and autumn, Osborne for Christmas and summer, and back to Windsor in early spring. For her efforts she received the same £30,000 dowry as had been granted to her sisters, but, to impecunious Alice's great annoyance, she also received a larger annuity of £6,000 and, of course, a free home.

Christian settled easily into his new life in England. With no official duties to occupy his time, he was perfectly content to loll about the gardens, puffing at his cigars until the Queen, watching him through the window, found his idleness disconcerting and, after sending a curt message telling him to find something useful to do, appointed him as Ranger of the Windsor Estate. Even then, the responsibilities were so undemanding that for the most part he occupied himself by caring for his children and shooting birds.

One day while out on a shoot, his brother-in-law, the Duke of Connaught, who was, ironically, a great marksman, accidentally shot him in the eye. Doctors rushed to the scene and after a careful examination informed Queen Victoria that the wounded eye would have to be removed. Whether or not Christian accepted the idea, the prospect of a one-eyed son-in-law so disgusted the Queen that she refused to permit surgery, which was, in her opinion:

> "...Quite unnecessary as formerly she knew several people with shot eyes who did not have it done and who did not become blind: that nowadays doctors were always taking out eyes; and in short [she] spoke as if [the doctors] wished to do it for [their] own brutal pleasure."[37]

Eventually, she relented and the damaged eye was removed, after which Christian acquired a large selection of different coloured glass eyes which he would display for the entertainment of guests.

A year after the wedding, Lenchen gave birth to her first son, Christian Victor (Christle) – 'a nice little thing' according to Vicky. Two years later, a second boy, Albert, was born, to be followed in May 1870 by Victoria Helena (Thora) and, in the summer of 1872, Marie Louise, whom the Queen had wanted to be named Georgina.

By the time of Marie Louise's birth the Christians had moved into the red brick Cumberland Lodge on the Windsor estate, where a third son, Frederick Harold, was born in 1876 but lived for only eight days.

The stresses of pregnancy weighed heavily on Lenchen's nerves and, following the birth of a stillborn child in 1877, she became increasingly convinced that she was suffering from all kinds of maladies, the symptoms of many of which were largely in her own imagination. Even her mother, while conceding that Lenchen was good and amiable, lost patience with her bouts of hypochondria and warned Vicky to show her less sympathy since she was, in the Queen's opinion, too inclined to coddle herself and was placing too great a reliance on her doctors.

To calm her nerves, Lenchen took up smoking (in secret, since her mother detested the habit and would not permit it in her palaces) and frequently badgered her doctors for prescriptions of laudanum. Eventually her addiction became so alarming and her behaviour so bizarre that the Queen and Prince Christian persuaded the doctors to prescribe her with placebos instead.

In spite of her personal problems, Lenchen diligently carried out her duties both as a princess and as a mother. She became the first president of the Royal School of Needlework, patronised various medical organisations, helped establish the Red Cross in England and played a major role in creating the Princess Christian Nurse Training Schools and the Princess Christian District Nurses, which proved so successful that, years later, her niece, Alix of Hesse, would establish similar institutions in Russia. Like her elder sisters, Lenchen took a passionate interest in music, religion and politics – a subject about which her elder daughter, Thora, would prove equally enthusiastic.

Like Uncle Louis in Hesse, Prince Christian, the avid gardener, taught his daughters to grow flowers; and, like Aunt Alice, Lenchen often invited the great performers of the day to sing for them. Princesses or not, the children did not always appreciate their mother's theatrical guests and were not above making occasional social gaffes, as happened when the renowned singer, Jenny Lind, appeared at Windsor:

> "She came up to the schoolroom," wrote Marie Louise, "and said she would like to sing to the 'dear children' - which she did...I went up to her when she had finished and said, 'Dear Madame Goldschmidt, must you always make such a noise when you sing?' All she said was 'Sweet child' - and kissed me."[38]

Devoted to her children, Lenchen raised them according to the broad educational principles established by her father. Her eldest son, Christle, was the first royal prince to attend a public school, while the girls, like their cousins in Darmstadt, were provided with an extensive curriculum and learned several languages from an early age. They spoke French to their maid and German to their father, who also taught them mathematics and inspired them with a love of poetry and music.

Living in such close proximity to their grandmother, the children were particularly close to Queen Victoria who was happy to take care of them while their parents travelled abroad. Christle, she said was 'handsome' and 'a splendid fellow' but she was not quite so taken by his younger sister. On one occasion while Lenchen was in the South of France, the Queen sent her a telegram reporting that:

"Children very well but poor little [Marie] Louise very ugly."[39]

Marie Louise's purported ugliness, which certainly was not in evidence as she grew older, did not prevent the Queen from taking a great interest in her granddaughters' upbringing. From their earliest years she instilled them with her belief in the value of simplicity and the necessity of treating members of the household with respect. Like their Hessian cousins, the girls were not permitted to expect servants to do for them what they could for themselves.

Respect for servants was one thing, but failure to live up to the standards expected of a princess was another. The Queen would never allow her granddaughters to forget the duties that their position entailed. Marie Louise recalled a dinner at Balmoral when she was fifteen-years-old:

"I was sitting next to the Lord Chancellor, feeling very shy and rather inarticulate. I was completely dumbfounded when a voice from over my head whispered in my ear, 'The Queen wishes the young princesses to remember that their duty is to entertain their neighbours at table.' After this, before coming down to dinner, I used to rehearse little bits of conversation so as to carry out my grandmother's injunction."[40]

Though firmly established in England, the girls spent much of their youth traipsing after their mother through the spas of Germany and France in search of a cure for her various rheumatic and psychosomatic ailments. The continental tours not only inspired Marie Louise with a great love of travel that would remain with her throughout her life, but also brought her and Thora into frequent contact with their German cousins in Potsdam and Hesse. Intelligent, gentle and unassuming, they were welcome guests in Berlin and Darmstadt, where they soon discovered they had a great deal in common with Princess Alice's daughters. Similar in age to the younger Hessian children, they too had been raised simply, cleaning their own rooms, wearing inexpensive clothes, and assisting their mother in her many nursing projects. With so much in common, it was unsurprising that Marie Louise and Alix of Hesse, born within two months of one another, soon became close friends.

Back in England, life in Cumberland Lodge passed serenely for Lenchen's daughters. They continued their lessons, cared for their pets, and played happily together by the lake or in the woods of Windsor.

> "Few sisters were really so different in temperament and perhaps character as [Thora] and I," wrote Marie Louise, "yet I do not think that any two sisters have been quite such close and intimate companions and friends as we were. I always referred to her in everything. She had such wonderful judgement, was so clear-headed and wise, and was so loyal and strong in her affection. With it all, she was very humble and very diffident about her own gifts."[41]

Their gentleness and good sense endeared them to their Wales cousins, though time had done nothing to ease Princess Alexandra's prejudice towards Prince Christian. While Queen Victoria delighted in having the little princesses so close at hand, the Princess of Wales could never forgive their father's part in the Schleswig-Holstein campaign and she was not above making childish and cruel remarks about the girls. Overlooking the plainness of her own frail daughters, she mocked their appearance, referring to Thora as 'the Snipe' – a nickname chosen by her brothers because of her long nose and thin features.

If the Christians were aware of her jibes, they might have known better than to take her words to heart. After all, their aunt could be equally cutting in her descriptions of the most flamboyant of all the royal cousins: the daughters of 'Uncle Affie,' Duke of Edinburgh.

Chapter 6 – After All They Are English

Edinburghs
Affie: Alfred, Duke of Edinburgh; second son of
Queen Victoria.
Marie: Duchess of Edinburgh, Affie's wife;
daughter of Tsar Alexander II
> Children of Affie & Marie:
> Young Affie (Alfred)
> Missy (Marie)
> Ducky (Victoria Melita)
> Sandra (Alexandra)
> Baby Bee (Beatrice)

Waleses
Bertie: Albert Edward, Prince of Wales
Alexandra: 'Aunt Alix' Princess of Wales
> Children of Bertie & Alexandra:
> Eddy (Albert Victor)
> George
> Louise
> Toria (Victoria)
> Maud

By the time of Lenchen's wedding Queen
Victoria's second son, Prince Alfred (Affie), Duke
of Edinburgh, was causing his mother almost as
much consternation as his elder brother, Bertie, had
done. A rough-speaking, hard-drinking sailor, Affie
first shocked the Queen by enjoying an affair with a
woman in Malta before developing an infatuation
with his sister-in-law, the Princess of Wales.

For a brief spell in early 1868 the Queen saw a possibility of redemption. That spring Affie spent six months touring Australia as the first member of the British Royal Family to visit the continent. The tour was beset by a series of misfortunes – during a firework display, three boys were burned to death; in the middle of a military display, a soldier's hand was blown off; and a hall, named in honour of the prince, caught fire and was destroyed. Nonetheless, the prince was well-received and the tour was deemed a success until Affie fell victim to a would-be assassin

Prince Alfred (Affie)

named O'Farrell, who shot him in the back. Fortunately, thanks to the ministrations of a group of Florence Nightingale's nurses, who had arrived in Australia the previous week, the prince made a full recovery; and Queen Victoria hoped that the realisation that God had spared him from death might bring about a change of character. She was quickly disillusioned. The good wishes he received increased his arrogance, and his behaviour became so brash that the Queen could hardly bear to be in his company.

"I am not as proud of Affie as you might think," she told Vicky, "for he is so conceited himself."[42]

As ever, she saw no alternative but to adopt her typical remedy for the treatment of errant princes and set about finding him a wife. Various brides were suggested and rejected until, at a gathering in Denmark, Affie came across twenty-one-year-old

Grand Duchess Marie Alexandrovna, daughter of Tsar Alexander II.

The Princess of Wales was quick to promote the match; she had received favourable reports of the Grand Duchess from her own sister, Dagmar, who was married to Marie's brother, the Tsarevich Alexander. Princess Alice, too, spoke highly of the Grand Duchess who, as a first cousin of Alice's husband, Louis, had been a regularly visitor to Darmstadt:

> "[She is so] dear and nice, with such a kind fresh face, so simple and girlish...She is very fond of children, and of a quiet country life – that is the ideal she looks for."[43]

But, for all their flattering descriptions and Affie's enthusiasm for the match, the notion of an Anglo-Russian alliance was received very badly in both St. Petersburg and Windsor.

While the Tsar doubted that a rough sailor prince, nine years her senior, was worthy of his only daughter, Queen Victoria could not have been more disgruntled had Affie said he intended to marry his Maltese mistress. Since the Crimean War she distrusted the Russians and considered the Romanovs far too decadent and ostentatious. The prospect of an Orthodox princess tripping through her palaces surrounded by chanting priests was more than she could bear and, as usual, it was Alice who took the brunt of her rage. This time she was accused of spoiling Affie and giving him 'grand ideas' during his visits to Darmstadt.

In an effort to distract him from Marie, Queen Victoria frantically searched for alternative candidates but Affie, dazzled by the prospect of an exotic bride and the immense wealth that she would bring from St. Petersburg, refused to be impressed.

Rejecting all other suggestions, he became so obnoxious, loitering gloomily about the palace and insulting the servants that at last Queen Victoria yielded. After a great deal of haggling with the Russian court about the correct protocol, she eventually allowed Affie to depart for Russia where the lavish wedding took place in St. Petersburg in January 1874.

When the couple returned to England, Queen Victoria saw her new daughter-in-law in a different light. She found her charming, 'a treasure,' and, if not conventionally beautiful, she had a 'pretty bust.' Moreover, unlike the Princess of Wales, the Duchess of Edinburgh had no desire to fritter away the hours in endless entertaining but enjoyed the more studious pursuits that appealed to the Queen.

Though it was true that she surrounded herself with icons and chanting priests, her devotion to Orthodoxy did not impinge on the rest of the family.

"Scrupulously respecting the [Protestant] faith we were christened in," wrote her eldest daughter, "she rather shunned speaking of religion with us, fearing perhaps to influence us in, any way."[44]

Nor was she as materialistic as Queen Victoria had anticipated. Members of the court were shocked to discover how little attention she gave to her appearance within her own home. On formal occasions, however, dripping in priceless jewels, she made her English in-laws appear dowdy in comparison.

Marie made an equally favourable impression on the British public. Shortly after the wedding, *The Ladies' Treasury* reported that:

"The Grand Duchess speaks English better than most English girls; she has a most pleasing manner, and a presence singularly ladylike and distinguished."[45]

Unfortunately, Marie could not reciprocate the English sentiments. Life at the English court was exceedingly tedious after the ostentation of St. Petersburg. The late nights were tiring; the food bland; and her home, Clarence House, uninteresting. Her mother-in-law's constant interference was bothersome and it irked her that she, an Imperial Highness and daughter of the Tsar, should come lower in the order of precedence than her sisters-in-law, who were mere Royal Highnesses.

Nor, as she learned to her cost, was the taciturn Affie an ideal prince. Disliked by the servants, to whom he was often rude, his favourite occupation was drinking to excess and entertaining his guests with discordant tunes on his violin until it came as a relief to Marie that he spent much of his time at sea. Nevertheless, the marriage produced five children: one son and four daughters.

Nine months after the wedding, the Queen was delighted at the birth of 'young Affie,' but relations between mother- and daughter-in-law were less cordial a year later when it came to a second confinement. Queen Victoria, no doubt recalling Vicky's traumatic experiences in Prussia, was convinced that English obstetricians were far more skilful and delicate than any of their foreign counterparts. It both annoyed and alarmed her that, when Marie retired to her country house, Eastwell Park in Kent, she insisted on being attended by German doctors. In spite of the Queen's vociferous objections, Marie remained adamant in her choice of accoucheurs, and a perfectly healthy daughter, was born on 29th October.

The christening at Windsor Castle on 15th December brought further disagreements. Although delighted by her new granddaughter, Queen Victoria was most put out that the child was not to be called Victoria, but rather Marie Alexandra Victoria – though, within the family, she was known as 'Missy.' When Marie went further and insisted on breast-feeding the baby, Queen Victoria realised that, despite her disgust at the process, she had no option but to resign herself to the inevitable, with the stipulation that the fact should not be made public.

Whether or not Marie knew of the Queen's aversion to breast-feeding, she was already growing weary of her overbearing mother-in-law's constant meddling in all her affairs, and she looked forward to an imminent escape from England. At birth, Affie had been chosen as successor to his uncle, the Duke of Coburg, and the family would eventually settle in Germany'. In the meantime, his appointment as Commander of the Mediterranean fleet provided an opportunity to move to Valetta in Malta. There, in the secluded freedom of the San Antonio Palace the Duchess of Edinburgh came into her own for she was able to live:

> "...entirely according to her desires, uncontrolled by Grandmama Queen and uncriticised by those who were inclined to find her ways foreign and out of keeping with British traditions."[46]

In Malta a second daughter, Victoria Melita (Ducky) was born on the evening of Saturday 25th November 1876 and christened in the San Antonio

---

* By rights, following the death of Prince Albert and his elder brother, the Duchy of Coburg would have passed to Bertie, the Prince of Wales, but since he was heir to the British throne, his parents deemed it more sensible to let Affie inherit the title. The family moved to Palais Edinburgh in Coburg in 1889.

Palace on New Year's Day 1877. Three weeks later, leaving their children in the care of governesses and nannies, the Duke and Duchess of Edinburgh embarked on a tour of Greece.

Two years were to pass before Marie's third daughter Alexandra (Sandra), was born in Coburg; and in 1884, she gave birth to her youngest child, Beatrice (Baby Bee), at Eastwell Park.

Just as Vicky had become increasingly determined to protect her children from the Prussian influence, so Marie, disenchanted with England, resolutely ensured that her children would be free from the English influence. Bearing in mind that her son would one day become Duke of Coburg, she dispatched him at the earliest opportunity to the military academy in Potsdam. Her daughters, too, were to be raised as Germans, attended by a German governess, who spoke no English and, as Marie also refused to speak to them in English, German became their first language causing the Danish Princess of Wales to carp:

> "It is a pity those children should be entirely brought up as Germans. Last time I saw them they spoke with a very strong foreign accent - which I think is a great pity as after all they are English."[47]

With her great love of all things German, the Queen might have been content, but their visits to England became so infrequent that she complained that she hardly knew the 'darling...lovely children' and wished she might see more of them. Vicky and the Princess of Wales were even more disgusted when Missy and Ducky were confirmed in the German Lutheran Church.

Histrionic and intriguing, the granddaughters of two of the most powerful monarchs in the world grew up with a love of adventure, an awareness of their own charisma and a Russian pride inherited from their mother. From their father, whom the Queen claimed they worshipped, they learned a complete disregard for convention, bordering on eccentricity.

Though strict and exacting, and less demonstratively affectionate towards her children than her sisters-in-law were, the Duchess of Edinburgh did everything possible to encourage her daughters to develop their many talents. Beautiful Missy, a gifted artist, sculptress and writer, was equally proficient at riding and dancing, and the mere sight of her was enough to make Cousin George of Wales's heart race. She was deeply attached to her younger and taller sister, Ducky. Like their cousin, Victoria of Hesse, the girls had a passion for riding fast horses and they galloped apace through the Maltese fields on the ponies that their father had brought over from England or their mother had obtained from her brother in Russia, dispelling the tension in the household as their parents grew further apart.

Compared to her adventurous sisters, Sandra, having neither their healthy constitutions nor strength of will, appeared dull. Even her mother considered her 'uninteresting' but her more placid temperament provided a stabilising influence among the siblings and made her an easier companion than the youngest Baby Bee, who would later 'almost lose her mind' in the throes of unrequited love.

If the Wales children gaped in wonder at their fascinating cousins, the Edinburghs must have been equally baffled by the frailty of the English girls. No two families could have differed more starkly. While the Princess of Wales' daughters fell ill at the slightest whim, the Duchess of Edinburgh insisted that her daughters must maintain their dignity and bearing in the face of tragedy or illness. Basically, they were not allowed to be ill; they must eat, without complaint, everything set before them and throughout their childhood they were encouraged and expected to participate in adult conversations.

Far from being coddled in sheltered nurseries, the Edinburghs were forced from their earliest years to confront the very real scandals and perils faced by many monarchies of the age. Not only were the girls aware of their parents' unhappy marriage but they had also undoubtedly heard stories of their Russian grandfather's affair with a woman thirty years his junior, who bore him four children. His wife, the sickly and consumptive Tsarina Marie, unable to tolerate the cold Russian winters, frequently repaired to the warmer climes of her native Darmstadt. In her absence the Tsar installed his young mistress in the Winter Palace in St. Petersburg and there, to the horror of the Imperial Family, the young woman remained, giving birth to his child even as his unhappy wife lay on her deathbed. With inordinate haste after the Tsarina's death, the Tsar secretly married his mistress. The whole of Europe was shocked, sympathising wholeheartedly with the late Tsarina who had, in Vicky's opinion, died of a broken heart.

Within the Russian Imperial Family a feud ensued that would remain unresolved for many more years than the brief spell that the Tsar enjoyed with his young bride.

One afternoon in March 1881, when Missy was barely six years old, her grandfather, Tsar Alexander II, was returning from a meeting at the Mikhailovsky Palace in St. Petersburg when a bomb exploded beneath his carriage. Miraculously, the Tsar emerged from the wreckage unharmed but as he turned to tend to his wounded guard, a second terrorist rushed forward hurling another device that exploded at his feet. Disfigured and bleeding, he was rushed to Winter Palace where, as his young wife fell hysterically upon his mangled body, he died in agony.

Marie hurried to St. Petersburg for the funeral and even the Russophobe Queen Victoria was aghast at the news. The shock waves rippled across the continent and nowhere were they felt more keenly than in the quiet Grand Duchy of Hesse-and-by-Rhine, where Princess Alice's daughters were already struggling to come to terms with a tragedy of their own.

Chapter 7 - Grandmama Will Try To Be a Mother to You

Hessians
Alice: Queen Victoria's second daughter
Louis: Alice's husband, heir to the Grand Duchy of Hesse
    Children of Alice & Louis:
    Victoria
    Ella
    Irène
    Ernie
    Alix
    May

Hohenzollerns (Prussians)
Vicky: Queen Victoria's eldest daughter; Crown Princess of Prussia.
Fritz: Vicky's husband, Crown Prince Frederick of Prussia.
    Children of Vicky & Fritz:
    Willy (Wilhelm, William)
    Charlotte
    Henry
    Moretta (Victoria Moretta)
    Waldemar
    Sophie
    Mossy (Margaret)

Throughout the 1870s it was clear to Princess Alice that the effort she had put into her children's upbringing was bearing fruit. High-spirited and boisterous as they were, she confidently informed her mother, that they were also considerate, well-behaved and 'very unspoilt in their tastes, and simple and quiet children, which I think is of the greatest importance.'[48]

While the younger girls, Irène, Alix and May remained in the nursery in the charge of a kindly English nanny, Mary Anne Orchard (Orchie), their elder sisters, Victoria and Ella were making rapid progress in the schoolroom. Victoria's enthusiasm for learning was undiminished and her mother was soon observing that she was 'immensely grown and her figure is forming. She is changing so much – beginning to leave the child and grow into the girl.'[49]

For Victoria, on the brink of adolescence, life in Darmstadt was also on the brink of change. In March 1877, the death of Louis' father cast a cloud over the New Palace and brought him one step nearer to inheriting responsibility for the Grand Duchy. A month later, the gloom was broken by a visit from Vicky and the Hohenzollern cousins – an event which the Hessian princesses had anticipated with excitement. It was some time since they had met and they 'wished they knew [their cousins] better' but it not did not take long to realise that Charlotte was no more companionable now than she had been seven and a half years earlier in Cannes.

With an air of assumed sophistication, Charlotte strolled flirtatiously through the New Palace, puffing at her cigarettes; her show of worldly-wisdom and boasts of her imminent marriage making her appear far older than her sixteen years. More disturbing for twelve-year-old Ella was the sudden, excessive attention shown her by Charlotte's brother, Willy, a student at the University of Bonn. As they played tennis or boated on the lake, Willy found the days in Darmstadt 'happy beyond description'[50] but Ella was more unnerved than flattered by his growing adulation and promises that he would visit more often.

Barely had the Prussians left, when Alice and Louis were urgently summoned to Seeheim where Louis' uncle, Grand Duke Louis III, was dangerously ill. With great trepidation they set out from Darmstadt, fearing the worst:

> "I am so dreading everything," Alice wrote to the Queen, "and above all the responsibility of being the first in everything and people are not being 'bienveillant.'"[51]

By the time they reached Seeheim the eccentric old man was dead, leaving Louis and Alice as the new Grand Duke and Duchess of Hesse-and-by-Rhine. Along with the title and responsibilities came several castles and hunting lodges and, for the first time since their marriage, they had money to spare. Typically Alice threw herself with greater devotion than ever into her new responsibilities, establishing the Alice Nurses and a home for unmarried mothers, while struggling to support her husband into his new role. The work load was immense and years of childbearing, depression and commitment to her numerous charities frequently left the thirty-four-year-old princess exhausted.

> "I have been doing too much lately," she confessed to her mother that autumn, "and my nerves are beginning to feel the strain, for sleep and appetite are no longer good. Too much is demanded of one; and I have to do with so many things. It is more than my strength can stand in the long run."[52]

By New Year, 1878, Alice was too exhausted to travel to Berlin for Charlotte's wedding˙. It was clear that she desperately needed a holiday and so, in

---

˙ see Chapter 9

the summer, Louis decided to use his new-found wealth to take the whole family on a Grand Tour of Europe. After paying another visit to Vicky, the Hessians enjoyed a restful cruise through the Baltic with the Duke and Duchess of Baden. When they arrived in England in July, Queen Victoria was delighted by Alice's 'truly beautiful children' but was deeply disturbed by how pale and drawn their mother appeared. The Queen hoped that the fresh sea air at Eastbourne and the Isle of Wight might help restore her daughter's vigour but even a month later she had to concede that Alice still looked very weak and delicate.

In autumn, when the Hessians had returned home, Alice enjoyed a series of visits from her brothers and sisters, and life appeared to be settling into its usual routine when suddenly the unthinkable happened. One evening in early November, as Victoria was reading to her sisters, she became aware of a swelling in her throat. What was initially believed to be a cold or mumps was soon diagnosed as diphtheria. One of the great killers of the age, the disease spread rapidly through the family, affecting each of the children in turn. Only Ella was spared and for her own protection she was sent to stay with her paternal grandmother in nearby Bessungen. Throughout Hesse, prayers were said for the children's recovery and a series of telegrams flew to England, keeping Queen Victoria informed of their progress.

Night and day, Alice nursed her children, adhering to the doctors' instructions that, in order to prevent the spread of the contagion, she must neither touch nor kiss them. In spite of Alice's tender care, four-year-old May, died in mid-November.

"The pain is beyond words," Alice telegrammed her mother, "but God's will be done!"[53]

By now Louis, too, had contracted the illness and a heart-broken Alice had to attend their daughter's funeral alone. Such was her grief that, having prayed by the tiny coffin, she could not bear to see it carried from the house and watched only through a mirror. The strain was enormous and, as Queen Victoria read the reports from Darmstadt, she could only praise her daughter's resignation and courage, while fearing that worse was to follow.

Victoria and her father recovered but the younger children remained dangerously ill and when Ernie asked daily for reports of May's progress, his mother could not bring herself to tell him that his little sister had died. Only when he began to improve did she break the sad news. Ernie was so distraught that Alice could restrain herself no longer and, disregarding all precautions, took him in her arms to kiss him. It was, as Disraeli later told the British Parliament, 'the kiss of death.' Within days she too, had succumbed to the disease.

As soon as the news of Alice's illness reached England, Queen Victoria dispatched her own doctor, William Jenner, to Darmstadt but, worn out by weeks of worry and sorrow, the princess had no strength left to fight.

"At times," wrote her sister, Lenchen, "she spoke in a most touching manner about her household, also enquiring kindly after poor and sick people in the town. Then followed hours of great prostration."[54]

Whispering her final instructions for her children's upbringing, she lapsed into semi-consciousness and died at the age of thirty-five on

Saturday 14ᵗʰ December 1878 – the seventeenth anniversary of Prince Albert's death. Her final words were a whispered, 'Dear Papa!'

As the rest of the family gradually recovered, Ella returned to Darmstadt to find the household in mourning. From an upstairs window, she and her sisters watched their mother's coffin draped in the British flag, carried through the streets of Darmstadt, followed by their father, Uncle Leopold, Uncle Christian, Uncle Bertie and crowds of weeping Hessians.

Messages of condolence poured in from all over the world, from Prussia to Russia, and from Canada to England, where a devastated Queen wrote of her terrible grief at the loss of her beloved child. All past disagreements forgotten, in a letter to Vicky she paid Alice the finest compliment she could give: a comparison with her angelic father:

> "She had darling Papa's nature, and much of his self-sacrificing character and fearlessness and entire devotion to duty!"[55]

Across the British Empire flags flew at half-mast, public houses were closed, curtains were drawn across the windows of Buckingham Palace, political engagements were cancelled and bells tolled in the churches in Windsor.

Noticeable for her absence among Alice's mourners was her closest sister and confidante. To Vicky's great sorrow, her father-in-law, the Kaiser, fearing she might bring the contagion back to Berlin, forbade her to go to Hesse for the funeral. In the event, the Kaiser's precautions proved futile. Within months, the epidemic had spread through Prussia, claiming Vicky's son, eleven-year-old Waldemar, among its victims.

Waldemar's illness, coming so soon after the death of Alice and May, was a great blow to his family. The brightest and most loveable of the Hohenzollern brothers, his cheerful good nature had been an endless source of amusement for his parents and siblings. Now, only too aware of the fate of their aunt and cousin in Darmstadt, they could only wait and pray for his recovery.

The Crown Princess, nursing her son herself, adopted all the precautions that Alice had taken. She wore protective clothing, bathed him in carbolic and sprayed herself with disinfectants before leaving the room. For a while he seemed to be improving: 'The doctors feel quite cheerful about him,' she told her mother on the 26th March, 'but of course all cause for anxiety is not over yet!'[56]

The note of caution was well-founded. At three-thirty the following morning, Waldemar died. 'The grief of my parents for the loss of this splendid son was unspeakable;' wrote Willy, 'our pain deep and cruel beyond words.'[57]

Even so, the Prussian journalists used the tragedy to further denigrate the Crown Princess. Accusing her of neglecting her children, one newspaper went so far as to state that God had sent her this tragedy as a punishment for her cold-heartedness. At least, as her second son, Henry, now a sailor in the Prussian Navy, hurried home from Hawaii, she could find some consolation in the knowledge that her often-divided family was for once united in grief.

From the moment that Queen Victoria was told of Alice's death, her heart went out to her Hessian granddaughters. For all her complaints about Alice, she knew that she had been a devoted mother whose absence would be keenly felt in the happy Hessian household, and she promised that from now on she would try to be a mother to the children.

When the gloomy Christmas was over and the family was well enough to travel, the Queen invited the Hessians to Osborne for an extended holiday. The sea air, she hoped, might aid their recuperation and the meeting would give her the opportunity to prove that her promise was more than mere words.

Irene, Victoria, Ella & Alix of Hesse

In January 1879, when the young princesses arrived with their father and brother on the Isle of Wight, the effects of the loss of Princess Alice were immediately apparent. Victoria, thrust from childhood into the role of mother to her younger siblings, prepared to take over many of the Grand Duchess's duties and within a short time would adopt many of her charities. Ella, too, had taken to heart her grandmother's exhortation to walk in Alice's footsteps in the service of others; but it was six-year-old Alix who seemed most deeply affected by the tragedy. The child whose exuberance had earned her the pet name *Sunny* was suddenly withdrawn and tormented by nightmares.

"The first months after her mother's death were untold misery and loneliness for Princess Alix...Long afterwards [she] remembered those deadly sad months when, small and lonely, she sat with old 'Orchie' in the nursery, trying to play with new and unfamiliar toys (all her old ones were burned or being disinfected). When she looked up, she saw her old nurse silently crying. The deaths of her beloved Grand Duchess and of Princess May had nearly broken her faithful heart."[58]

Queen Victoria, the doyenne of mourners, empathised completely with her bereaved son-in-law, Louis. Her own grief at the death of the Prince Consort had almost led to a nervous breakdown and rendered her virtually incapable of carrying out her duties as monarch. Now, seeing Louis wearily wandering around the island where sixteen years earlier he had spent his honeymoon, the Queen began to have doubts about his ability to raise adolescent daughters unaided. The girls, she decided, needed a mother and therefore Louis must remarry as soon as possible.

Of course, the bride would have to be carefully chosen; she must not only be prepared to continue Alice's educational programme, but she must also be willing to ensure that the girls spent a good deal of time under their grandmother's supervision in England. Casting her eyes around the court, it did not take long for the Queen to select an ideal candidate: her own youngest daughter Princess Beatrice.

Since Beatrice was only five years older than her eldest Hessian niece, and twenty-one years younger than her prospective groom, the suggestion was hardly appealing. Louis had never shown the least romantic interest in Beatrice and it must have come as a relief to them both to discover that the Church of England forbade marriage between a brother and sister-in-law. Aggrieved that her scheme had been thwarted, Queen Victoria petulantly suggested that the rule could be altered but her proposal was tactfully declined and grudgingly she had to abandon the plan. Beatrice remained at home with her mother and, in time, Louis consoled himself with a mistress – a Polish divorcée, Alexandrine de Kolomine – and a new hunting lodge at Wolfsgarten, about an hour's drive from Darmstadt, which would soon become the scene of many happy family reunions.

Before the Hessians returned to Darmstadt at the end of February 1879, the Queen appointed them a new governess who had strict instructions to keep her informed of every detail of their progress and development. Uncle Leopold joined them on their homeward journey and, after a break of several weeks at Wolfsgarten, they returned to the New Palace to face the reality of life without Princess Alice.

Although life had changed dramatically for the family, Louis did his utmost to continue to raise his children according to the plans laid down by their mother. The girls could also rely on the unwavering, and occasionally unwelcome, support of Queen Victoria, who adhered to her promise to be a mother to them. She wrote regularly to Victoria with instructions to pass on to her sisters. The pages were filled with assurances of her affection and practical guidance on all manner of subjects. In one letter she could advise them about table manners and diet, before reminding them of the necessity of hard work and the importance of spiritual reading. The Queen was particularly sensitive to Victoria's position as the eldest child, and frequently urged her to ensure that her younger siblings did not neglect their lessons – particularly Ernie who, according to his tutor, was becoming rather lazy.

Not content to watch their progress from a distance, Queen Victoria encouraged other members of the family to make regular visits to Darmstadt and each year she invited the Hessians for extended holidays in England where her affection and admiration for each of them deepened. Victoria's good sense and intelligence constantly impressed her; Irène was dear and good; Ella was sensible and most lovely; and Alix was beautiful beyond words.

When it came to considering the girls' future, the Queen was equally determined to intervene. In 1880, she wrote to Victoria, warning her not to rush into marriage and yet she herself was already reviewing prospective husbands for the young princesses. She was happy to hear from Vicky that her son, Henry, was displaying a marked affection for Irène, and his twenty-year-old brother, Willy, was paying a great deal of attention to her elder sisters.

While launching Victoria on her lifelong addiction to cigarettes (no doubt concealing the fact from his mother and grandmother, both of whom detested the habit), Willy was even more attentive to Ella. As a student, he continued to make regular excursions from his university in Bonn to Darmstadt and soon, in his typically impulsive fashion, he was declaring his love for his pretty young cousin.

Vicky was pleased to hear it. During his early adolescence, alternating between despising and adoring his English mother, Willy had developed an unhealthy fixation with her and had taken to writing her letters filled with passionate descriptions of his dreams about her. While his mother made little of his strange obsession, she was relieved to discover that had fallen in love with someone eminently more suitable. Queen Victoria, too, was elated: who better to calm the reckless boy than his gentle cousin, Ella?

Fourteen-year-old Ella was aghast. More horrified than thrilled by his overbearing attention, she confessed to her elder sister that she thought him 'absolutely horrid'. Yet she was too polite to be openly rude to him and, the more she demurred, the greater became his ardour. He followed her everywhere, hanging on her words, gazing at her and writing her romantic poems; but Ella was not to be swayed. When at last Willy realised that his suit was hopeless, he could not forgive her. Even years later he could hardly bear to remain in the same room as her but to the end of his life he kept her photograph beside that of his beautiful Aunt Alix, Princess of Wales, on his desk.

For Willy's paternal grandmother, Queen Augusta, Ella's refusal was seen as a personal insult for which there was no excuse. In response, she voiced loud criticisms of Alice's daughters and on one occasional snubbed them in public. Queen Victoria, though equally disappointed to the extent that years later she would sigh when she thought of 'what might have been,' accepted Ella's decision and consoled herself with the thought that her granddaughter's Hessian good looks and charming manner were sure to win the attention of several other equally eligible suitors.

With so many children and grandchildren across Europe, it was impossible for the Queen to attend every family celebration but for Princess Alice's daughters she made an exception. In 1881, she was in Darmstadt for Victoria and Ella's confirmation – a ceremony that also marked a girl's entry into society. The following year, Ella arrived in England for her first social season and, as she accompanied her grandmother to the theatre and ballet, British newspapers were eagerly speculating on the marriage prospects of the beautiful princess. Aware of the dangers facing stunning but naïve and motherless young women, the Queen advised them not to mix too freely with young people outside the family and was gratified when Victoria replied that she and Ella were content in each other's company, enjoying the delights of the opera at Wolfsgarten and attending to their mother's charities, and considered themselves too young to attend balls. Victoria, as tomboyish as ever, preferred galloping on fast horses and watching or even participating in the shoot, to consider a future outside Darmstadt. In spite of their repeated reassurances, however, it was clear to Queen Victoria that it could not be long before such beautiful girls would be receiving proposals of marriage.

Chapter 8 - My Beloved Leopold

Connaughts
Arthur: Duke of Connaught & Strathearn; Queen
Victoria's third son.
Louischen (Louise): Duchess of Connaught.
> Children of Arthur & Louischen:
> Daisy (Margaret)
> Arthur
> Patsy (Victoria Patricia)

The Albanys
Leopold: Duke of Albany; Queen Victoria's
youngest son.
Helen: Duchess of Albany.
> Children of Leopold & Helen:
> Alice
> Charles Edward

The cloud of sorrow that descended over Osborne and Windsor following Princess Alice's death was alleviated the following spring by the cheerful preparations for the wedding of Queen Victoria's favourite son: Prince Arthur, Duke of Connaught and Strathearn.

Healthy, handsome and untainted by scandal, twenty-nine-year-old Arthur was his mother's ideal of a prince. Even as a child he had outshone his brothers in her esteem. 'He is really the best child I ever saw,'[59] she told Vicky when he was eight years old, and the passing of time only added to the charms of this 'angel of goodness,' on whose many virtues Queen Victoria loved to dwell.

The godson of the Duke of Wellington, after whom he was named, Arthur had always taken a keen interest in the army and it was only to be expected that he would pass through the Royal Military Academy at Woolwich with distinction. Following his commission in the Royal Engineers, he had played an active part

Prince Arthur

in several expeditions and earned promotion through personal displays of courage. His lack of affectation and insistence upon being treated like any other officer, had won the respect and affection of the troops and, in his subsequent appointments, he made a favourable impression on the peoples of India, Canada and Ireland. Noble in every sense, he so resembled his father that he could not have pleased Queen Victoria more.

"Dear boy!" she had written, "He is so good, and innocent, so amiable and affectionate that I tremble to think to what his pure heart and mind might be exposed. There is no blemish in him…"[60]

In fact, Arthur seemed so perfect and so utterly chaste that she saw no reason for him to marry at all and was taken aback when he returned from a wedding in Potsdam in February 1878, to announce that he had chosen a bride.

With her preference for German spouses, the Queen might have been overjoyed that her favourite son had proposed to Louise (Louischen) of Prussia, but for a cloud that shaded the princess's background. Her father, a cruel and vindictive man, inflicted so many inhuman tortures on his children that his wife had deserted him, bringing disgrace upon the family. To nineteen-year-old Louischen, the dashing English soldier must have appeared like a knight in shining armour rescuing her from a terrible past. Though she was not the most beautiful of princesses, her devotion captured Arthur's heart.

In spite of her initial shock, Queen Victoria could deny her favourite son nothing and, though she suggested he would do well to consider other more beautiful brides before rushing into marriage, she raised no objections to the match. After all, she could hardly complain of Louischen's unfortunate background since it was not so different from that of her own beloved husband. When Prince Albert was a child, his mother had likewise deserted an unfaithful husband for another man and for her sins she was never permitted to see her children again.

Louischen was duly invited to Windsor where she made a pleasing impression upon everyone, despite shocking the Queen by riding unchaperoned with Arthur to Frogmore.

Even the recent death of Princess Alice was not permitted to impinge on the wedding celebrations, which took place on 13th March 1879 in St. George's Chapel, Windsor. The occasion was commemorated in a rather tedious and verbose poem by the Poet Laureate, Alfred, Lord Tennyson, dedicated and addressed to Princess Alice:

"Dead princess, living power, if that which lived,
True life live on – and if the fatal kiss
Born of true life and love – divorce thee not
From earthly love and life...then perhaps...

* See Appendix III

99

...this March morn that sees
Thy soldier brother's bridal orange-bloom
Break thro' the yews and Cyprus of thy grave,
And thine Imperial mother smile again,
May send one ray to thee!"[61]

Such was the Queen's devotion to Arthur that, rather than disappearing after the service, she attended the wedding feast. It was the first family party she had attended since the death of Prince Albert.

The Connaughts moved into Buckingham Palace before settling into the newly-built Bagshot Park in Surrey where, on 15th January 1882, their first daughter, Margaret (Daisy), was born. A year later the Duchess gave birth to a son, Arthur, at Windsor Castle; and her youngest child, Victoria Patricia, (Patsy) was born on the feast of St. Patrick, 17th March, 1886, in Buckingham Palace, where her godparents included Aunt Lenchen and Cousin Willy of Prussia.

Queen Victoria was fond of Louischen, and visitors found her affable and charming with a pleasant sense of humour. Within her own home, however, the Duchess adopted an almost militaristic discipline that often left her daughters trembling in terror. Fortunately for the girls, their parents often travelled abroad leaving them in the care of their doting and indulgent grandmother. Freed from the Duchess's restraint, Daisy showed all the boisterousness of her Hessian cousins and her antics so delighted the Queen that she made allowance for her cheeky vivacity. So fond was the Queen of Daisy that when Arthur, as Commander-in-Chief of his regiment, was posted to India in the autumn of 1886, she declared that the climate was unsuitable for a child of her age, and she should be left in England.

Patsy ('such a beauty and so good') was still a babe-in-arms at the time of her father's posting, and therefore deemed too young to be left behind. Instead, she travelled to Bombay with her parents, remaining under the strict and unyielding discipline of her mother. Though as pretty as her sister, and a gifted linguist and water colour artist, Patsy quailed under her mother's authoritarian regime, which gradually destroyed her confidence. Quaking in her hand-me-down dresses and too tight shoes, Patsy would have preferred to sink into the background with the whispering Waleses than effervesce with the Edinburghs. It was a handicap that would remain with her throughout her childhood and adolescence.

In 1888, Daisy joined her family in India and, following their return to England, the Connaughts settled again into Bagshot Park from where they made frequent visits to Windsor and Osborne. Their travelling days were far from over, however. In 1899, Arthur was posted to Dublin as Commander-in-Chief of the troops in Ireland. He and his family were provided with an official residence in the city and a house in Phoenix Park, loaned to them by a member of the Guinness family:

> "It was a lovely house," the Queen's Equerry recalled, "with oak and tapestry and the Duchess of Connaught and Princess Patsy preferred it to the official house."[62]

Regular visits to Windsor, Osborne and Balmoral continued and the Queen found constant delight in Arthur's 'darling and lovely' daughters.

By the time of Arthur's wedding, Queen Victoria's fourth and youngest son, Leopold, longed more than ever to find a wife and a life of his own. Princess Alice's recent death had come as a great

Prince Leopold

blow to her brother, who had spent many happy holidays in Darmstadt, becoming a particular favourite of his Hessian nieces. Haemophiliac himself, he had fully understood Alice's concerns for her son, Frittie, and, after the little boy's death, he had gloomily assured his sister that death was often preferable to a life that would bring nothing but suffering.

Leopold's own childhood had been blighted as much by his mother's near-neglect as by the agonizing effects of his illness. Although he was certainly the cleverest of her sons, Queen Victoria thought him the 'ugliest and least pleasing child of the whole family...' and there were times when she could hardly bear to look at him. When he was only five years old she complained to Vicky that he was clever but 'an oddity' and, as episodes of bleeding left him crippled, she found his bearing and his behaviour still more unattractive.

That Leopold was sometimes a badly-behaved little boy was largely the Queen's own doing. While his family travelled around the country, he was often left in the care of governors and doctors, whose over-protective supervision made him rebellious and difficult. His father, who might have understood his frustration, died when he was only eight years old, and the Queen became too absorbed in her own grief to expend much energy on the ugly duckling in her nest.

In spite of his physical difficulties, however, Leopold's intelligence was quickly becoming apparent. By the time he was fifteen, even his mother was aware of his abilities, and his tutors, recognising his considerable intellect, eventually succeeded in persuading her to allow him to attend university from where reports of his excellent progress convinced her that he was indeed a very gifted young man. So impressed was she by his achievements that, once his studies were complete, she took him into her confidence, allowing him access to government papers and relying on his advice in much the same way as she had once relied on the Prince Consort. While his elder brother, the Prince of Wales, remained firmly excluded from affairs of state, Leopold was even granted a much-coveted key to the Queen's cabinet boxes.

Yet, while she appreciated his intelligence and trusted him implicitly, Queen Victoria, fearful for his health and determined to keep him by her side, continued to treat him as a child. In 1877, at the age of twenty-four, he begged her to allow him to represent her at an exhibition in Australia but she refused. Later, he would ask to be appointed Governor of Victoria but again his request was denied.

Stifled and frustrated, Leopold dedicated much of his time to worthy causes, in particular institutes for deaf children, and he escaped from his duties at court at every possible opportunity. In spite of his mother's early misgivings he had grown into a handsome young man and his health did not prevent him from enjoying the pleasures of Paris and Monte Carlo, or the company of the 'fast set' at Marlborough House. He became a close friend of his sister-in-law, Marie, Duchess of Edinburgh, and a firm favourite with all his nieces; but the devotion of his extended family could not alleviate Leopold's dissatisfaction and his intense longing for independence with a wife and children of his own.

It took Queen Victoria some time to accept that her frail son was not content to devote his entire life to her service and, considering the fragility of his health, she despaired more of his ever finding a bride than she had of Lenchen ever finding a groom. Nevertheless, moved by his evident unhappiness, she agreed to help where she could. To add weight to his position, she created him Duke of Albany, granted him the moderate freedom of his own home, Claremont House at Esher near London, and encouraged him to seek out a bride among the numerous German princesses.

Shortly before Arthur's wedding, she packed him off to Darmstadt with his Hessian nieces, from where he could visit an old friend, Frederica, daughter of the blind King of Hanover. The visit was unsuccessful. Fond as she was of the prince, Frederica had to admit that she had fallen in love with someone else, and Leo, accepting her refusal with good grace, returned home disappointed.

The following winter Queen Victoria invited Daisy, the seventeen-year-old stepdaughter of Lord Rosslyn, to Windsor with a view to inspecting her as a prospective daughter-in-law. She was sufficiently impressed to recommend the girl to her son but again the plans again came to nothing since neither Leopold nor Daisy was attracted to the other. Within months, Daisy had announced her engagement to Lord Brooke, the future Earl of Warwick. For Leopold, perhaps it was a lucky escape; the flighty 'babbling Brooke' became renowned for taking numerous lovers, among them Leopold's brother, the Prince of Wales.

In the autumn of 1880, an idea occurred to Queen Victoria: twenty-year-old Princess Helen of Waldeck-Pyrmont lived in Arolsen not far from Darmstadt. She was intelligent, well-educated and well-travelled and would certainly be worth a visit. Leopold made the journey and was sufficiently impressed to inform his mother that here was a woman he would be more than happy to marry. He thought her pretty and she came with the highest recommendation from his Hessian nieces. To the Queen's surprise, the princess was equally enamoured, and her genuine delight in their happiness was made all the greater by her admiration for the spirited Helen. Unlike most newcomers to the court, Helen was not in the least overawed in the presence of the Queen and, although her appearance was unremarkable, her charm and grace immediately endeared her to the household.

The wedding took place in St. George's Chapel, Windsor, on 27th April 1882, a fortnight after Leopold's twenty-ninth birthday. Though the prince had hurt his leg and was forced to lean on a stick throughout the service, it was a happy occasion made all the brighter by obvious elation of the young couple.

The Albanys moved into Claremont House where Helen proved a devoted wife, nursing her husband through his numerous episodes of bleeding and paralysis.

If his mother was pleasantly surprised that Leopold had at last found the happiness he craved, she was still more astonished to hear that, only a month after the wedding, Helen was pregnant. Queen Victoria had not believed her frail son capable of fathering a child but a perfectly healthy daughter was born at Windsor on 25ᵗʰ February 1883, and named Alice after her late aunt. Uncle Louis of Hesse and Aunt Vicky were among her godparents, as was Queen Victoria herself who, for once, was able to enthuse about the 'beautiful, plump child' with beautiful brown eyes, which were something of a rarity in the family.

Delighted by his little daughter, Leopold continued his duties and charitable works, but there was no relief from his medical condition. A year after Alice's birth, he was troubled by a particularly painful swelling in his joints and his doctors recommended a trip to the warmer climes of the south of France. By then Helen was again in the early stages of pregnancy and not well enough to accompany him to Cannes. Although his life had often hung in the balance, as she watched him depart she had no idea that she would never see him again.

One afternoon, he slipped on the tiled floor of his hotel and banged his knee. A painful swelling ensued and the subsequent haemorrhage was so severe that he did not recover. After less than two happy years with Helen, he died in Cannes on 28ᵗʰ March 1884.

"My beloved Leopold!" Queen Victoria wrote, "That bright clever son who had so many times recovered from such fearfull [sic] illnesses, and from various small accidents has been taken from us! To lose another dear child, far from me, and one who was so gifted and such a help to me, is too dreadful."[63]

Later, in a more tranquil moment, the Queen reflected that death had come as a blessing, for so often in his hours of agony Leopold had cried out that death would be preferable to his suffering.

The Scottish poet William McGonagall, wrote a dreadful ode in his honour, which begins:

"Alas! Noble Prince Leopold, he is dead,
Who often has his lustre shed:
Especially by singing for the benefit of Esher School,
Which proves he was a wise prince. and no conceited fool."[64]

The ditty continues through a further seventeen equally painful stanzas.

Although Leopold's haemophilia had prevented him from entering the armed forces, he was given a full military funeral on the 12th April. His coffin, having been returned to England aboard the Royal Yacht *Osborne*, was carried by eight Seaforth Highlanders and laid in the vault in St. George's Chapel, Windsor, to the strains of one of the Queen's favourite hymns: John Newman's *Lead Kindly Light*.

As ever in a crisis, Queen Victoria's heart went out to the twenty-two-year-old widow and she insisted on being present at Claremont House when, six months later, the Duchess gave birth to a son, Charles Edward. It was heart-breaking to see little Alice deprived of her father, and, as with her Hessian granddaughters, she promised to do all she could to help in her upbringing.

To Alice, her grandmother was nothing like the prudish old lady of popular myth; she found her so kind, approachable and loving.

"She was wonderful," Alice told an interviewer, shortly before her death, "always very nice. When we lost our teeth, she always used to give us a pound...One time, I hadn't seen her for some time and I had lost three and

I was awfully keen to show her. She said, 'Oh dear, that's very expensive.'"

Alice's affection was returned in full, and the Queen's admiration for Helen's cheerfulness and lack of self-pity was boundless. In fact so great was the Queen's attachment to the Albanys that at times it aroused a little jealousy among other members of the family. On one occasion the Queen felt obliged to ask Vicky to persuade the Duchess of Connaught to be a little kinder to her.

Like so many other members of the family, the Duchess of Albany devoted much of her time to charitable works. She took an interest in nursing and, together with Princess Beatrice, the Duchess of Connaught and the Princess of Wales, she obtained a first aid qualification from the recently formed St. John's Ambulance Brigade. The Duchess, too, paid special attention to the fate of 'fallen women' and established an institute in Deptford Market for the improvement of the slaughterhouse girls, providing them with regular meetings for Bible reading, singing, sewing and an occasional treat. She came to know each of the girls by name and, in time, won their affection and respect.

The loss of her father at such an early age had none of the dramatic effects on little Alice that the loss of their mother had on her cousins in Hesse. Inheriting the strong spirit of both parents, she was a confident, vivacious child. While the Queen thought her 'pretty,' 'merry' and 'good,' visitors were not always so impressed by her precocity. Following a meeting with the six-year-old Alice, the author Lewis Carroll wrote to a friend:

> "The little Princess I thought <u>very</u> sweet but liable, under excitement, to betray what is <u>called</u> 'self-will' (it's really <u>weakness</u> of will)

and that selfishness which is the besetting sin of childhood. Under weak management, that child wd, I should fear, grow up a terror to all around her."[65]

Fortunately, Alice was brought up under the strong management of her mother and grandmother and Carroll's fears were not realised.

The death of Prince Leopold had drastically reduced the Duchess' income and as a result Alice, like her Hessian and Christian cousins, was raised in relative simplicity and not allowed to become inflated by her royal status. Two years after their first meeting, Lewis Carroll's opinion of little Alice changed considerably. She was, he thought:

"...improved...not being so unruly as she was two years ago: they [Alice and her brother, Charles] are charming children. I taught them to fold paper pistols, and to blot their names in creased paper..."[66]

While Alice and her brother were young, their mother spent many hours in their nursery, reading to and playing with them. As they grew older she encouraged them to study a wider range of subjects alongside the usual accomplishments of riding, music and dancing, and even arranged for Alice to travel into London to attend extra classes.

Like her cousins, Alice was fortunate in having so many relations across the Continent with whom she could spend happy holidays. Among the chief pleasures of her childhood were the visits to her mother's native Arolsen where many happy family reunions involved cousins squabbling over toys and running boisterously through the woods. Usually among the guests was her mother's widowed sister, Emma, Queen Regent of the Netherlands, with her little daughter, Queen Wilhelmina.

Apart from visits to Arolsen, the Albanys often holidayed in France with the Queen, who was present with them in Cannes in 1898 for Alice's confirmation in a chapel built as a memorial to her father.

PART II
"A Very Doubtful Happiness"
Happy & Unhappy Marriages

Chapter 9 – Nature Has Made Her So

Hohenzollerns

Vicky (Victoria): Queen Victoria's eldest daughter; Crown Princess of Prussia

Fritz (Frederick): Crown Prince of Prussia

Charlotte: Eldest daughter of Vicky & Fritz; Princess of Saxe-Meiningen

Bernhard: Charlotte's husband.

Willy: Eldest son of Vicky & Fritz

Dona: Augusta Victoria of Schleswig-Holstein; Willy's wife.

In spite of her own blissful, if occasionally stormy, years with beloved Albert, Queen Victoria had a particularly pessimistic view of marriage. She had dreaded her daughters' weddings, unable to bear the thought of handing her innocent girls over to a man to become 'bodily and morally his slave.' By the time that her granddaughters had reached marriageable age, her opinion had altered little. People married 'far too much', she claimed, and for a women marriage was 'a very doubtful happiness.'

Her gloomy reflection proved accurate in the lives of several of her granddaughters: one married a notorious womaniser and at least two others were shocked by their husbands' infidelities; three discovered that their husbands were alleged to be homosexual; and others became embroiled in scandals, two of which ended in divorce. Even those princesses who were fortunate enough to fall in love with loyal and devoted husbands often found themselves in foreign courts, far from their families and isolated in unfamiliar surroundings.

There were, of course, love matches but inevitably within weeks or even days of their wedding, the majority of the young and naïve princesses found their new-found freedom curtailed by the 'unecstatic state' of pregnancy with all the risks and restrictions that entailed.

Yet, while the Queen frequently insisted that unmarried people were often happier than those who were married, few of her granddaughters could envisage any other future than that of her a wife. For nineteenth century princesses, as for most Victorian women, the only alternative to marriage was to become a piteous maiden aunt and dutiful daughter – an unpaid companion to aging parents. Faced with such a choice, even the prospect of a loveless marriage was preferable to enduring the stigma of spinsterhood and when suitors were not forthcoming, princesses sometimes panicked. At least one rushed into marriage with the first available prince, while another pleaded desperately with her parents to find her an appropriate *parti*.

Most of the Queen's granddaughters married young – often *too* young in their grandmother's opinion – and it was predictable that the Queen's eldest and probably most difficult granddaughter, Charlotte of Prussia, should be the first to announce her engagement, if only to assert her independence and escape from her parents' domination.

The years since the holiday in Cannes had done nothing to alleviate Vicky's anxieties about her eldest daughter's appearance or behaviour. At the age of fourteen Charlotte had, in her mother's opinion, not 'an atom' of a figure and showed no evidence of growing into maturity. By the time she visited Darmstadt two years later, Vicky was still more disconcerted by her ill proportioned body with its short legs and 'immense breasts and arms.'

Nor had the onset of adolescence improved Charlotte's demeanour or manners. She had always been moody and difficult but now became so flirtatious and untruthful that her mother genuinely feared for her future. Her childish nervousness had given way to bizarre attention-seeking behaviour and, while outsiders delighted in listening to her revelations about the goings-on at the Prussian court, the slanders and secrets she divulged were causing untold damage, not least to her mother's reputation.

Coquettish, materialistic and addicted to smoking, Charlotte seemed very much in danger of causing a scandal. Then suddenly, at the age of sixteen, with the impulsiveness so characteristic of her elder brother, she announced to her startled parents that she intended to marry. Her chosen fiancé, Prince Bernhard of Saxe-Meiningen, an officer in the prestigious Potsdam regiment, was a cousin on her father's side into whose arms she had literally been thrown when the switchback train on which they were travelling suddenly jerked to a halt.

Few, if any, of the family believed that she was in love and it was widely rumoured that she was marrying simply to escape from her mother. Nevertheless, the Crown Prince and Crown Princess, believing that a studious husband nine years her senior might calm their wayward daughter, gave their consent, hoping, as Vicky told Queen Victoria, that Bernhard would prevent her from causing any more harm.

The optimism was premature. No sooner was the engagement announced than the flabbergasted Crown Princess was complaining to Queen Victoria that the younger generation had lost all sense of propriety since Charlotte did not even bother to tell her when she was writing to Bernhard! Queen Victoria wholeheartedly agreed and bemoaned the fact that young people had lost all modesty and decorum. Even in those far off days, she suspected the American influence.

The wedding took place in Potsdam in February 1878, beginning with the civil ceremony in the drawing room of her parents' home before continuing through a long service and series of celebrations in the old Schloss. Dressed in a silver silk-moire train, with myrtle and orange decorating the veil, Charlotte looked 'very pretty' in her mother's opinion, and, in spite of her reckless behaviour and all the anxiety she had brought her parents, Vicky secretly wept at her departure.

"When I came back last night and looked into her little empty room and empty bed where every night I have kissed her before lying down myself I felt very miserable. However it must be so and she looks very happy and shed not a tear yesterday, and Bernhard dotes upon her…I am sure she is thankful the wedding ceremony is over! It all went off very well we may say, and that is a thing to be thankful for…"[67]

After a brief honeymoon, the couple moved into a house near Berlin, provided by the bride's grandfather, the aged Kaiser Wilhelm I. Charlotte, now mistress of her own home, delighted in her new-found freedom and immediately dispelled all her parent's hopes that that Bernhard might be a calming influence on her. She had no intention of allowing marriage to restrict her behaviour; on the contrary, freed from her mother's influence, she threw herself with greater fervour than ever into the life of what Queen Victoria called the fast set. She and Bernhard purchased a car and a villa in Cannes, which soon attracted all the most fashionable people in society.

> "...the great love of amusement is much to be regretted," wrote Queen Victoria, "and then I blame her husband very much if he allows what you say?"[68]

Parading around in her Parisian gowns, drinking copiously, chain-smoking and alternating

between bouts of illness and self-indulgence, Charlotte revelled in cultivating friendships with foreign kings and dignitaries by encouraging them to believe that she could supply them with private information about the intrigues of the Hohenzollerns and the Prussian court. Even at home, she delighted in shocking the court with her revelations and tales

Princess Charlotte

of her imaginary affairs.

When she wished, she could be charming; Ella of Hesse, who throughout her life earned a reputation for seeing the best in everyone, preferred Charlotte to her elder brother, Willy, and liked her enough to send her gifts. Unfortunately, more often than not Charlotte used her charm to manipulate others into believing the most preposterous lies and it did not take long for the rest of the family to see through her pleasant façade. Even her mother commented that her pretty appearance concealed the most 'dangerous' traits.

To her younger cousins, Missy and Ducky of Edinburgh, Charlotte's air of confidence and sophistication were so fascinating that they were delighted to receive an invitation to her home in Berlin. Their idol promised to entertain them lavishly and introduce them to all her fashionable friends, and the excitement leading up to the visit made the reality all the harder to bear. Charlotte was so engrossed in her own flirtations that she had 'hardly a look or word' for her young guests and treated them so disdainfully that, years later, Missy recalled that the visit was 'one of the most painful memories of my young life.'[69] Charlotte had fallen from her pedestal and had become instead:

> "One of the most fickle and changeable women...with a single word she could shrivel up your ardent enthusiasm, make your dearest possession appear worthless or rob your closest friend of her charm."[70]

Queen Victoria had long defended her eldest granddaughter and throughout Charlotte's unruly adolescence had urged Vicky to be a little less strict in the hope that praise might prove more successful than criticism. Yet even the Queen had to concede that Charlotte lifestyle was unseemly and wondered why her husband did not keep her in check. Queen Victoria knew too, that Charlotte was not to be trusted and she worried about her visits to England for fear of whom she might meet. When Charlotte claimed she had asked her grandmother to present a gift to her regiment of dragoons stationed in Berlin, the Queen understood Vicky's need to clarify the matter, as they could never be sure whether or not she was lying.

Moreover, as her mother was quick to point out, Charlotte had a habit of interfering in matters that were not her business, and never was her interference more acerbic than when it came to the marriage of her elder brother, Willy.

In 1881, Willy secretly proposed to the plain but pious and well-meaning Princess Augusta Victoria (Dona) of Schleswig-Holstein – a first cousin of his cousins, Thora and Marie Louise. News of their secret engagement caused something of a furore in the Prussian Court. As the daughter of a mere countess, Dona lacked the ideal provenance of a future Empress and neither her dowdy appearance nor aloof manner endeared her to the rest of the family.

Vicky, ever willing to welcome newcomers and set them at ease, assured Queen Victoria that she was 'sweet,' 'amiable' and would 'win all hearts' but the Queen was not convinced. While conceding that she had good teeth, she replied in her typically candid manner that she did not consider her pretty at all

'Insipid and boring' according to one of Queen Victoria's ladies-in-waiting, Dona's zealously evangelical opinions and obsession with etiquette often infuriated other relations. To Willy, however, still smarting from the sting of Cousin Ella's refusal, her fawning adulation had a definite allure. Unlike his Hessian cousin and even his own sisters, Dona eagerly agreed with everything he said and so boosted his ego that he repeatedly beseeched his grandfather to permit him to marry so malleable a bride. Eventually the Kaiser gave his consent and the wedding took place in Potsdam in early 1881.

From their earliest meetings Vicky went out of her way to welcome her new daughter-in-law to the somewhat forbidding Prussian court but it did not take long for her kindness to backfire. Dona's arrival did little to enhance court life and her self-righteous deference to her husband exacerbated rather than eased the tension between Willy and his mother.

> "Dona enjoys her position intensely and her whole face expresses the most intense satisfaction," Vicky complained. "She is convinced that all William and she do and think and say is perfect, and this is certainly a state of beatitude. She meddles in everything the family does, every little trifle is reported to her, and she orders and directs in a way very galling for the others from so young a person."[71]

More distressing for Vicky was Dona's refusal to allow her to play any part in the upbringing of her grandchildren and her apparent intention of alienating them from her. Repeatedly Vicky tried to understand Dona's antipathy, making excuses for her behaviour and hoping that time might ease their relationship; but if the Crown Princess was prepared to make allowance for her 'parvenu' daughter-in-law, Charlotte was not.

Irked that the lower-born Dona would now take precedence over her, Charlotte had no qualms about belittling her future Empress and treating her as little more than the butt of her cruellest jokes. Family gatherings became tense occasions when both women were present as no one could be sure what mischief Charlotte would make next.

In February 1883, Vicky and Fritz celebrated their Silver Wedding anniversary – a month later than planned due to a recent family bereavement. Vicky, whose love for her husband had deepened with each year of marriage, had gone to great lengths to ensure that the festivities in Berlin would be worthy of the occasion. Invitations were extended across Europe and a wide variety of artists and actors were called to the palace to present an Elizabethan pageant. One of the highlights of the celebrations was a performance of a play staged by the Crown Princess' children and members of her suite. It was a tradition that Vicky had brought with her from childhood when Queen Victoria and Prince Albert delighted in such family entertainment and, with a touch of nostalgia, she anticipated the performance with excitement.

Unfortunately, Charlotte had other plans. Disregarding her mother's feelings, she used the occasion to humiliate her sister-in-law by drawing attention to her poor acting skills, deliberately upstaging and publicly ridiculing her[72].

Later, following Willy's accession to the throne, Charlotte's behaviour became even more outlandish. Initially she went out of her way to ingratiate herself with the new Kaiser, siding with him against their mother whom she blamed for not having given Willy his rightful position during Queen Victoria's Golden Jubilee procession; but her façade of devotion did not last long. Her vindictive jokes about Dona continued unabated and she frequently appeared unannounced and uninvited at formal functions with the sole intention of causing trouble. On one occasion when the Kaiser was attending a prestigious hunt, he was horrified to see his sister, obviously the worse for drink, clumsily mount a horse in a cruel impersonation of the Kaiserin.

There was even a suggestion that Charlotte was involved in a more serious scandal when Willy, Dona and various government ministers received a series of pornographic photographs and letters detailing accounts of their alleged misdemeanours. Willy ordered a full investigation of the matter and eventually a court official was imprisoned but, when the scurrilous letters continued, it was obvious that there had been a miscarriage of justice and the unfortunate official was released. The content of the letters made it clear that they had been written by someone with inside knowledge of the court and, though there was no evidence to implicate Charlotte, her brother felt sufficiently suspicious of her involvement to advise her to leave Germany for a while.[*]

In 1896 she settled in Roumania, ingratiating herself with the German-born King Carol and his wife, the eccentric Queen Elizabeth, and deliberately spreading malicious gossip about her cousin Missy of Edinburgh.[♦]

A little over a year after her wedding, Charlotte gave birth to a daughter, Feodora (Feo), and, declaring she would have no more children, promptly returned to her fashionable friends and foreign holidays, leaving the little girl in her mother's care. For Vicky, whose fondness for children was so great that Queen Victoria had accused her of baby-worship, such indifference was incomprehensible and she could only gaze askance at Charlotte's complete lack of maternal feeling.

Sadly for Vicky, as Feo grew older it became increasingly apparent that she had inherited many of her mother's less attractive characteristics. The similarity in their temperaments made the relationship between Charlotte and her daughter

---

* Recent research has suggested that the letters were, in fact, sent as blackmail by an abandoned mistress.
♦ See chapter 18

even stormier than that between Charlotte and Vicky.

In 1898, eighteen-year-old Feo announced that she was engaged to be married to man fifteen years her senior. Charlotte, forgetting that she had treated her own parents in an identical manner, was outraged that she had not been consulted. Virtually disowning her daughter, she turned her malicious tongue upon the unfortunate girl with greater venom than ever. When Feo fell ill with a series of mystery symptoms, Charlotte even spread the rumour that she had contracted venereal disease from her husband. In response Feo refused to visit her for several years.

The true cause of Feo's illness was never fully recognised or disclosed during her lifetime but research by John C.G. Rohl, Martin Warren and David Hunt[73] shows that both she and Charlotte were suffering from the hereditary malady, porphyria˙. The diagnosis would account for much of Charlotte's bizarre behaviour and consistently poor health and perhaps excuse some of her more outrageous activities.

Surprisingly, perhaps, in spite of Charlotte's difficult temperament and often unaccountable behaviour, her marriage was not the disaster that some members of the family had anticipated. Her husband, Bernhard, shared her enjoyment of life among the fast set and together they zipped across Europe as leading lights in the fashionable world of high society. Whether or not there was any truth in her boasts of her numerous lovers, Bernhard cared for her during her increasingly frequent bouts of illness and, unlike many of her more stable cousins,

---

˙ See chapter 28

there is no evidence to suggest that she ever had cause to regret her decision to marry so young.

Chapter 10 – Great Marriages Do Not Make
Great Happiness

Hessians:
Louis: Grand Duke of Hesse; widower of Princess Alice
> Daughters of Louis & Alice:
> Victoria
> Ella

Battenbergs
Alexander: Prince of Hesse
Julia, Princess of Battenberg: morganatic wife of Alexander
> Sons of Alexander & Julie:
> Louis: husband of Victoria of Hesse
> Sandro (Alexander): Sovereign Prince of Bulgaria
> Liko: Henry

Hohenzollerns (Prussians)
Vicky: Queen Victoria's eldest daughter; Crown Princess of Prussia
Fritz: Vicky's husband, Crown Prince Frederick of Prussia
> Children of Vicky & Fritz:
> Willy (Wilhelm, William)
> Charlotte
> Henry
> Moretta (Victoria Moretta)

Not far from the New Palace in Darmstadt lived four handsome young cousins of Grand Duke Louis of Hesse-and-by-Rhine. Ambitious and charming, the young men's striking good looks were enough to capture the hearts of several European princesses and their marital prospects would have been excellent but for the unfortunate circumstances of their parents' marriage.

Their father, Prince Alexander of Hesse, had once been a rising star in the Russian court where his sister, Marie, was married to the future Tsar Alexander II. The dashing young Hessian made such an impression in St. Petersburg that he seemed destined for a brilliant future until a scandal in 1851 brought his glittering career to a sudden and dramatic end. Alexander had committed the terrible faux pas of marrying a commoner: his sister's lady-in-waiting, Julia Haucke.

Stripped of his commission and expelled from Russia, Alexander and his morganatic wife eventually returned to Hesse, where the Grand Duke conferred on Julia the title Countess of Battenberg. Though treated with disdain throughout most European courts, the couple settled happily into the Alexander Palace in Darmstadt and produced a daughter, Marie, and four sons: Louis, Alexander (Sandro), Henry (Liko) and Franz Josef (Franzjos), all of whom took their mother's Battenberg title.

In spite of their inauspicious origins, the ambitious young princes soon made their mark on the world. For some years Sandro had served in the Russian army until, following the Congress of Vienna, he was chosen, with the backing of his uncle, Tsar Alexander II, as the Sovereign Prince of Bulgaria. With the help of Princess Alice and Prince Alfred, Sandro's elder brother, Louis, obtained a position in the British Navy where he quickly proved his worth as a sailor.

---

* The wife and children of a morganatic marriage are not allowed to inherit the husband's rank or titles.

"[He] has passed a first-rate examination." Princess Alice wrote to her mother in 1874, "The parents are so happy, and the influence of the good conduct and steady work of the elder brother has on the younger [ones] is of great use as they wish to follow him and be as well spoken of and please their parents as he does."[74]

His naval career took him far afield. He served with the Duke of Edinburgh and became a close associate of the Prince of Wales by whose mistress, Lillie Langtry, he was rumoured to have fathered a child.

Whether or not the rumours penetrated the walls of the New Palace in Darmstadt, Victoria of Hesse was delighted when Louis returned to the Grand Duchy in June 1883. Throughout her childhood, she and her sisters had been regular visitors to the Battenbergs' romantic summer residence, Schloss Heiligenberg, where among the leafy avenues and hazel groves, she had been entranced by the debonair young prince. Now, fresh from a voyage to the Holy Land, the tales of his romantic adventures added to his charm and when he appeared equally enamoured of her, Victoria could hardly contain her excitement. That summer when the Queen issued her annual invitation to Balmoral, the princess was unusually reluctant to leave Germany, and her sister Ella was convinced that this was because she was about to become engaged.

Victoria did not go to Scotland, Louis proposed and, as Ella had predicted, Victoria accepted him.

When Ella and her father broke the news to Queen Victoria, the fond grandmother was initially alarmed. In spite of her personal fondness for Louis, Victoria's first duty, she believed, was to her widowed father who needed help in running the Grand Duchy and caring for his younger children. Moreover, much as she detested the snobbery that made other monarchs disdainful of the Battenbergs, Louis was not a wealthy man; would he be able to support a wife and family?

Level-headed Victoria reassured her on both counts: as a serving sailor her husband would often be away at sea leaving her plenty of time to attend to her duties in Darmstadt. As for money, she had inexpensive tastes and was convinced that Louis' steady income would prove sufficient. Grandmama was satisfied and, though expressing her regret that she would be unable to attend the wedding in Darmstadt, she gave the couple her blessing and secured Louis a position on her own royal yacht, *Victoria and Albert*, so that in the early months of his marriage he would not be separated from his wife by long sea voyages.

Content as she was, the Queen was not so naïve as to believe that everyone would be so accommodating.

"Of course," she wrote prophetically to Vicky, "those who like great matches will not like it, but great matches do not make great happiness."[75]

Vicky was only too aware that the Prussians certainly did not like it, for at the very moment that Louis was pursuing a princess in Darmstadt, his younger brother, Sandro, was similarly occupied in Berlin.

The assassination of his uncle and patron, Tsar Alexander II, had severely jeopardised Sandro's hold on the precarious Bulgarian throne. The new Tsar, Alexander III, looked down on his Battenberg cousin and, irritated by Sandro's refusal to act as his puppet in Bulgaria, was secretly stirring the Bulgarians against their Sovereign Prince. Sandro realised that he would have to look elsewhere for European allies and, in the summer of 1883, his quest took him to Berlin.

The appearance of the romantic prince caused a stir in the Kaiser's court, not least in the heart of Vicky's seventeen-year-old daughter, Moretta. At the sight of the suave and much talked about hero, the shy young princess, entranced by accounts of his escapades in the Balkans, fell head over heels in love. Whether or not Sandro was equally attracted to Moretta, he recognised the benefits of a dynastic alliance and, with the Crown Princess' encouragement, hinted at marriage.

Vicky, almost as enamoured as Moretta was by the dashing prince, was delighted and could hardly find superlatives enough to describe him to her mother. Queen Victoria, with a keen eye for a handsome young man, particularly one who was prepared to stand up to the 'nasty' Russians, could not have agreed more and was equally happy to encourage the match. Bertie, the Prince of Wales, too, encouraged the budding romance – but, sadly for Moretta, the response in Berlin was far less obliging.

The Prussian court was incensed. The aged Emperor, outraged by Battenberg's impertinence, made it perfectly clear that he would never sanction a match between a Hohenzollern princess and the son of a commoner. Willy, choosing to forget that his own marriage had caused such commotion, was equally quick to pour scorn on the idea; and even Moretta's father, the liberal-minded Crown Prince Fritz, refused to consider a Battenberg prince as a prospective son-in-law. For once, the Crown Prince saw eye-to-eye with Chancellor Bismarck, who claimed that such an alliance would damage Germany's relations with Russia. Privately, Bismarck was seeking to enhance his own standing in Prussia by marrying his son, Herbert, to Moretta.

In the midst of such antagonism, the news of Cousin Victoria's engagement brought Moretta a glimmer of hope. If one German princess should marry a Battenberg, would she not set a precedent for another? It was a naïve hope. The Prussians gasped in horror at Victoria's foolishness and declared that if she insisted on marrying Louis Battenberg, the Hohenzollerns would boycott the wedding.

The absence of bombastic Willy and his suite would probably have suited the bride but Queen Victoria refused to stomach such an insult. Furious at the Prussians' arrogance and determined to show her support for her granddaughter, she immediately rearranged her schedule to make the journey to Hesse. If the 'grandmother of Europe' saw fit to attend the wedding, who would dare to refuse an invitation?

In April 1884, the 'royal mob', as Queen Victoria referred to her extended family, descended en masse upon the little Grand Duchy. Never before had the Hessians seen such a gathering of royalties in Darmstadt. From England came Princess Beatrice and the Prince and Princess of Wales with their three 'royal shynesses,' Louise, Toria and Maud. From Russia came the Grand Dukes Serge and Pavel, younger brothers of Tsar Alexander III; and from Prussia came the disgruntled Hohenzollerns, among them the lovelorn Moretta, and Charlotte with her

129

three-year-old daughter, Feodora. The local people turned out in their hundreds to show their appreciation to the British Queen who, delighting in the warm reception she received, was still more gratified to discover that the room in which Princess Alice had died six years earlier remained untouched as a shrine to her memory.

Perhaps for the first time since Princess Alice's death, the New Palace echoed to the sounds of laughter and rejoicing.

"The young Princesses were so much excited by the event that this first break in their family circle had no sadness in it, particularly as Princess Victoria promised to return to Darmstadt whenever her sailor husband was at sea."[76]

In fact, so great was Victoria's excitement that, leaping about in joy, she sprained her ankle and for several days was too agitated to eat. When she finally feasted on lobster, the night before her wedding, she promptly made herself sick. Only the prompt assistance of Queen Victoria's doctor, James Reid, ensured that she was sufficiently recovered in time for the ceremony.

Victoria of Hesse

The wedding took place 30th April 1884 and, if the Prussians gritted their teeth through the service, the celebrations were passing without incident, when suddenly the bride's father made an announcement which stunned the entire gathering. Excitedly he announced that his second daughter, Ella, had accepted the proposal of the Russian Grand Duke Serge Alexandrovich – a severe blow to Cousin Willy and a tragedy for the Russophobe Queen. As if that were not enough to rile the Prussians, a far more shocking revelation soon began to emerge:

> "There is a scandal being whispered about here," wrote the Queen's doctor, Sir James Reid, "...that the Grand Duke is going to marry a Polish lady of rather doubtful reputation, who is divorced from her husband a Russian baron. The Queen does not yet know all the trouble, but she will be furious..."[77]

The rumours were true. That very evening, Louis secretly married his long-time mistress, Alexandrine de Kolomine. It was three days before the news was confirmed and, if the Grand Duke had hoped for congratulations, he was quickly disillusioned. The Hohenzollerns were thrown into paroxysm of indignation and no sooner did the German Emperor hear what had happened than he ordered the entire Prussian party to return at once to Berlin.

The scandal threatened to ruin not only Victoria's wedding celebrations but the reputation of the entire Hessian family and again it was left to Queen Victoria to save the situation. Though as shocked as everyone else by her son-in-law's aberration, she refused to abandon her granddaughters in their hour of need. Outwardly, she continued as though nothing had happened, while behind the scenes ordered the Prince of Wales to arrange an immediate annulment of the mésalliance. The Grand Duke yielded meekly and, as Victoria and Louis Battenberg set off for their honeymoon at romantic Heiligenberg, the hapless Mme. Kolomine left for Poland, paid off with a hefty sum from the Queen's own coffers.

After a brief honeymoon, Victoria and Louis set sail for England. They leased a house, *Sennicotts* – a pretty regency villa in Chichester, close enough to Portsmouth for Louis to continue his service aboard the *Victoria and Albert*, and close enough to Windsor to allow the Queen to keep a fond maternal eye on Victoria.

The mother of nine children was only too aware of the almost unavoidable state in which young wives soon found themselves and was anxious to be on hand to help her motherless granddaughter when the occasion arose. Before the wedding she had delicately hinted to Victoria that she must always turn to her grandmother for advice concerning 'her health' and a month later she was exhorting the young bride to avoid riding if there were any possibility that she might be pregnant.

Her advice was timely; within weeks of the wedding Victoria was expecting a child and the news prompted another barrage of letters from the Queen inquiring into every detail of her condition. By then, Victoria had returned to Darmstadt to help her father in the running of the Grand Duchy but the Queen, recalling Vicky's terrible experiences of childbirth at the hands of German doctors, recommended only English doctors and midwives; better yet, Victoria should return to England for the birth so that her grandmother could be on hand to comfort and support her.

Victoria answered the summons and arrived at Windsor Castle in the winter of 1884-5. The Queen, discarding the pressing affairs of state, remained at her side, stroking her hand throughout the long labour and nostalgically recalling that, twenty-two years earlier, she had sat in the same room with Princess Alice when Victoria herself was born. Out of deference to her mother, Victoria named her daughter Alice.

In early spring, the Battenbergs returned to Darmstadt where the baby was christened, and where Victoria was soon was receiving further admonitions from her grandmother. Before the wedding, the Queen had given her a good deal of advice about marriage. A woman's first duty, she said, was to her husband whom she must obey and look up to and in whom she must confide everything. Now, the Queen noted, Victoria seemed to be spending an inordinate amount of time attending to her father's affairs, and the Queen felt obliged to warn her not to neglect her husband. Victoria accepted the reprimand with good grace and assured her grandmother that she and Louis were devoted to one another. Even so, as the Queen observed with concern, it was four years before a second child, Louise – 'a rather miserable little object' – was born at the Heiligenberg, and a further three years before the girls had a brother, George. In 1900, at the age of thirty-seven Victoria gave birth to her youngest child, Dickie, the future Lord Louis Mountbatten, at Broadlands in Hampshire.

While raising her young family, Victoria lived a rather peripatetic existence, following her husband's naval postings and migrating from Darmstadt and Portsmouth to Valetta in Malta, but the endless travelling did not prevent her from taking personal responsibility for her children's education and upbringing just as her own mother had done. Accepting the Queen's advice, she appointed respectable nannies and when she discovered that her eldest daughter, Alice, was deaf, she even succeeded in teaching her to lip read in several languages.

Victoria's love of learning continued throughout her life. Without neglecting the many charities which her mother had founded, she continued to travel extensively, earning the respect and love of her family.

Victoria's might not have been 'a great match' but it proved a long and happy marriage, and she would live to see the wedding of her grandson, Philip, and Queen Elizabeth II.

Chapter 11 – A Jubilee Baby

Battenbergs
Victoria (of Hesse): wife of Prince Louis Battenberg
Beatrice: youngest daughter of Queen Victoria
Liko (Henry): Prince of Battenberg; Beatrice's
husband.
     Children of Beatrice & Liko:
     Drino (Alexander)
     Ena (Victoria Eugenie)
     Leopold
     Maurice

A week after Victoria's wedding, Queen Victoria returned to Windsor with Grand Duke Louis in tow. Though her son-in-law's unhappiness and the prospect of Ella's imminent departure for Russia preyed on her mind, she could rest satisfied by her part in averting the Hessian scandal and had no idea that an even greater thunderbolt was about to strike her.

At the Darmstadt wedding, while she had been distracted by the Grand Duke's folly, her youngest daughter, Princess Beatrice, had been busily falling in love with the bridegroom's younger brother.

At the age of twenty-seven, 'Baby' Beatrice seemed destined for a life of spinsterhood. Since the plans to marry her to Louis of Hesse had come to nothing, the Queen had decided that her youngest daughter should remain single as her constant support and companion. By the age of twenty-two Beatrice had only ever spent ten days away from her mother and she appeared so content with her lot that no one, least of all the Queen, believed her capable of falling in love. Just in case she should have other ideas, handsome young men were discouraged from paying her any attention and guests were forbidden to mention marriage in her presence.

The sudden disclosure that Beatrice wished to marry the dashing Prussian cavalry officer, Henry (Liko) Battenberg, took the Queen by complete surprise. She had no objection to the

Princess Beatrice

Battenbergs *per se* – she was still encouraging Moretta in her hopeless pursuit of Sandro – but what angered and shocked her was the fact that Beatrice had dared to fall in love at all! Offended that the daughter on whom she depended could consider leaving her side, she dismissed the suggestion as ludicrous and adamantly refused to discuss the matter. The more Beatrice persisted, the more obstinate her mother became until she would not speak to her at all and for several months they communicated only by note.

Beatrice was not without allies. Vicky, tactfully pointed out that her younger sister was no longer a child and if the Queen were to persist in her opposition, who could tell what scandals may follow? She might even follow Grand Duke Louis' example and marry in secret! Grudgingly the Queen began to give way. Yes, she would consent to the marriage on condition that Liko resigned his Prussian commission and agreed to come and live with her in England.

Liko hesitated. Unlike Lenchen's husband, Prince Christian, he was young, energetic and active, and the prospect of exchanging the exciting life of the Prussian Cavalry for one of servitude to a demanding mother-in-law lacked appeal; but Liko's brothers favoured the match and, when Louis and Victoria invited him to their Chichester home, they succeeded in winning him over. He agreed to resign his Prussian commission and remain under the Queen's roof for the duration of his marriage. Faced with such compliance, the Queen raised no further objections.

While Beatrice rejoiced, republican journalists bewailed the arrival in England of another 'German pauper' who would have to be kept at public expense. Adopting the Queen's simile of 'the rabbits in Windsor Park', they complained of the expected surfeit of 'Battenbunnies' and made cruel suggestions as to how they might be disposed of. In Parliament, too, there was discord as republican members objected to Beatrice's marriage settlement.

The muttering in England was nothing compared to the furore in Berlin. That Victoria of Hesse had married a Battenberg was galling enough but that the Queen of England should allow her own daughter to do the same was positively unpalatable. In a typical about turn, Queen Victoria flew to Liko's defence. Elevating him from Serene to Royal Highness, she berated Vicky's husband, Fritz, for voicing his opinion that Liko was not 'of pure blood,' and was even more furious that Willy dared to criticise what she had sanctioned. After all, she was quick to point out, Willy's wife, Dona, was a 'parvenu', whom the family had accepted in spite of her less than regal origins.

At least Vicky's younger son, Henry, proved more compliant. Since he was busily courting Irène of Hesse, it would not do to belittle her brother-in-law's family. When he heard that Irène and her younger sister, Alix, had been chosen as bridesmaids, he was even prepared to brave Willy's scorn to attend the wedding.

As the wedding day drew nearer, Queen Victoria's misgivings returned. The prospect of handing over her baby to a man was even more traumatic than the marriages of all her elder daughters. If a girl knew in advance what marriage entailed, she said, she would refuse to approach the altar. In Beatrice's case she could only hope that there would be 'no results' – in fact there would be four: three sons and a daughter.

The wedding took place at Whippingham Church not far from Osborne House, and, after the briefest of honeymoons, the couple returned to take up permanent residence with the Queen. They holidayed with her in the south of France or the Italian Riviera and followed her annual rotation between Osborne, Balmoral and Windsor where their first son, Alexander (Drino) – a very pretty child, in Queen Victoria's opinion – was born in the autumn of 1886. Within months Beatrice was pregnant again and would soon give birth to Queen Victoria's youngest granddaughter: the 'jubilee baby'

In June 1887, as Londoners prepared to witness the greatest pageant of foreign royalties the capital had ever seen, Queen Victoria saw her well-ordered court thrown into disarray. She understood that so many of her relatives wished to participate in the celebrations for her fifty years on the throne, but, at the age of sixty-eight, her distaste for entertaining the royal mob was stronger than ever. While hundreds of officials planned the route, the festivities and the service, the Queen was preoccupied with arranging the order of precedence.

Still more troublesome was the problem of where to house her numerous guests, ensuring that those who did not get on were placed far enough apart. Willy was being bothersome. Seeming to relish the fact that his father was unwell, he suggested that the Crown Prince should stay in Prussia so that he could glory in the limelight of representing the Kaiser. His behaviour had become so objectionable that Queen Victoria was loath to invite him at all and only Vicky's pleading on his behalf had led her to change her mind. Even so, he could not be relied upon to treat the Battenberg princes with respect and therefore, to avoid any unpleasantness, it would be necessary to keep him as far from Louis and Liko as possible.

Then there was Charlotte. Not only was she actively encouraging Willy's bombastic demands, but the Queen knew her well enough to realise what trouble her tales could cause and would have preferred her to stay in Prussia. There was no space for her at Buckingham Palace, the Queen explained to Vicky, and it would not be advisable to allow her to stay with the fast set at Marlborough House.

Osborne was so overcrowded that Princesses Alix and Irène of Hesse were forced to share a bed; and, if that were not enough, there was the unwelcome prospect of entertaining the Russians. Delighted as Queen Victoria was to see 'dear lovely Ella', not least to grill her about her marriage, the prospect of meeting her Russian husband was far less enthralling. The Queen could only hope that Ella's sister, Victoria, who had recently been struck down by typhoid, would be sufficiently recovered to

---

* see chapter 16

attend and would do her utmost to keep the Grand Duke well away from her.

Hitches and bickering apart, the celebrations began in the evening of 20th June 1887 when the Queen travelled to London to entertain the foreign guests at a banquet at Buckingham Palace.

The next day, as a warm summer morning dawned, the royal cousins were taken to Westminster Abbey for a Service of Thanksgiving. Shortly before eleven-thirty, bugles sounded the National Anthem to announce the arrival of the sparkling procession of princesses who made their way to their seats to the left of a raised dais. Their titles were as ancient and illustrious as their surroundings: Princesses Victoria Moretta, Sophie and Margaret of Prussia; Grand Duchess Elizaveta Feodorovna; the Hereditary Princess Charlotte of Saxe-Meiningen; Princesses Helena Victoria and Marie Louise of Schleswig-Holstein; Princess Louise of Wales; Princesses Alix and Irène of Hesse; and Princesses Marie and Victoria Melita of Edinburgh.

As the chatter of sisters and cousins echoed on the abbey walls, the Queen's landau left Buckingham Palace preceded by a procession of princes. Enthusiastic crowds lined the streets to cheer the impressive pageant of royalties. The Queen's grandsons and grandsons-in-law rode at the head of the procession, followed by the Kings of Denmark, Greece and Saxony, and the Princes of Prussia, Portugal, Austria and Sweden. From the farthest reaches of the Empire came the Maharajas of Morvi, Gondal, Holkar, Indore, and Queen Kopiolani of Hawaii.

At the entrance to the abbey, the princes, arrayed with the emblems of their Orders, dismounted and made their way to the right of the dais on which the tiny Queen would sit during the service.

When the prayers were completed, the princesses, some with tears in their eyes, stepped forwards to curtsey to their grandmother, who embraced and kissed each of them in turn. As the royalties emerged from the abbey, enthralled crowds cheered the magnificent procession, hailed their monarch and waved their flags, oblivious of Willy's grumbling that his wife came lower in the order of precedence than the black Queen Kapiolani of Hawaii. For the first time since the death of Prince Albert, the British public turned out in their thousands to demonstrate their affection for the Queen. Later, a grand formal dinner was held, during which the Queen granted the Order of the Bath to several of her grandsons and awarded each of her granddaughters the Jubilee Medal and brooch. In the evening royalties gathered in the gardens of Buckingham Palace to watch a magnificent firework display.

As was to be expected, the Poet Laureate produced a rather sycophantic poem for the occasion:

> *"Fifty times the rose has flower'd and faded,*
> *Fifty times the golden harvest fallen,*
> *Since our Queen assumed the globe, the*
> *sceptre.*
> *She beloved for a kindliness*
> *Rare in fable or history,*

Queen, and Empress of India,
Crown'd so long with a diadem
Never worn by a worthier,
Now with prosperous auguries
Comes at last to the bounteous
Crowning year of her Jubilee."[78]

The celebrations continued for several days, during which the Queen frequently appeared in public with her granddaughters. There were opportunities, too, for small family gatherings. The Queen bounced little Alice of Albany on her knee; she took tea at Frogmore with Alix and Irène of Hesse, whose engagement to Cousin Henry of Prussia had recently been announced. She drove through Windsor with five-year-old Daisy Connaught, visited Prince Albert's tomb with Marie Louise, entertained Charlotte at a large family dinner and, beneath the trees at Windsor, plied Ella with questions about her Russian marriage.

By the time the celebrations were over and the guests had returned home, Queen Victoria could rest contentedly knowing that, in spite of her years of seclusion, her popularity was greater than ever, and the family reunion had passed off without incident. By autumn, she believed she had earned a rest at her favourite retreat, Balmoral, and there, in October, Beatrice's jubilee baby was born.

The confinement was not easy. After a prolonged labour, the child was removed by forceps, leaving Beatrice prostrated for several weeks. The baby, however, was a healthy, sturdy daughter who, according to her grandmother, bore a strong resemblance to her cousin, Ella of Hesse. As the first princess to be born in Scotland for many centuries, she was feted by the Scots and much was made of her baptism in the Presbyterian Crathie Kirk, where she was christened Victoria Eugenie after her godmother, the Roman Catholic Empress Eugenie of France. In the family, however, she was always known by her third name, Ena.

Boisterous and lively, the young Battenbergs brought a breath of youth to the English palaces and revived in the Queen a jollity that she had rarely displayed since the death of Prince Albert. Servants and guests alike were amazed to hear her laughing so freely with the children whom she claimed to love 'as much as their parents do.'

When Ena was two years old, a second brother, Leopold was born, and two years later he was followed by a fourth child, Maurice. To accommodate the growing family an extra wing, the Durbar Wing, was added to Osborne House and there, in the freedom of the Isle of Wight, the children learned to cycle and swim.

Raised in a family of boys, Ena was a wild unruly child and, though the Queen was extremely indulgent with her, there were occasions when she found it necessary to give the little girl a slap.

"She runs about all over the place," wrote her cousin, Moretta of Prussia, "& the Indians & nurses after her, try to get her back, she is so strong."[79]

Another cousin, Marie Louise, was also enchanted by her naughty little cousin and recognised that she possessed such 'great qualities' that 'great possibilities' lay ahead of her.

Ena's adventurousness rivalled that of her brothers and on one occasion almost resulted in tragedy. One Saturday afternoon in February 1894, the six-year-old princess was riding at Windsor when her pony stumbled and threw her before rolling on top of her. The little girl managed to walk home but on reaching the palace was violently sick before lapsing into unconsciousness. Fearing a brain haemorrhage, the Queen's physician, Sir James Reid, remained in attendance all night but by the following morning the 'splendid child' began to show the slightest signs of recovery.

"The little princess is much better than she was, but I am still anxious about her," wrote Sir James. "She is quite conscious when awake but rambles a little when asleep...I trust the improvement may go on steadily but I tell them that she is not yet out of danger and I watch her very closely both when she is asleep and awake."[80]

After so serious an accident, it came as a relief to see her gradually becoming 'obstinate and troublesome' again, and Ena remained as fearless as ever. In fact, as she later confessed, the most daunting aspect of her childhood was the terror she felt when her grandmother grilled her about her Bible studies.

Chapter 12 – If You Love Him Set Him Free

Hohenzollerns (Prussians)
Vicky & Fritz: Crown Prince and Crown Princess of
Prussia; then Emperor and Empress Frederick
    Children of Vicky & Fritz:
    Willy
    Charlotte
    Henry
    Moretta
    Sophie
    Mossy

Irène of Hesse: daughter of Princess Alice; wife of
Henry of Prussia

Battenbergs
Sandro: Alexander of Battenberg; deposed
Sovereign Prince of Bulgaria

From Berlin, Moretta could only gaze in
wonder at the evident bliss of Aunt Beatrice and
Cousin Victoria with their Battenberg husbands
while happiness with Sandro continued to be denied
her. Though her mother urged her not to give up
hope, the Kaiser remained intransigent and by 1886
the chances of the Hohenzollerns accepting Sandro
into their clan had reached their nadir. Undercover
agents sent by the Tsar stirred the Bulgarians against
the prince and, before the end of the year, after a
series of swashbuckling adventures and heroic
escapades, he had been ousted from his throne.
Eventually, he returned home to Darmstadt so
disillusioned and depressed that, even when the

people begged him to return, he refused, declaring that he would not set foot on Bulgarian soil again.

His fall from power made little difference to lovelorn Moretta, who dramatically claimed that if she could not marry Sandro she would kill herself. Distraught, Vicky pleaded more fervently on her behalf but her efforts merely strengthened the Prussians' resolve. Infuriated by her 'meddling', Bismarck initiated a whispering campaign to discredit both the Crown Princess and Sandro. The prince, it was said, had contracted syphilis; he was decadent; he was homosexual; the Crown Princess was so eager to promote the match because she wanted the handsome young man for herself. When Vicky continued to plead Sandro's case, the Kaiser stated that if the wedding ever took place, he would disown both Moretta and her mother.

For a further year, the saga dragged on. Sandro waited, Moretta languished, and her mother struggled for a solution but by spring 1887 Vicky and her daughters faced a more immediate concern.

On Tuesday, 22nd March, Fritz's father, Emperor Wilhelm I, celebrated his ninetieth birthday with a banquet in Berlin at which Queen Victoria was represented by Bertie and Lenchen. During the dinner, Fritz was to toast his father and formally announce the engagement of his son, Henry, to Cousin Irène of Hesse – an event that the shy Hessian princess anticipated more with trepidation than excitement – but when Fritz rose to speak, his voice was barely audible.

Throughout the winter, he had been troubled by a sore throat and hoarseness, which did not improve as expected with the coming of spring. Assuming that the illness was an after-effect of his recent bout of measles, the Crown Prince initially paid little heed to the symptoms but as they persisted he finally accepted his doctors' advice and agreed to take a cure. In April, following the confirmation of his younger daughters, he and Vicky travelled with Moretta, Sophie and Mossy to the fashionable spa town of Ems. Away from the capital, he seemed a little better but when the family returned to Berlin in May there was no evidence of any great improvement.

Further medical investigations uncovered a series of growths on his larynx, which the doctors attempted to excise in a brutal and painful procedure, carried out without anaesthetic. The Crown Prince patiently bore the ordeal but no sooner were the growths removed than others appeared. At Bismarck's suggestion, Vicky consulted a renowned British throat specialist, Dr Morell Mackenzie, who recommended an immediate biopsy and arranged for a further examination when the Crown Prince visited England for the Queen's Golden Jubilee celebrations.

To avoid the smog of London, Vicky and Fritz stayed in the outskirts at Upper Norwood but it was clear to the guests that, despite the Crown Prince's noble bearing in the jubilee procession, he was seriously ill. When the jubilee celebrations were over, Mackenzie removed another growth and recommended an extended period of convalescence. Vicky, Fritz and their three younger daughters enjoyed a visit to the Isle of Wight and a brief sojourn with the Queen at Balmoral before travelling to the Austrian Tyrol. As the autumn chill set in, they moved on to the warmer climes of St. Remo in Italy where 'the *gentilezza* of the young princesses captured all hearts.'[81]

Far from the damp, dust and stresses of Berlin, Fritz's condition appeared to be improving. He was happy in Italy with Vicky and their daughters who, he told a friend, 'surround us with their loving tenderness.' His recuperation seemed so effective that by October, Mackenzie was able to report that:

> "...when I saw him at Baveno he was going on very well. There never has been anything at all characteristic of malignant disease as far as (the naked eye) appearance goes..."[82]

Though he added a note of caution, Vicky was sufficiently confident to write to the Queen that she was certain of his recovery.

Within a month however, larger growths appeared and this time Mackenzie had no doubt that they were malignant.

> "Without rising from my chair I informed His Imperial Highness that a very unfavourable change had taken place in his throat.
>
> "He said, 'Is it cancer?' to which I replied, "I am sorry to say, Sir, it looks very much like it.'...The Crown Prince received the communication with perfect calmness. After a moment's silence, with a smile of peculiar sweetness, which so well express the mingled gentleness and strength of his character, he grasped my hand and said, 'I have lately been fearing something of the sort. I thank you, Sir Morell, for being so frank with me.' In all my long experience, I have never seen a man bear himself under similar circumstances with such unaffected heroism."[83]

Crown Prince Frederick
(Fritz)

The Crown Prince's condition worsened throughout the winter but by February 1888, news reached him that his father was dangerously ill and it was vital he should return to Berlin to take up his duties.

It was impossible, Vicky said, for Fritz to go back to the dusty capital before Mackenzie had re-examined him, and she immediately summoned the doctor to Italy. This time Mackenzie was forced to confirm to the family what Fritz had known all along: the tumours were cancerous and nothing could be done.

While Vicky struggled to come to terms with the devastating news, rumours ran rife through Berlin. The Crown Prince's lengthy absence and the reported use of mercury in his treatment led to speculation that he was suffering from syphilis contracted during his visit to Egypt in 1869. Disputes between Mackenzie and the German doctors exacerbated the situation until stories spread that the Crown Princess and her English doctors were deliberately killing him or alternatively keeping him alive just long enough to secure her position as Empress. Vicky's determination to maintain a cheerful appearance for Fritz's sake did nothing to allay the gossip; her smiles merely confirmed to her critics that she cared nothing for her husband and had already taken other lovers.

The German doctors recommended immediate surgery but, when Mackenzie warned that Fritz would not survive the operation, the Crown Prince

---

* Mackenzie was in fact Scottish.

declined further treatment. At the height of the tension, Willy rushed to Italy demanding a full account of the prognosis so that he might report back to the dying Kaiser. Disgusted by his bombastic manner, Vicky refused him access to his father and he returned to Berlin angry and offended, openly stating that Mackenzie was killing the Crown Prince. To Vicky's despair, Charlotte and Henry agreed and, likewise, urged their father to ignore the advice of British doctor and opt instead for surgery.

By February 1888, the tumours had grown so large that Fritz had no alternative but to undergo a tracheotomy to enable him to breathe. A month later, on 9th March 1888, a telegram arrived at his villa in Italy informing him that his father had died and he was now Emperor.

For thirty years, Vicky had been preparing for this moment. The miseries of life in Prussia had been made bearable only by the thought that one day Fritz would succeed his father and implement numerous reforms. His accession had come too late. While Fritz wept for the dead Emperor, Willy heartlessly declared that it was impossible for a man who could not speak to rule Germany and suggested that his father should abdicate in his favour. Hearing of his outburst, a disgusted Queen Victoria angrily dispatched a letter telling Vicky to send Willy and his 'odious, ungrateful wife' away to 'find their level.'

In spite of the warm welcome he received at each station, the long journey to Berlin in appalling weather exacerbated Fritz's condition, and by the time he reached the Charlottenburg Palace in the middle of a snowstorm, he was utterly exhausted. Despite his earnest pleading, Mackenzie eventually succeeded in preventing him from attending his father's funeral but he could not keep him from carrying out the necessary affairs of state, and the weight of his new responsibilities quickly took their toll.

On 24th May 1888, he struggled to attend Henry and Irène's wedding but the service exhausted him and, though he put on a brave appearance, the guests were only too aware of his pallor and the laboured whistling of his breath through the tracheotomy tube.

Within days, his health deteriorated even more alarmingly. In April, Queen Victoria, deeply saddened by the news, paid a visit to Charlottenburg to offer what comfort she could but she knew as well as anyone that there was little hope of a recovery.

Unable to implement the reforms of which he and Vicky had dreamed for so long, Fritz at least had the opportunity to grant one of his wife's dearest wishes by consenting to the marriage of Moretta and Sandro. Realising that he was dying, Fritz composed a will in which he included a message for his son and successor:

"I wish to have set in evidence as my unbiased personal opinion that I entirely acquiesce in the betrothal of your second sister with Prince Alexander of Battenberg. I charge you as a filial duty with the accomplishment of this my desire, which your sister Victoria [Moretta] for so many years has cherished in her heart. I count upon your fulfilling your duty as a son by a precise attention to my wishes, and as a brother by not withdrawing your co-operation from your sister."[84]

After reigning for only three months, the fifty-six-year-old Emperor Frederick III died at the Friedrichskron Palace, his favourite home in

151

Potsdam, surrounded by his family on 15th June 1888.

"Thus," wrote Morell Mackenzie, "passed away the noblest specimen of humanity, it has ever been my privilege to know...No one could know him even slightly without loving him...He has gone down to the grave leaving us the memory of a stainless life and a beautiful death."[85]

As his widow and daughters sat weeping at the bedside, however, Willy virtually snatched the crown from his dead father's hands. Even as Fritz lay dying, his heir had ordered a battalion of guards to surround the Friedrichskron and, the moment that Fritz breathed his last, he ordered them to prevent anyone from leaving the building. While the new Kaiser Wilhelm II ransacked his father's desk in search of incriminating documents, soldiers forbad his mother from even going into the garden to pluck flowers for her dead husband.

Willy's heartless behaviour at his father's deathbed marked only the beginning of the trials that Vicky and her younger daughters were to suffer at his hands in the early months of their bereavement. Initially Willy agreed to abide by Fritz's request that no post-mortem should be carried out on his body but, when he was approached by the German doctors seeking to discredit Mackenzie, the new Kaiser changed his mind and ordered an autopsy, after which the unceremonious funeral was carried out in such haste that few foreign royalties were able to attend. Still more distressing for his mother, Willy immediately demanded that she should send him Fritz's uniforms and effects; and for the Empress Frederick and her daughters worse was to come. Not only did he adamantly refuse to permit Moretta and Sandro to marry, but he also curtly informed his mother that she and her daughters must leave the Friedrichskron Palace, which had been the girls' home all their lives. In a deliberate attempt to erase his father's memory, he announced the palace was to revert to its original unimaginative name the New Palace. Refusing his mother's requests for various alternative accommodations, he offered her instead the smallest mansion in Potsdam.

Broken-hearted at her loss, and despairing at her son's unfilial behaviour, Vicky's sole comfort came from her younger daughters and from an empathetic mother in England. No one knew the extent of a widow's grief better than Queen Victoria, and, as usual in a family crisis, her kindness came to the fore. While urging Vicky to 'struggle on bravely' for the sake of her 'three dear girls', she offered to send a small sum of money to help them to purchase a country house, as well as extending her customary invitation to England. Grieving, ousted from their home and facing the galling prospect of having to show obeisance to their haughty and self-righteous sister-in-law, Vicky and the young princesses leaped at the chance of escaping from Berlin and gratefully accepted their grandmother's invitation.

In mid-November 1888, Moretta, Sophie and Mossy arrived with their mother for a tearful reunion with the Queen. The genuine warmth and concern with which the British people welcomed Vicky, their Princess Royal, almost tempted her into accepting Queen Victoria's offer of making England her permanent home. For three months, she and her daughters remained at Osborne and Windsor with the Queen who was 'kindness itself' but, by the time they moved on to Sandringham House in March,

Moretta could only wonder at her grandmother's evident change of attitude towards the possibility of marriage to the Battenberg prince.

Alexander of Battenberg
(Sandro)

The Queen had always championed Sandro's cause and claimed that his unceremonious ousting from his throne had turned him into 'a martyr as well as a hero.' Yet now it seemed to Moretta that her grandmother's enthusiasm had cooled. It was impossible, the Queen explained, for Moretta to disregard the will of her new Emperor and, since Willy remained obdurate, she must resign herself to life without her prince. Not until she returned to Berlin, did Moretta discover the true reason for her grandmother's change of heart.

Liko had informed the Queen that his brother's passion had waned. Waiting in Darmstadt and losing hope of ever being allowed to marry into the Hohenzollern family, Sandro had become involved with an actress in the Darmstadt theatre to whom he would soon propose.

When a heartbroken Moretta eventually discovered the truth, she rushed back to England for comfort, where 'Grandmama' held and kissed her as they wept together.

Sandro Battenberg married his actress and Moretta had no option but to reconsider her future.

Chapter 13 – Happiness Is Not To Be Hers

Hohenzollerns (Prussians)
Vicky: Queen Victoria's eldest daughter; the
widowed German Empress Frederick
> Vicky's children and their spouses:
> Willy: German Emperor - Kaiser Wilhelm II
> Dona: German Empress - Willy's wife
> Charlotte: Princess of Saxe-Meiningen
> Bernhard: Prince of Saxe-Meiningen
> Henry: Prince of Prussia
> Irène of Hesse - Henry's wife
> Moretta: Princess of Schaumburg-Lippe
> Adolph: Prince of Schaumburg-Lippe;
> Moretta's husband.
> Sophie : Crown Princess of Greece
> Tino: Crown Prince Constantine of Greece
> Mossy

Greeks
George: King of the Hellenes; brother of the Princess
of Wales.
Olga: Queen of the Hellenes.

When Empress Frederick and her daughters
returned to Germany in the spring of 1889, their
immediate priority was finding a suitable home. The
former Crown Prince's Palace in Berlin, which Willy
now offered, was too close to court to appeal to the
Empress, who spent several months viewing more
appropriate properties. One place in particular
attracted her: an old country house set in the
beautiful countryside of Krönberg in the Taunus
Mountains, not far from Homburg and Frankfurt.

Appealing as it was, the building was dilapidated and Vicky doubted she had sufficient funds for a complete renovation until a stroke of good fortune finally came her way. An old friend, the Duchess of Galliera, had recently died, leaving Vicky a large legacy which gave her the financial independence to rebuild the property.

It was a slow and time-consuming project but Vicky, utilising her artistic talents to the full, delighted in the task which distracted her not only from her recent bereavement but also from the militaristic regime that her son appeared to be espousing in Berlin. Employing only the finest artists and craftsmen, she intended to make her new home a fitting tribute to Fritz's memory, and the eventual outcome was Friedrichshof – a name chosen by her daughter, Moretta – the home that the Empress Frederick would occupy and love to the end of her life.

"The house is very like an English country house," wrote Frederick Ponsonby, "...Herr Ihne, the architect who built it, was half English, and fell in at once with the Empress Frederick's idea of making it like an English country house. The bedrooms seemed quite English except for the stove. Otherwise the house was like a museum filled with a collection of works of art and curiosities." [86]

The absorbing venture, however, did not distract Vicky from her children's futures and, throughout the summer of 1889, she was preoccupied with the imminent wedding of her daughter, Sophie.

While Moretta languished in a desperate search for a husband, her younger sister had long seemed destined for a throne. At one time, she had

Sophie of Prussia

been considered as a bride for the Russian Tsarevich Nicholas but, while visiting Marlborough House during Queen Victoria's Golden Jubilee celebrations, she met and fell in love with the Princess of Wales' nephew, the Duke of Sparta, Crown Prince Constantine (Tino) of Greece.

Queen Victoria was among the first to see the possibilities of a match between her 'very sweet' granddaughter and the attractive young soldier. Though she realised he was not the cleverest of men, she was sufficiently impressed by his looks and charm to ask Vicky if there were any possibility of a match.

Two months later, the engagement was announced and a date set for an autumn wedding, the following year. Vicky's delight at the prospect of seeing her daughter as future Queen of the Hellenes was tempered by the thought of having to part with 'dear little' Sophie but at least she could take comfort in Queen Victoria's assurance that, although Greece was far away, Sophie would surely be happy there.

Practical matters, too, concerned the Empress Frederick as Sophie prepared to leave for Athens. As she reflected upon the inadequacies of the Greek medical services, she recalled her own traumatic first childbirth and was determined to spare her daughter the same ordeal. Knowing from bitter experience how strongly foreign courts resented outside intervention, she conceived a plan to include an English midwife disguised as a lady-in-waiting in Sophie's entourage.

At four o'clock in the afternoon October 25th 1889, Sophie, her mother, sisters and the midwife arrived to a rapturous welcome in Athens. The buildings between the Royal Palace and Cathedral were draped with flags and banners and the crowds turned out in force to greet their future Queen, who 'bore herself so nicely, and was gentle, quiet and composed.' Royalties arrived from all over Europe: Tino's grandparents, the King and Queen of Denmark; the Russian Tsarevich Nicholas; the Prince and Princess of Wales; and eventually the new Kaiser and Kaiserin, accompanied, to everyone's surprise, by their own chaplain.

King George of the Hellenes (the Danish born brother of the Princess of Wales) had gone to great lengths to ensure that the wedding would pass smoothly and, as Sophie and Tino had agreed that the service would be conducted according to both the Orthodox and Lutheran rites, he had appointed his own personal chaplain to preside over the Protestant ceremony.

The arrangement suited everyone except the bride's brother, Willy. Hardly had he set foot ashore when he announced that he and his strictly evangelical wife were unhappy with the Greek King's choice and insisted that their own dogmatic chaplain should lead the service instead.

Regardless of Willy's interference, and the tears of Sophie's sisters, the wedding took place on the 27th October 1889 and passed without incident. The bride wore a white satin gown with a covering of cloth of silver, garlanded with orange blossom and myrtle. The train was also white satin, embroidered with silver thread. Unfortunately, someone had forgotten to include the bridal veil in her trousseau and she had to make do with a tulle substitute, fasten by diamond pins.

The bride and groom moved into an Athenian villa, which was to be their official residence for the next twenty-four years. In the summer heat, they were able to escape to their favourite home: a small cottage in the mountainous Tatoi Woods – 'a tiny place, smaller than Osborne Cottage (a good deal), but light and cheerful and comfortable arranged like a little French villa'[87] – where Sophie, almost as much an Anglophile as her mother, had the rooms decorated in 'the English style.' There, she and Tino followed the English routine of a good breakfast in the early morning, a light luncheon at midday and, after a siesta, afternoon tea. Far from the stiff formality of the Prussian Court, the Crown Prince and Crown Princess lived a relatively simple life, swimming in the sea, tending their gardens, planting trees and growing flowers.

Vicky's foresight in appointing the English midwife proved necessary sooner than anticipated. Eight months after the wedding, in the sweltering heat of July 1890, Sophie gave birth to a premature son, George.

Vicky and her younger daughters, who had hoped to be present for the birth, arrived too late, and by the time they reached Athens in August, they were horrified to find Sophie in a very poor state of health. In spite of the presence of the English midwife, she had suffered terribly at the hands of three inexperienced doctors who, it was rumoured, had deliberately brought on the labour so that the child might be born before Sophie's family arrived. On hearing of the events, a squeamish Queen

Victoria warned Vicky to keep Sophie's sisters from the 'unedifying and alarming details' in case it should frighten them.

Three years later, a tragic event in her household threatened Sophie's second pregnancy. Among her staff was a young nursery maid named Marie Weber, whom Vicky had recommended and sent to Greece from Germany. One afternoon, the unhappy Marie climbed to the top of the Parthenon and threw herself to the ground. She died later that evening. It was left to Sophie's youngest sister, Mossy, to break the news to Marie's parents.

Sophie, though distressed, was unharmed and five months later gave birth to a second son, Alexander. For him and for her subsequent children – Helen, Paul, Irene and Katherine, born at irregular intervals, between 1896 and 1913 – she employed only English nannies.

With Vicky's encouragement Sophie dedicated herself wholeheartedly to her duties as Crown Princess. In true family fashion, she established schemes to improve the medical services and implemented forestation programmes to aid agriculture but, for all her good intentions, her efforts were not always well-received. While she despaired of the Greeks' lack of enthusiasm for her projects, they found her stiff Prussian temperament overbearing and she lacked the personal magnetism to win great popularity.

More wounding for Sophie was the realisation that Tino was not quite the faithful and 'very good husband' that Queen Victoria had envisaged. Having been raised by parents who were totally devoted to one another, it came as a shock to discover that Tino thought nothing of entertaining mistresses and embarking upon several affairs.

The disappointment of Tino's infidelity and the lack of warmth shown her by the Greeks soon smothered much of Sophie's early enthusiasm. Her pessimism and gloom increased with age, so much so that her cousin, Missy of Edinburgh, wrote succinctly: 'she bored me.' Perhaps Missy had little patience with her cousin's complaints, for by then, in her own idiosyncratic fashion she had found a far more effective way of dealing with a husband's infidelities."

Returning to Germany after Sophie's wedding, Vicky knew that Moretta would not settle contentedly into what her grandmother piously called a state of 'blessed singleness.' Moretta could envisage no other future than marriage, and the trauma of Sandro's departure spurred her on a desperate quest for a husband. Cousins and courtiers were persuaded to assist in her search. For political reasons, Bismarck advocated the son of the Portuguese King but, since that would entail converting to Catholicism, Moretta declined. Queen Victoria examined the possibility of a match with a Swedish prince but, receiving reports of his unsuitability, concluded that he was too young.

Her aunt, Marie of Edinburgh, was eager to help and recommended two of her Russian cousins: Grand Dukes Sandro Mikhailovich and Pyotr Nikolaevich. In spite of her aversion to all things Russian, Queen Victoria raised no objections, and Moretta was delighted by the prospect of meeting the dashing Sandro Mikhailovich – 'the sailor boy'. Sadly, as with the earlier Sandro, her dreams met with disappointment. Her hopes of an encounter were repeatedly dashed and it soon became clear that

*See chapter 18

the Grand Duke had already set his sights on the Tsar's daughter, while Pyotr Nikolaevich was courting a Montenegrin princess.

Various other princes were mentioned and forgotten and, as one after another they slipped from her grasp, an increasingly despondent Moretta became convinced that she was too fat and too ugly to attract a mate. In despair, to her mother's great consternation, she launched herself on a drastic diet, exercising to extremes and virtually refusing to eat anything.

With typical good sense, Queen Victoria decided to take her anorexic granddaughter in hand. In June 1889, she invited her to England where she kept a close eye on her, even allowing her to share her own sleeping carriage on the train to Balmoral from Windsor – a privilege which, until then, had been reserved for her daughter, Beatrice. She regulated Moretta's diet and encouraged more moderate exercise but by then even a fond grandmother was coming to believe that it was unseemly and degrading to go on frantically pursuing false hopes. To Moretta's chagrin, she advised that, after so many disappointments, it would be better to abandon the pursuit of a husband and resign herself to spinsterhood. To make matters worse for Moretta, the presence of Sandro's brother and sister at Balmoral revived old wounds, and the announcement of the engagement of her younger cousin, Louise˙ added to her despair.

_____

* see chapter 15

At twenty-three years old, Moretta believed she was growing beyond marriageable age. Her elder sister, Charlotte, and three of her Hessian cousins had married before their twenty-second birthdays and even her own younger sister, Sophie, was already married.

Victoria Moretta of Prussia

"I shall never, never marry – all my relations, sisters, friends do, except my stupid self," she wailed to her mother. "I am too ugly and nobody will have me..."[88]

She tried briefly to put all hopes from her head but, finding the state of singleness anything but blessed, her thoughts repeatedly returned to her unhappy plight. Everywhere she looked, she saw men with whom she dreamed she might be happy, and redoubled her relentless pursuit of love so frenetically that Willy rather cruelly observed that she would marry 'anyone who was manly.' His comment was not entirely unjust. Even Vicky was afraid that Moretta might throw herself at any available young man who showed an interest in her, while Queen Victoria warned against allowing her to mix too freely with 'unsuitable' people, and both were relieved when a minor German Prince, Adolph of Schaumburg-Lippe, arrived in Homburg and seemed quite taken with the lonely princess.

The somewhat scruffy soldier prince was neither well-educated nor well-travelled but he had good health and a respectable reputation and when, within days of their first meeting, he proposed Moretta accepted him.

The following June, Adolph was whisked off to Windsor for inspection by his future grandmother-in-law. In spite of the satisfactory if somewhat uncouth impression he made upon the English court, Moretta herself was hardly enthusiastic about her prospective groom. It was not a love-match; it was widely rumoured that Moretta did not even like her husband and was marrying solely 'for the sake of marriage' but at least she would be free of the stigma of spinsterhood and could look forward to raising a family of her own.

On the evening of 19th November 1890, wearing the veil that her mother had worn to her own wedding thirty-three years earlier, Moretta made her vows in a civil ceremony in the old Schloss in Berlin before moving on to the chapel for the religious service. An observer noted:

> "The Bride looked lovely and if, as people said, she was marrying a man whom she disliked, she did not allow people to know it by her face."[89]

Though attended by numerous foreign royalties including the Crown Princes of Greece and Roumania, it was a relatively simple affair by royal standards as many of the traditional festivities were curtailed by Empress Dona's pregnancy. Even so, according to one guest, Moretta's cousin, Marie Louise, the celebrations lasted long enough to become monotonous:

> "There was of course, a wedding feast and afterwards the traditional torchlight procession, when the bridegroom, preceded by pages, holding in their hands candelabra…had to lead

each princess right round the room bowing to the Emperor and Empress. The best man then led the bride around the room in the same manner, and all the princes and princesses did likewise. You can imagine how long this took and how very bored we became."[90]

As Marie Louise found distraction elsewhere·, a weeping Moretta prepared to say goodbye to her family. The prospect of leaving her mother cast a shadow over the celebrations, and her leave-taking was not made any easier when Willy entered into a dispute with his sister, Sophie, which would take five years to resolve.¨

Late in the evening, amid many tears the couple left for their honeymoon in Egypt.

If Moretta was not in love with her husband, she at least had the joy of discovering that by the end of her extended holiday she was pregnant. After long years of failed romances it seemed that at last the future was bright and, in early February, three months after her wedding, she cheerfully set out from Cairo to take the good tidings to her sister, Sophie, in Athens.

A holiday of several weeks had been planned and Sophie eagerly awaited her sister's arrival with a view to showing her all the splendours of Greece. Moretta had been in the city for only an hour and a half when she suddenly announced that she and Adolph must leave at once for Homburg. The following day Vicky received a 'frantic' telegram from Sophie, telling her that Moretta was urgently rushing home.

The cause of the sudden departure soon became apparent. Moretta had suffered a miscarriage

---

· see chapter 17
✦ see chapter 21

and, while the sympathetic Queen advised her to 'have some rest' before 'beginning again,' it emerged that Moretta would never be able to have children. It must have seemed at that moment that her desperate longing for a husband and family had been jinxed from the start and further disappointments were soon to follow.

Adolph's native principality, Lippe, on the borders of Hanover and Westphalia had been ruled for twenty years by the childless Prince Waldemar. The prince's brother and rightful successor was so hopelessly insane that he was incapable of ruling and so, in a secret decree, Waldemar had appointed Adolph to act as regent after his death.

Following Prince Waldemar's death in 1895, Adolph prepared to take up his new role and he and Moretta arrived in the picturesque capital, Detmold, where they received a warm greeting from the crowds who gathered to welcome them to the city. The quaint little town with its medieval buildings was surrounded by beautiful forests, and both Adolph and Moretta envisaged a happy future there – but again their hopes were dashed. Other branches of the extended Lippe family were dissatisfied with Waldemar's secret arrangement and contested his decree. A prolonged court hearing ensued which took almost two years to resolve until, in the summer 1897, the court found in favour of the contesters, forcing Adolph and Moretta to leave the town.

It was yet another blow for Moretta but it drew her and Adolph closer together, so much so that by the following year Queen Victoria's lady-in-waiting, Marie Mallet, thought them 'a devoted couple and she has changed much and for the better in her personal appearance, being now a graceful good-looking woman.'[91]

The same year, they settled into a villa in Bonn, which they had rebuilt in the style of an English country house on the banks of the Rhine.

Settled into her new home, Moretta's life sank into a stagnant routine. Daily she wrote to her mother, bemoaning her childlessness, but, although she had not discovered the 'grand passion' of her dreams, she had at least found a faithful husband, leaving Vicky free to turn her attention to her one remaining daughter.

Chapter 14 – My Benjamin

Vicky: German Empress Frederick
Mossy (Margaret): Vicky's youngest daughter

Eddy: Prince Albert Victor, Duke of Clarence &
Avondale, eldest son of the Prince of Wales.
Eddy's sisters:
> Louise
> Toria
> Maud

Alix of Hesse: Youngest surviving daughter of
Princess of Alice
Ella: Grand Duchess Serge of Russia; Alix's elder
sister

Lenchen: Princess Christian; Queen Victoria's third
daughter.
Thora: Lenchen's daughter

By 1893, the Empress Frederick had
completed her work on the Friedrichshof and settled
comfortably into her new home with her youngest
daughter, Mossy. Between riding, reading and
writing interminable letters, she devoted much of her
time to philanthropic activities. In Krönberg, she
founded and regularly visited a hospital, built alms-
houses and established a school, but her chief
concern, as ever, was her family. Reluctant as she
was to part with her youngest child, whom she
referred to as 'my Benjamin[*]', it was time to find an
appropriate husband for Mossy.

Already several suitors had been suggested,
among them the young Tsarevich Nicholas, but he,

---

[*] A reference to the youngest and most beloved child of the Biblical Jacob.

in love with Mossy's cousin, Alix of Hesse, declared he would rather become a monk than marry the Prussian princess. Mossy, moreover, had no intention of converting to Orthodoxy, as was required of a future Tsarina.

In 1891, Queen Victoria proposed a more suitable candidate: Mossy's cousin, Eddy, Prince Albert Victor, Duke of Clarence and Avondale. As the eldest son of the Prince of Wales, Eddy was second-in-line to the throne, and Queen Victoria had little doubt that princesses would be queuing up to ascend to 'the highest position there is.' It came as a shock to discover that she had overestimated her beloved Eddy's attraction.

In truth, though his mother and sisters adored him, none of his cousins was drawn to the young prince. A very poor scholar, listless and lethargic, he was so dependent upon his younger brother that even when he spent a brief stint in the navy, George was sent with him. In fact, much of his supposed lack of intelligence was undoubtedly due to the deafness which he had inherited from his mother, but in his lifetime, and still more since his death, many false rumours were spread about his lack of interest in affairs of state and his relentless pursuit of pleasure.

The fact that one of his associates was involved in the Cleveland Street scandal*, led to speculation that the prince was bisexual, and by the late 1880s, it was said that he had contracted syphilis. There is little evidence to substantiate the rumours and, even if they were true, the stories must have escaped the Queen's notice or she would not

---

* The scandal involved a police raid of a male brothel on Cleveland Street, allegedly patronised by many aristocrats. The government was accused of covering up the scandal to protect the wealthy and influential clients.

have been so keen to promote a match between Eddy and one of her favourite granddaughters.

In spite of the Prince Consort's warnings of the need to bring new dark blood into the family, Queen Victoria favoured marriage between first cousins. After all, she and Albert had been cousins and, since their progeny crowded the courts of Europe, there were few available royalties who were not somehow related. Of all Eddy's cousins none seemed, in Queen Victoria's eyes, better suited to the role of future Queen Consort than the intelligent and devout Princess Alix of Hesse.

Since her mother's death, Alix had spent a good deal of time at the English court and held a particularly high place in her grandmother's affection. Her Hessian good looks were sure to appeal to the sensuous Eddy and, more to the point, in the Queen's view, betrothal to her cousin would distract her from the handsome Tsarevich, to whom she had lost her heart while visiting her sister, Ella, in Russia.

For Ella, who was busily promoting *that* match, the idea that Alix should marry the hapless Eddy was 'absolutely ridiculous.' Apart from his physical frailty, he was 'quite stupid' in Ella's opinion and, though his genuine kindness had its appeal, he held no real attraction for Alix. For several months under sustained pressure from both families, Alix wavered until at last, she gently refused his proposal.

It was not the first time that one of her Hessian granddaughters had thwarted the Queen's plans for a family wedding but she resigned herself to the outcome and wasted little time with regrets. There were other granddaughters of the right age and temperament: Mossy of Prussia, for instance.

Unlike Cousin Alix, Mossy was not, in her grandmother's opinion, 'regularly pretty' but she had 'a pretty figure' and a great love for England.

The prospect of her daughter happily settled in her own childhood home delighted Vicky and when she received a letter from Mossy's sister, Sophie, praising Eddy's gentle kindness, she needed no further assurance. In February 1891, Mossy accompanied her mother to Paris where French journalists wrote several complimentary descriptions of the svelte, blonde, Prussian princess. From France they journeyed to England for a holiday at Sandringham in the hope that Mossy and Eddy might fall in love.

The plan was doomed to fail. By then Eddy had become infatuated with the daughter of the deposed French Emperor, Hélène of Orleans, and Mossy was in the throes of an unrequited passion for a German cousin, Max of Baden. It soon became apparent there was even less chance of pairing Eddy with Mossy than there had been with Alix of Hesse.

It was probably just as well. The Princess of Wales would never have approved of a Prussian daughter-in-law and much preferred the Catholic Hélène, whom Eddy was meeting regularly at the home of his sister, Louise. Eventually, at his mother's prompting, he even went so far as to propose to the French princess before rushing her off to the Queen to announce their engagement. Touched as she was by the romance, Queen Victoria was powerless to intervene. The law prevented the heir to the throne from marrying a Catholic and even when Hélène offered to seek a papal dispensation to convert to Anglicanism, ministers pointed out that it would be impossible to receive the deposed Emperor's daughter without damaging England's relationship with Republican France. Eddy resigned himself to the inevitable and within a year had proposed to, and been accepted by, his childhood friend, Princess May of Teck.

Queen Victoria was satisfied with the outcome and considered May sensible, pretty and reliable but not everyone in the family shared her delight. Vicky considered her 'rather stiff' and lacking in charm, while Eddy's sisters mocked her dullness. The jealously protective Princess of Wales, while conceding that May would make a reliable wife, was reluctant to hand over her precious son to any other woman, and in Cumberland Lodge Aunt Lenchen was most put out that Eddy had chosen the lower-born May before her own eligible daughter, Thora.

In the event, the complaint was immaterial. During the bitterly cold January of 1892, the Waleses gathered at Sandringham for Eddy's birthday. It was hardly going to be the most thrilling event: his brother, George, was recovering from typhoid, frail Toria was in bed with influenza and most of the rest of the family had colds. On the day before his birthday, while out shooting with his father, the prince became ill and returned to the house to join the other invalids. The following morning he managed to make a brief appearance to open his presents but was too weak to participate in the planned festivities. That evening influenza was diagnosed and for the next few days, while his anxious mother and sisters sat mopping his brow, he drifted in and out of consciousness, repeatedly whispering 'Hélène,' until, in the early morning 14th January 1892, he died surrounded by his family. Even the sheltered world of the Waleses was not immune to tragedy.

Meanwhile, in the Friedrichshof, Mossy, recovering from her infatuation with Max of Baden, met and fell in love with the scholarly Frederick (Fischy) a brother of the Landgrave of neighbouring Hesse-Kassel. He may not have been the most illustrious of princes, but Vicky, more concerned with Mossy's happiness than her position, was delighted.

Queen Victoria's response was typically guarded. Although she had recently been pressing for a match with Prince Albert Victor, she now decided that it would be better for Mossy to remain single to devote her life to the service of her widowed mother. Happily, Vicky had no intention of putting the same pressure on Mossy as the Queen had once put on Beatrice, and, putting aside her own feelings, willingly gave them her blessing.

The usual gathering of royalties arrived for the wedding in Potsdam on 25th January 1893. From England, Queen Victoria sent a ring and other gifts for the bride. Willy, despite his complaint that a mere Landgrave was unworthy of the Kaiser's sister, behaved himself well, and only the brother of the straight-laced Empress Dona marred the occasion by entertaining the visiting Tsarevich with dancing girls and plying him with so much drink that he could barely stand.

Margaret of Prussia (Mossy)

Mossy and Fischy moved into the peaceful Schloss Rumpenheim – an ancient castle given to them in trust by Fischy's elder brother – and began what was to be probably the happiest marriage of any of Vicky's daughters. The Queen's fears that Vicky would be lonely once Mossy had left home proved largely unfounded. Mossy and Fischy regularly stayed at Friedrichshof where their cordiality impressed all who came to visit. Vicky's admiration for her studious son-in-law increased by the day; he shared her love of art and architecture, and repeatedly in her letters to Mossy, she *wished* that Fischy could have been with her to share a particular experience, a scenic view or an impressive building. She trusted his judgement so implicitly that she came to rely on his advice in political and family matters.

Within days of the wedding Mossy conceived her first child, causing her grandmother to worry that the draughty old Schloss was unsuitable for a woman in such a condition, but in October 1893, Mossy's gave birth to a healthy son, Friedrich. The following year a second son, Max, was born, to be followed in 1896 by twin boys, Philipp and Wolfgang – an event which delighted the Queen who 'laughed very much and is rather amused at the list of her great grandchildren being added to in such a rapid manner.'[92]

A second set of twins Christoph and Richard were born in 1901. Like their parents, they were gentle studious boys who had no appetite for militarism. Alice Topham, the English governess to Willy's daughter, recalled a visit they made to Berlin in 1903. Standing beneath a painting of a great Prussian victory, eight-year-old Max said:

> "My father says war isn't like that at all. He says it's not so clean and bright and that shells tear the men and horses to pieces and it's horrible."[93]

In little over a decade, Max and his brothers would realise the tragic accuracy of their father's words.

Chapter 15 – It Really Is Not Wise To Leave These Girls Dans la Vague

Waleses
Bertie & Alexandra: Prince & Princess of Wales
    Children of Bertie & Alexandra:
    Louise, Duchess of Fife
    Toria (Victoria)
    Maud
    George, Duke of York

May of Teck: Duchess of York
Carl: Prince of Denmark; nephew of the Princess of Wales

Christians
Lenchen (Helena): Queen Victoria's third daughter
Christian: Lenchen's husband
Thora: Elder daughter of Lenchen & Christian

Content that her daughters were finally settled, Vicky could only gaze askance at her Wales nieces confined in their childhood home with no apparent desire to escape.

Leaving the sheltered world of the nursery was no easy matter for the daughters of the Princess of Wales. Awkward in company and shy among strangers, none of them hoped for a great match in the court of a foreign king, and yet, as they watched their cousins precede them to the altar, even the 'whispering Waleses' harboured hopes of the limited independence that marriage might bring.

Unlike Moretta, they had neither an obstinate Kaiser nor an arrogant court to contend with; for the Waleses the chief obstacle was their mother's reluctance to break up her happy family. With a possessiveness surpassing even that of Queen Victoria, Princess Alexandra clung to her children, carelessly dismissing their pleas to find them suitable *partis* before it was too late.

Louise of Wales

Louise was the first to strain at the apron strings though her manner of escape raised a few eyebrows at court. As the eldest daughter of the heir to the British Empire, the twenty-two-year-old princess might have married one of several foreign princes but home-loving Louise opted instead for a forty-year-old friend of her father's, Alexander Macduff, Earl of Fife.

Although immensely rich, the uncouth and ill-mannered Macduff was certainly no great catch in the eyes of the aristocracy but to shrinking Louise he offered the possibility of vanishing into the luxurious obscurity of his several Scottish estates. In spite of the age difference, Louise was delighted by his proposal and one member of her household observed that 'there was never anyone more in love.'

Since Macduff shared his passion for racing and shooting, the Prince of Wales approved of the match, and even Louise's mother was content, knowing that her daughter would not have to leave the country. Queen Victoria, with her fondness for Scotsmen, was equally content and as part of her wedding present elevated Macduff from Earl to Duke of Fife.

After an engagement lasting less than a month, the wedding took place in July 1889 in the flower-bedecked chapel of Buckingham Palace, where Cousins Thora and Marie Louise of Schleswig-Holstein acted as bridesmaids. The wedding dress enhanced Louise's features, and observers commented on how graceful and charming she appeared. The Queen was less impressed, observing that, as Louise whispered her vows and fumbled with the wedding ring, she looked very pale and unbecoming.

Marriage revitalised Louise. Spending much of her time at Macduff's London home, Sheen Lodge, or travelling around his Scottish estates far away from her mother's pampering, her health improved dramatically. Though a stillborn baby blighted the early years of her marriage, Louise found happiness with her fatherly husband and in May 1891 she gave birth to a healthy daughter whom she dutifully named Alexandra after the Princess of Wales. The baby was christened at Windsor with her Aunt Toria among the godmothers. Eighteen months later, Louise was excusing herself from a visit to Windsor for Christmas, because, she was once more *enceinte.*

A second daughter, Maud, 'a pretty little thing but very small', was born the following April.

The Princess of Wales might complain that she saw too little of her grandchildren but Louise was happy. She took up fishing and cycling and according to one observer, even her appearance improved.

The same could not be said for her younger sisters.

Gloomily recovering from their brother's death and traipsing around after their mother on her many foreign jaunts, Toria and Maud were finding the state of singleness increasingly onerous. As Cousin Moretta had already discovered, it was humiliating to attend so many family weddings while their mother firmly refused to make any effort to encourage appropriate suitors.

"It is really not wise to leave these dear girls *dans la vague*," Vicky warned Queen Victoria, who drew the matter to the attention of their father. The Prince of Wales' response was discouraging. He understood Vicky's concern, he said, but his wife was reluctant to part with the girls, both of whom he believed were quite happy to remain single.

The Prince of Wales was mistaken. Toria felt her spinsterhood as keenly as any of her cousins. Though her health had not improved with age – she had even felt faint at Cousin Sophie's wedding and had to miss some of the celebrations – she had every reason to remain optimistic. Many royalties would have been delighted at the chance of becoming a son-in-law of the future King, and various gentlemen of the court and foreign princes had been mentioned as prospective candidates but the Princess of Wales stubbornly dismissed each suggestion.

Stifled and frustrated, Toria's health deteriorated under the strain, so much so that, during a visit to England in 1894, the Tsarevich Nicholas recorded that she had become much thinner and did not look well.

Her younger sister, Maud, on the other hand, gained weight and fell into a 'malheureuse passion' for the handsome but wayward brother of the Duchess of York, Prince Francis of Teck. 'Frank' did not reciprocate her feelings and when it was discovered that he that was conducting an affair with an older, married woman, any hope of a possible match came to a sudden end.

While Toria fretted and fainted, Maud refused to lose heart and persistently pleaded with her mother to find her an eligible prince. She briefly entertained the idea of marrying the much-sought-after Max of Baden but he showed little interest in her, and her efforts to meet him were repeatedly dashed. At last, shortly before her twenty-sixth birthday, a suitable candidate appeared in the person of her first cousin, Prince Carl of Denmark, the second son of Princess Alexandra's brother, the future King Frederick VIII. Though he was two years Maud's junior, and looked much younger, he was charming and handsome and, being Danish, even the protective Princess of Wales had no objections to the match.

The engagement was announced on 28th October 1895 after which Carl departed for a five month tour of the West Indies, leaving Maud time to fret about the trauma of leaving the fairy tale world of her childhood. His return in the spring restored her spirits and the wedding took place in the private chapel of Buckingham Palace on Wednesday 22nd July 1896, where the bridesmaids included Maud's sister, Toria, Cousin Thora of Schleswig-Holstein, the two Connaught princesses, Daisy and Patsy, and Alice of Albany.

As a wedding present, the Prince of Wales gave his daughter Appleton Lodge on the Sandringham estate so that she might return home whenever she wished. Even so, it was almost six months before Maud could bear to tear herself away from her family. Shortly before Christmas 1896, she said her tearful goodbyes and set sail for

Copenhagen, which was to be her home for the next nine years.

It was a happy marriage, marred only in its early years by Maud's failure to conceive. Seven years passed before she gave birth to her only son, Alexander.

Maud's departure for Denmark left Toria lonelier and more desperate to make a life of her own. At the same time it strengthened her mother's resolve to cling to her one remaining daughter.

Victoria of Wales (Toria)

Increasingly deaf, the Princess of Wales had become so reliant on Toria's company that she barely allowed her out of her sight and was rarely seen anywhere without the dowdier princess trailing like a puppy at her heels.

Humiliated by the stigma of spinsterhood and compelled to endure the tedium of her mother's endless Danish excursions, the sight of her numerous married cousins only increased her pain. As if her loneliness were not enough, every year the Princess of Wales thoughtlessly invited many of Toria's married friends to her birthday parties; but for the unhappy princess, the most wounding blow of all was her mother's refusal to consider a proposal of marriage from the widowed Prime Minister, Lord Rosebery, with whom she had fallen in love. Notwithstanding the fact that Louise had already married a commoner, the Princess of Wales argued that Rosebery was unworthy of a daughter of the future King. It was Toria's last chance of escape from her mother's domination and, that having failed, she gave way to her numerous psychosomatic ailments and became increasingly resentful and unpopular with the younger members of the family.

The death of Prince Albert Victor dramatically altered the eligibility status of his younger brother, George. Now his wife would eventually assume what Queen Victoria had called 'the greatest position there is' and again the hunt was on for an appropriate bride. Reputedly more intelligent than his brother, George was popular with his cousins. Sophie thought him 'such a dear & so awfully amusing,' while in later years Marie Louise would describe him as:

> "...one of the kindest and most generous men you can imagine. Under that rather gruff manner was the most considerate of hearts. He carried out in full the principle of not letting his right hand know what his left hand did. His generosity, unknown to the outside world, was perfectly wonderful."[94]

But it was Marie Louise's sister, Thora, who began an earnest quest to win his heart. Her mother, Lenchen, was determined that this time her daughter would not be overlooked and encouraged twenty-two-year-old Thora to make herself noticed. Hovering in George's presence and offering him her photograph, the naïve princess succeeded only in incurring Aunt Alix's ridicule. The Princess of Wales had still not forgiven Prince Christian's part in the Schleswig-Holstein affair, and dismissed the possibility of his daughter marrying George, in a sarcastic letter to her son:

"So the Xtians have been following you about with their lovely Snipe! Well it will be a pleasure to expect that beauty as your bride – when may we expect the news? You see she is quite prepared to take you by storm already offering you her contrafeit (sic) in a frame."[95]

Even without the Princess of Wales' acid comments, Thora had little hope of attracting the prince. George had already fallen under the spell of another cousin, five years her junior: Affie's eldest daughter, Missy of Edinburgh.

During his naval days, George had often stayed with the Edinburghs at San Antonio in Malta where he and Missy had become great 'chums.' The young princess appreciated his friendship and enjoyed his company but his reserved manner was no match for her passionate nature. Nor was Missy's mother, the Duchess of Edinburgh, enthralled by the prospect of her daughter as future Queen of England – a country she had come to despise. When George eventually summoned the courage to propose, Missy refused him.

Affronted and angry at the refusal, the Prince of Wales blamed Missy's father for the outcome, while the Princess of Wales scathingly remarked that her Edinburgh niece was still a mere 'baby, barely out of petticoats.' Baby or not, within months, the seventeen-year-old princess announced her engagement to Ferdinand of Hohenzollern-Sigmaringen, the twenty-seven-year-old heir presumptive to the throne of Roumania.

The following year the problem of George's marriage reached a happy conclusion. Since Eddy's

---

* see chapter 18

death, he had grown close to his late brother's fiancée, May of Teck, and there seemed no reason why she should not transfer her affection from one brother to the next. There had been a precedent in royal circles: the Princess of Wales' sister had once been engaged to the then Tsarevich, and, following his early demise, happily married his younger brother, the future Tsar Alexander III.

May was willing, but undemonstrative George, fearful perhaps of a second refusal, dithered until his sister, Louise, decided to take the matter in hand. In March 1893, she invited George and May to her home, Sheen Lodge in Richmond, in the hope that he would propose. Still he tarried until, thanks to Louise's cajoling, he eventually dared to broach the subject with May, who instantly consented.

The wedding took place in July 1893. Nine of Queen Victoria's granddaughters acted as bridesmaids: George's sisters, Toria and Maud; the three younger Edinburgh girls, Ducky, Alexandra and Baby Bee; Daisy and Patsy Connaught; and six-year-old Ena of Battenberg. The ninth, with remarkable good grace in view of the snub she had received, was Thora of Schleswig-Holstein.

There were many at court who believed Thora to have been an excellent contender for 'the highest position there is.' Though she may not have been as pretty as some of her cousins or her younger sister, Marie Louise, her common sense and gentleness endeared her to all the family and there were some who believed she would have made an ideal bride for the future Tsar Nicholas.

But Thora was cautious when it came to choosing a husband. As far back as 1890, Aunt Vicky wished 'someone nice' could be found for her and, four years later, after the embarrassment of George's rejection, suggested a minor German prince, Ernst of Hohenlohe-Langenburg, a grandson of Queen Victoria's half-sister, Feodora. Nothing came of the plan and Ernst later married Thora's cousin, Alexandra of Edinburgh. Almost a decade passed and no suitable candidate appeared. In 1899, there was a vague possibility of a match with a minor Catholic prince but, in spite of her advanced age, the twenty-seven-year-old princess was wary in view of the disparity between their religions.

Helena Victoria (Thora)

Again, the plans came to nothing and Thora settled happily into a life of 'blessed singleness' devoting her attention to her brothers, her parents, her grandmother and her mother's charitable causes. Far from being stifled in a loveless marriage, the intelligent and open-minded princess enjoyed her freedom and travelled widely, visiting her cousins in Germany and Russia. Her two brothers also remained single and, though both Christian Victor, who served in the British Army, and Albert who served in Germany, were often away on active duty the family remained very close.

Thora also enjoyed the company of her grandmother whom she saw almost daily as she and her mother followed the annual migrations between Osborne, Balmoral and Windsor. Living in such close proximity to the Queen, she was a regular participant in state dinners where, conversing with politicians and statesmen, she developed her own firm views about politics and world affairs, some of which brought her into conflict with her equally politically-minded mother.

Unlike Toria of Wales, Thora was content, justifying the Queen's claim that single people were often far happier than married people, many of whom were enslaved in loveless relationships.

The Queen was speaking from experience: by the turn of the century she was convinced that several of her granddaughters were suffering such a fate.

Chapter 16 – All I Can Repeat Is That I Am Perfectly Happy.

Ella: Grand Duchess Serge of Russia; second daughter of Princess Alice
Serge: Grand Duke Serge Alexandrovich; Ella's husband; younger brother of Tsar Alexander III.
Victoria: Ella's sister; Princess Louis of Battenberg

When Victoria of Hesse married Louise Battenberg in April 1884, Queen Victoria had more on her mind than the aberration of the bride's father and the unforeseen romance between Beatrice and Liko. Though, of course, she had been informed in advance, the announcement of Ella's engagement to a Russian Grand Duke sent a shiver of terror down a fond grandmother's spine.

Since her formal entry into society three years previously, nineteen-year-old Ella might have had her pick of several European princes. Renowned as one of the most beautiful women in Europe, word of her charm, intelligence and gentleness brought proposals from many quarters. While Cousin Willy was still smarting at her rebuttal, Prince Leopold entreated her father not to throw her away on a dull Scandinavian prince who was earnestly seeking her hand. Ella herself had turned down the son of the Duke of Manchester, and in 1883 Queen Victoria was mildly disappointed to hear that she had declined the proposal of her childhood friend, Fritz of Baden. The Queen's disappointment turned to horror when she discovered that Ella had rejected him in favour of 'a Russian!'

Apart from his great wealth, there was little to commend Grand Duke Serge Alexandrovich to the Queen. Not only was he a Russian and a Romanov –

a younger brother of Tsar Alexander III – but his highly-strung nature and unyielding reactionary views had created many enemies in his native St. Petersburg. His natural reticence gave him a haughty air and the assassination of his father, Alexander II, had filled him with such a deep hatred of revolutionaries that he would mercilessly oppose any reform that might undermine the Romanov autocracy.

Nor was the Grand Duke's appearance particularly appealing to a Queen. His niece, Ella's cousin, Missy of Roumania, thought him strikingly handsome, but noticed, too, the coldness in his steely-grey eyes. The French Ambassador, Maurice Paléologue observed that his face was disagreeable,

Grand Duke Serge Alexandrovich

'distinguished by greyish-white eyebrows and a hard look.'[96] Tall and extremely thin, he accentuated his gaunt figure by wearing whalebone corsets that showed through his clothes.

As if that were not enough to disenchant the Queen, she might well have heard the more insidious rumours, emanating from St. Petersburg.

"Try as I will," wrote his cousin Sandro Mikhailovich, "I cannot find a single redeeming feature in his character...obstinate, arrogant, disagreeable, he flaunted his many peculiarities in the face of the entire nation, providing the enemies of the regime with inexhaustible material for calumnies and libels."[97]

Stories of his alleged peculiarities were to haunt the Grand Duke all his life. As a young man, his devotion to the officers of his beloved Preobrazhensky Regiment led to speculation that he was homosexual and his apparent reluctance to marry added further fuel to the rumours.

What, Queen Victoria wondered, could attract 'dear lovely Ella' to such an unpleasant man? It was true that Princess Alice had been fond of the shy little boy who, throughout Ella's childhood, had often accompanied his consumptive mother on her recuperative visits to her native Hesse-Darmstadt. It was equally true that he was very different from the bombastic Willy, and Ella had responded with affection to his friendship; but now, surrounded by so many more sparkling suitors, the aloof Grand Duke

Ella of Hesse

seemed a most unlikely choice. He had made little impression upon Ella when he accompanied his mother on her final visit to Darmstadt in 1879, and she had even confessed to her sister that she found him rather boring. Yet, when he returned to Hesse after his father's assassination, her opinion changed dramatically.

Perhaps it was his heartfelt sorrow at the loss of his father that convinced her that his brittle exterior concealed a more sensitive nature. Having lost her own mother, Ella empathised with his grief and, spending more time in his company, gradually came to realise that, in spite of their disparate political and religious opinions, they shared the same aesthetic interest in music and art, inspired by a deeply spiritual temperament.

Gossip spread quickly through the family and, by the time of Victoria's engagement, word of Ella's growing attachment to the Russian had reached a horrified Queen Victoria in Scotland. Summoning her granddaughter to Balmoral, the Queen earnestly attempted to dissuade her from the match. Princess Alice, she claimed, would never have wanted her daughter to marry a Russian. The vast Romanov wealth would 'turn Ella's head'; the country was unstable and St. Petersburg society, immoral. The thought that Ella might be led astray by the 'unscrupulous' Russians was more than the Queen could bear; and if that were not disconcerting enough, Ella need only think of the cold Russian climate, which that would ruin her health, as it had that of several German princesses including Serge's own mother.

Chastened by the lecture and unwilling to distress her grandmother, Ella assured the Queen that she had no intention of marrying Serge and that she would 'hate to live in Russia.' She returned to Darmstadt in the early autumn determined to put him from her mind and when Serge proposed, she refused him. Though the Russians, including Serge's sister, the Duchess of Edinburgh, considered the refusal an insult, the relieved Queen was filled with admiration for her granddaughter's independence and strength of character. She had yet to discover quite how independent Ella could be.

Serge's proposal had come at a time of great upheaval in Darmstadt. The New Palace was buzzing in preparation for Victoria's wedding and her father was on the point of marrying Madame de Kolomine. Within a month of Ella's departure from Scotland, the Queen was alarmed to hear that Serge had received a further invitation to Hesse and could only pray that, in his presence, Ella would not yield.

Her hopes were in vain. Whether it was the sense of romance in the air, or she had truly fallen in love, when Serge proposed for a second time Ella accepted him. It was left to Victoria to break the news to the Queen, before Ella dared pick up her pen to write to 'dearest Grandmama' with some trepidation:

> "...I am afraid this letter will not give you as much pleasure as I should wish but as it concerns my happiness and you have always been so kind to me, I wish you to know what I think about Serge...though he may have opinions you do not like, do you not think, dear Grandmama, that I might do him good?
> ...I shall try to keep to the right path and will always keep those I love in my mind and follow their good example...I think I know what I'm doing and if I am unhappy, which I am sure I never will be, it will all be my doing, as you know. Please forgive me if you are vexed with what I shall do, and although I will have to begin a new life, I will always cling to those who have been dearer to me than I can say."[98]

As Ella struggled to stand up in the numerous jewels which Serge lavished upon her at their engagement, Queen Victoria could only shake her head in despair.

Six weeks after Victoria's wedding, the royalties migrated to St. Petersburg where, on 15th June 1884, Ella and Serge were married according to both the Lutheran and Orthodox rites in the chapel of the Winter Palace. Cousin Willy, having made tactful excuses for his absence, missed the beautiful spectacle of his first love, draped in Russian Court dress and the jewels of Catherine the Great, walking down the aisle 'on the arm of haughty Sergei.' Even so, the Prussians managed to use the celebrations to humiliate the Battenbergs. Still angered by Moretta's attachment to Sandro, Bismarck whispered a word in Russian ears to ensure that during the wedding banquet Louis Battenberg was placed as far away as possible from the top table where his wife, Victoria, was seated near the bride.

After the wedding, the celebrations continued for a further ten days before Ella, now Grand Duchess Elizaveta Feodorovna, bade goodbye to her family. She and Serge travelled east for a honeymoon on his country estate, Ilinskoe, not far from Moscow, where her generosity and eagerness to learn everything about her new homeland quickly endeared her to the villagers. In the autumn, the couple returned to the magnificent Beloselsky-Belozersky Palace in St. Petersburg for the season, which ran from New Year's Eve to the first day of Lent, and Ella threw herself into the social life of the capital, winning admiration in the ballrooms and receptions of the aristocracy.

The winter days were filled with skating parties, theatre visits and balls where, dripping in the jewels that Serge lavished upon her, she often disappeared partway through the evening only to reemerge in an entirely new gown and another set of priceless gems.

> "To please her husband," wrote her lady-in-waiting, "she cultivated society, and society admired her. Radiantly beautiful she showed herself at balls, sparkling with jewels but on her calm brow, her vocation was already printed..."[99]

Devoted to her husband, popular at court and loved by the people, life appeared idyllic for the naïve Grand Duchess but, within months of her wedding, rumours began to surface, that would plague her for the next twenty years.

Marriage had done nothing to improve Serge's reputation. On the contrary, Ella's calmness and passivity contrasted so sharply with his shortness of temper and dictatorial manner that her very presence at his side seemed to highlight the flaws in his character. Observers, disgusted by the way he criticised and humiliated her in public, were convinced he must be still crueller when they were alone. It was said that he was so jealous that he spied on all her movements, refused to allow her to go out without his permission and that he even read all her letters.

While Ella could not deny that Serge made every decision affecting their lives – even to choosing her partners at balls – the rumours of his unkindness were greatly exaggerated and caused her far more pain than his supposedly cruel treatment of her; but, however vehemently she protested that she 'adored' her husband and was 'perfectly happy' in Russia, increasingly outlandish stories spread not only through Russia but via the large family network to all the courts of Europe. Within six months of her marriage German newspapers were reporting that she was about to be divorced.

Queen Victoria was deeply troubled. She had dreaded this marriage from the start and now the rumours that she heard convinced her that her fears were well-founded. Ella's letters repeatedly assured her that all was well but the protestations of happiness served only to increase the Queen's doubts.

What was more, as the Queen could not fail to observe, there was evidence enough that something was awry in the marriage: many months had passed since the wedding yet Ella showed no sign of conceiving a child. In a family where children were as numerous 'as the rabbits in Windsor Park' her childlessness proved to Serge's detractors that he was homosexual and had no interest in his wife. Increasingly salacious stories proliferated. Some claimed, without justification, that Ella refused to yield to Serge's 'unnatural' perversions while others, more charitably but no less humiliatingly, believed that the shock of his father's death had left him impotent.

It is possible that Ella was simply unable to have children. Since her adolescence, her grandmother had often commented on her frailty and, with her usual euphemistic references to her health, implied that as a young girl Ella suffered from gynaecological problems. Conversely, though Ella frequently went to great lengths to defend her husband, she never made any attempt to explain away her childlessness. It was not simply a matter of coyness – after all, her Aunt Louise, Queen Victoria's fourth daughter, also remained childless but had openly sought a cure in various European spas. Other members of the family were equally candid in their correspondence with the Queen, who, for all her professed distaste for the subject, was unduly inquisitive about the married lives of her daughters and granddaughters. Ella's refusal to discuss the matter seems simply to confirm what the gossips had surmised: due to some failing on Serge's part, the marriage remained unconsummated.

As the rumours continued unabated, the Queen seized every opportunity to cast a concerned eye over her precious granddaughter. When they met for a christening in Darmstadt in 1885, she observed that Ella and Serge seemed happy together but Ella had become particularly pale and thin. Two years later, when Ella arrived in London for the Golden Jubilee celebrations, she was totally unprepared for the grilling she was about to receive. It was humiliating enough to hear the rumours and 'disgusting lies' that circulated through St. Petersburg, but mortifying to discover that the most intimate details of her marriage were being discussed as far away as Windsor. Deeply embarrassed by the Queen's probing questions she could only reply with increasing desperation:

"All I can repeat is that I am perfectly happy."

Ella's heartfelt protestations were sincere. She loved Serge enough to endure a possibly celibate marriage, but with each passing year the pain of her childlessness became harder to bear. Ella loved children and longed for a child of her own. During a visit to Ilinskoe in 1886, her aunt (and sister-in-law), Marie of Edinburgh, noticed how readily she spoiled her eight-year-old cousin, Sandra, and she could not have been more thrilled to hear of the birth of her first niece, Alice. In Russia, too, she delighted in the company of her friends' children, whom she frequently entertained by hiding gifts and sweets for them to seek out in the rooms of her palaces. Among the many charitable organisations that she patronised, the dearest to her heart was the Elizabethan Society, which she had established to take care of orphans and neglected children. If, in the early years of her marriage, she entertained the forlorn hope that eventually something would change and she might have a child of her own, with each passing season her optimism gradually faded.

For an intelligent and well-educated woman dogged by scandalous rumours, the trivial hours in the ballroom soon lost their appeal. Ella had been raised to a life of service and duty but now she was little more than a beautiful ornament to a husband who showed her scant physical affection and denied her any say in the decisions affecting her life. Had she sought them, the beautiful and charming Grand Duchess would have had no shortage of lovers in the infamously decadent Russian court, but, believing that vows made before God were binding for life, Ella could not contemplate infidelity. Instead, like her mother before her, she devoted herself to her charities and, with ever greater fervency, to her religion.

Although tales of Serge's perversions and sadism continued until his death and beyond, Ella never spoke so much as one word of criticism against him. In the unlikely event that the rumours of his homosexuality were true, she accepted the situation without complaint or self-pity and remained convinced that he loved her. In that, at least, she found the comfort that was denied to one of her cousins, for out of all Queen Victoria's granddaughters none suffered greater humiliation at

---

* see chapter 21

the hands of her husband than the desperately unlucky Marie Louise of Schleswig-Holstein.

Chapter 17 – Tell My Granddaughter To Come Home To Me

Christians
Lenchen & Christian: Queen Victoria's third daughter and her husband
Marie Louise: Princess Aribert of Anhalt; younger daughter of Lenchen & Christian

Hohenzollerns (Prussians)
Willy: Kaiser Wilhelm II; eldest son of Queen Victoria's daughter, Vicky.

'Poor dear Lenchen,' dependent on laudanum and placebos, had never found life easy but her nerves were strained to the limit in the summer of 1900 when an alarming telegram arrived at Cumberland Lodge. The message tersely informed her that her daughter, Marie Louise, must return at once to the little German Duchy of Anhalt to face divorce proceedings. According to the message, her husband found life with her 'intolerable' and, since she had 'neglected her marital duties' and the marriage had never been consummated, her father-in-law, the Duke of Anhalt, intended to declare it null and void.

Reeling with shock, a frantic Lenchen rushed to Windsor Castle to bear the dreadful tidings to the Queen. Divorce under any circumstances was a scandal that Queen Victoria could not countenance and yet, in this case, knowing the full facts, the Queen had nothing but sympathy for her maligned granddaughter.

Ten years earlier, eighteen-year-old Marie Louise was living a sheltered existence in Cumberland Lodge, interspersed with frequent trips to German spas with her mother. Fair, slim and graceful with striking blue eyes, the princess had already attracted the unwelcome attention of Crown Prince Ferdinand of Roumania, but it was the dashing Prince Aribert of Anhalt-Dessau who caught her eye when she arrived in Berlin for Cousin Moretta's wedding. Bored

Marie Louise

by the interminable torch dance and flattered by Aribert's attention, Marie Louise was instantly infatuated.

> "He was very tall and good-looking, and a very striking personality," she recalled, "and I suppose to a young girl of eighteen, he was the *beau ideal* of a cavalry officer. I have no hesitation in saying that I fell completely under his charm – in others words, fell in love. He paid me a good deal of attention which both flattered and bewildered me."[100]

Her cousin, the Kaiser, was quick to encourage the romance and, bewildered or not, then and there Marie Louise decided that this was the man she would marry. Within a week of their meeting, Vicky was writing to the Queen in favour of the match.

Though Queen Victoria was disconcerted at the speed of events, Marie Louise's parents approved of Aribert and on 'a very cold snowy day' in December 1890 the couple were engaged at Cousin Willy's home in Potsdam. From there they made the three-hour journey to Anhalt where a nervous Marie Louise was to be formally introduced to Aribert's family.

The following month, Queen Victoria invited Aribert to visit Osborne for the obligatory inspection of future grandsons and found him entirely suitable. English journalists, however, were less convinced. Even before his arrival, newspapers hinted that there was something 'not quite right' about the 'youthful lover' but Marie Louise was enraptured and the family agreed that the extremely good-looking young man would make an ideal husband. With the Queen's blessing, plans were made for a July wedding at St. George's Chapel at Windsor.

The celebrations coincided with a state visit from the Kaiser who, proud of his part in bringing the couple together, was eager to attend the service. When the ceremonials were over, the bride and groom drove in an open carriage through the streets of Windsor, where crowds of Eton schoolboys, who had been given a day off in honour of the occasion, gave them a warm reception. The set out for a honeymoon in Cliveden in Buckinghamshire, and spent a further ten days in Marie Louise's childhood home, Cumberland Lodge, before embarking on a tour of Holland. In the autumn, Prince Aribert took his wife home to the quaint sleepy town of Dessau in eastern Germany.

For all her youth and naïveté, it did not take Marie Louise long to discern that her husband was not quite the 'nice amiable young man' of Aunt Vicky's imagination. It soon became clear that, as a serving officer in the German Cavalry, Aribert much preferred the company of his fellow soldiers to that of his wife. Abandoned to her own devices in the medieval atmosphere of Dessau, Marie Louise came to the sad and humiliating realisation that her handsome husband had married her solely to conceal his homosexuality and protect his reputation.

Marie Louise had undoubtedly heard the rumours surrounding Cousin Ella's marriage but at least Ella had the consolation of knowing that, in spite of his difficult nature, her husband loved her. Ella had enjoyed many splendid hours in the glittering ballrooms of St. Petersburg and won the affection of her husband's people, but Marie Louise, denied even that solace, found herself isolated and trapped by the thousand rules that governed the lives of princesses in Anhalt.

Every aspect of her existence was organised according to an ancient code of etiquette that had been in existence for centuries. She was not permitted to leave her rooms without the prerequisite number of attendants and, as she quickly discovered, if she dared to flout the rules there was always someone on hand to reprimand her. On one occasion, Willy's wife, the Empress Dona, was appalled to hear that Marie Louise had dared to venture out in an ordinary cab, unaccompanied by footmen and pages.

Marie Louise might have endured her husband's predilection for young men had he shown her the least consideration but Aribert not only preferred his male friends but made it clear that he resented her being there at all:

"I was not wanted, my presence was irksome to him, and we were two complete strangers living under the same roof. We occasionally met at meals and when we had guests, otherwise days might pass without our even seeing each other – and from the enthusiastic girl of eighteen, I became a disillusioned woman."[101]

Drawing on her cigarettes, the unhappy princess sought escape from Anhalt whenever possible. She paid regular visits to Aunt Vicky and her circle of interesting artists and intellectuals in Berlin, and, taking advantage of Aribert's apathy, indulged her lifelong love of travel in a series of tours. She visited Italy with her brother and Cousin Charlotte, before journeying further afield to meet with the Roman Catholic White Fathers in their African mission.

Her husband, meanwhile, squandered her dowry, sold her jewels and made her life so unpalatable that Marie Louise, disheartened and alone, fell ill.

As usual, the observant Queen Victoria was among the first to detect that something was amiss and in June 1898 she invited her granddaughter to England, where she observed how weak she had become. After eight years of a sham marriage, Marie Louise's spirits were sinking rapidly. She remained with her grandmother at Osborne throughout the summer, enjoying visits from Cousin Sophie and Tino of Greece. On the 12th August, she celebrated her twenty-sixth birthday on the Isle of Wight in the company of her sister, Thora, and her uncle and aunt, the Duke and Duchess of Connaught, receiving telegrams from her Wales cousins, who were staying aboard the Royal Yacht *Osborne*.

The peaceful respite in comfortable and familiar surroundings made Marie Louise's return to the gloom of Dessau all the more depressing, and the outbreak of the South African War intensified her unhappiness. The strength of anti-British feeling in Germany made life unbearable for an English princess, particularly one whose brother was serving with the Queen's forces.

Weary with the façade of her marriage and desperate to escape from Anhalt, Marie Louise, with Queen Victoria's encouragement, asked her husband's permission to take an extended break in America. Aribert, scarcely aware of her absence, was more than happy to agree.

For several weeks in the spring of 1900, she toured the United States and Canada, thoroughly enjoying the visit until the telegram from Anhalt brought an abrupt end to her holiday. To her horror, her father-in-law was summoning her back to Dessau. The same day, her parents received the letter informing them of Aribert's intentions to divorce her.

Queen Victoria, utterly indignant and appalled at Marie Louise's 'cruel treatment,' immediately dispatched a telegram to Lord Minto, the Governor of Canada: 'Tell my granddaughter to come home to me. V.R.'

After a gruelling and anxious sea crossing, Marie Louise returned to the solace of Cumberland Lodge where her bewildered parents and sister, Thora, were anxiously waiting to meet her. As a horrified Marie Louise listened to the list of 'obscene' charges that her husband levelled against her, her humiliation was absolute and she could only take comfort in the knowledge that 'there was one accusation which my husband did not bring against me, because he could not, and that was the charge of infidelity.'[102]

Only later did the princess learn the true reason for the urgent summons. In her absence, Aribert had been caught *in flagrante delicto* with a homosexual lover. To avoid bringing scandal on the family, his father demanded an immediate annulment of the marriage, laying the blame for its non-consummation squarely at his wife's feet. Rather than facing a prolonged and humiliating court battle, the Christians agreed to an annulment, and Marie Louise, though deeply distressed by the outcome, was finally released from a life that had brought nothing but disappointment and unhappiness.

She returned to her family and, having acquired rooms for herself in London, established a small studio where she made jewellery. Most of her time, however, was devoted to numerous charitable foundations, including the 'Princess Club' to assist the impoverished factory workers of Rotherhithe; centres for homeless people and former prisoners; and those connected with her mother's nursing foundations. Like Aunt Alice and her Hessian cousins, Marie Louise was often to be found in the homes of the poor, learning about lives which were very different from her own, and attempting to alleviate their suffering.

In spite of all she had suffered, Marie Louise shared Ella's belief that vows made before God were binding for life. She never saw her husband again but continued to wear her wedding ring and always considered herself a married woman.

"The reason I have never married again," she wrote towards the end of her life, "is because my marriage was according to the Church of England with its solemn and binding vows, and no arbitrary local family law could absolve me from these marriage vows."[103]

It was hardly likely that her passionate Edinburgh cousins, Missy and Ducky, would resign themselves so patiently to life with unfaithful husbands.

Chapter 18 – A Mere Child & Quite Inexperienced.

Edinburghs
Affie (Alfred): Queen Victoria's second son; Duke of Edinburgh and Coburg
Marie: Affie's wife
Missy (Marie): Eldest daughter of Affie & Marie

Hohenzollerns (Prussians)
Charlotte: Princess of Saxe-Meiningen; eldest daughter of Vicky

Roumanians
Ferdinand (Nando): Heir to King Carol of Roumania
Carol: King of Roumania
Elizabeth ('Carmen Sylva'): Queen of Roumania

In June 1892, members of Queen Victoria's household were shocked to read a newspaper announcement of the engagement of sixteen-year-old Missy of Edinburgh to the twenty-six-year old heir to the throne of Roumania. For some months there had been much speculation about the young princess's future; her name had already been linked with several continental princes, including 'the odious Gunther,' brother of the German Empress Dona, and by the summer of 1892 the Prince and Princess of Wales were under the definite impression that Missy was on the verge of accepting their son, George's proposal of marriage. The sudden announcement of her engagement brought a swift and unexpected end to all speculation.

"It seems to have come very rapidly to a climax," wrote a stunned Queen Victoria, "The country is very insecure, the Society dreadful & she is a mere Child & quite inexperienced."[104]

The Prince and Princess of Wales were incensed that George had been snubbed but, when they berated Missy's father for his part in settling the affair, they soon discovered that he had had no say whatsoever in the matter. His wife, the Anglophobic Duchess of Edinburgh, had engineered and arranged everything without so much as consulting her husband.

Marie of Edinburgh (Missy)

Her own unhappy marriage to unfaithful Affie, left the Duchess with a very low opinion of English princes and, determined to keep Missy from the overbearing influence of her grandmother, she had long ago decided that her daughter should marry a German.

Ferdinand of Hohenzollern-Sigmaringen, a German-born cousin of the Prussian Imperial family, suited the Duchess' purpose in every respect. Unassuming to the point of dullness, he was living a lonely existence in Bucharest as heir to his uncle, the childless King Carol of Roumania, where, according to Vicky, he was popular and behaved very well.

The Duchess had little doubt that her sparkling daughter, ten years his junior, would make an instant impression on the shy young man and arranged a meeting at the home of their mutual cousin, Charlotte of Prussia.

The first encounter was unpromising. Unaware of what was expected of her, Missy paid little attention to the prince, who concealed his nervousness by laughing and seemed far more engrossed in the scintillating conversation of the more sophisticated Charlotte. The Duchess refused to give up hope and immediately arranged a further meeting in Munich. Now, in a more romantic setting, Missy, uninhibited by Cousin Charlotte, found the opportunity to shine. Munich was, as she later recalled:

> "...the town of towns for this sort of thing...We were both young, there was love in the air, it was springtime and Mamma had a happy, expectant face."[105]

By the time they met again that summer at Cousin Willy's Potsdam palace, the brief courtship culminated in the prince's proposal. Eager to please her mother, Missy accepted him. While the Duchess rejoiced, the Kaiser gave a banquet in their honour, and Missy could only imagine what future awaited her.

If Queen Victoria was stunned by the news, her court was horrified. Apart from Missy's youth, stories of the strange goings-on in Bucharest, made the prospect of sending the innocent girl to Roumania appear even more unsavoury.

Ferdinand's aunt, Queen Elizabeth, was a somewhat eccentric figure who, writing under the pseudonym, Carmen Sylva, had earned a considerable reputation as an author. She surrounded herself with Bohemian friends who shared her literary tastes, among them a young poetess named Hélène Vavarescu. So alarmed was King Carol by his wife's extreme attachment to the mystical Hélène, that he had exiled the Queen from court and sent her back to her mother, the Princess of Wied.

Throughout her three-year banishment, Queen Elizabeth refused to abandon her protégée and actively encouraged her nephew, Ferdinand, to fall under her spell. Although Hélène was not the most stunning of women, the lonely prince fell unashamedly in love. Marriage to a mere poetess was out of the question for the heir to the throne, yet even at the time of his engagement, it was rumoured that Ferdinand's infatuation remained undiminished.

With her usual inquisitiveness, Queen Victoria decided to discover the truth for herself and invited Nando and Missy to Windsor for an inspection. Satisfied by the appearance and manners of the tongue-tied prince, she commented that Missy seemed very happy, and gave the couple her blessing.

Despite the Queen's wish that her granddaughter should marry in St. George's Chapel Windsor, it was decided that the wedding would take place in Nando's native Sigmaringen. In early January 1893, an excited if nervous Missy arrived in the town with her million franc dowry. In the presence of the usual gathering of royalties, including the Duke of Connaught, representing the Queen, the wedding ceremonies took place according to both the Protestant and Roman Catholic rites and the couple departed for their honeymoon in a country house just outside the town.

The wrench of leaving her family to begin a new life with a virtual stranger was heart-rending for the young bride, and her diffident groom did little to ease the tension. The wedding night proved disastrous and matters did not improve in the coming weeks.

When the brief honeymoon was over, the couple moved on to Bucharest where Missy quickly realised that her husband lived so much in awe of his uncle, King Carol, that he dared not contradict him in anything. When the King forbade the young couple from entertaining or attending social functions to avoid creating unpleasant rivalry among the Roumanian aristocracy, Ferdinand meekly yielded to his order. Missy's familiar ladies-in-waiting were dispatched home and the adolescent Crown Princess found herself isolated in a foreign country with a husband she barely knew.

Life in the gloomy and gaudy Byzantine palaces was intolerably tedious for such a high-spirited girl, and when, much to her surprise, she became pregnant within a fortnight of her wedding, her loneliness was more acute than ever. Contrary to her wishes that the baby should be born at her country estate, Sinaia, King Carol insisted that she remained in Bucharest and resolved to make all the arrangements even to the appointment of midwives and doctors.

Homesick and friendless, Missy could hardly wait for her mother's arrival but the appearance of the Duchess merely exacerbated the tension. Not only did the Duchess overrule all King Carol's plans, insisting that the baby should be born at Sinaia, but was equally determined to resist Queen Victoria's attempts to provide an English midwife. Whatever Missy made of her mother's disputes, she was at least grateful that the Duchess insisted that she should be given chloroform during labour.

Within months of the birth of a son, Carol, in October 1893, Missy was pregnant again and consequently denied the possibility of any social life whatsoever. What was more, as she suffocated in the stifling atmosphere of the court, her husband, she soon discovered, was happily enjoying affairs with various other women.

The return of the eccentric Queen Elizabeth did little to ease Missy's plight. With more than a hint of jealousy for the Crown Princess's youth and charm, the Queen went out of her way to crush Missy's spirit. Though childless herself, she constantly interfered in the upbringing of Missy's children, even appointing the nursery staff and giving them instructions to report to her any misdemeanour on the princess' part. Matters came to a head when Queen Elizabeth insisted on keeping a governess of whom Missy did not approve. At her wits' end, Missy went home to her mother in Coburg and refused to return until the woman was dismissed.

Such behaviour earned the Crown Princess the reputation of being neurotic and arrogant but with her 'instinctive sense of self-preservation' she refused to be crushed. By the time she returned to Bucharest, she was determined to take charge of her life and make use of her many talents. She had never doubted her own fascination and, if Ferdinand did not give her the attention she craved, numerous admirers were constantly on hand to flatter and reassure her.

Fuelled largely by the malevolent tongue of Cousin Charlotte, who had recently arrived in Roumania, rumours began to spread that Missy had embarked on an affair with a Russian cousin, Grand Duke Boris Vladimirovich. When the news reached her mother, the horrified Duchess demanded an explanation. Affronted by the accusations, Missy vehemently denied any wrongdoing but even she knew that her passionate personality could not long endure a disappointing marriage to a prematurely aging husband.

The romance with Boris might have been innocent but, unlike Sophie in Greece, Missy was not prepared to accept the prevalent view that there were different moral codes for men and women. She had done her duty by providing the country with an heir and now, aware of her husband's infidelities, she sought lovers of her own including a lieutenant in the Roumanian army and, allegedly, Waldorf Astor. Tales of her penchant for handsome young men circulated through the courts of Europe, leading Cousin Willy to refer to her later as a 'meddlesome little flirt' and 'English harlot.'

Though the rumours were exaggerated, Missy made little effort to conceal her affairs, and so complacent was her husband that he happily employed her long-term lover, the dashing Prince Barbo Stirbey, in his household. For her part, Missy often praised the beauty of Ferdinand's mistresses. Their mutual acquiescence suited all parties and allowed the Crown Prince and Crown Princess to become friends.

Whatever her opinion of her husband, Missy loved their six children: Carol, Elizabeth, Nicolas, Marie, Ileana and Mircea (the youngest of whom was probably fathered by Prince Stirbey). Thriving on adulation herself, she lavished praise upon them, refusing to reprimand them and spoiling them so terribly that the result would eventually be disastrous not only for Missy personally but also for the country.

Her relationship with her eldest son bore striking similarities to that of Aunt Vicky and Cousin Willy. At an early age, Carol was taken from Missy's care to be placed under the supervision of tutors appointed by the King. The most prominent and influential of his teachers was a repressed homosexual who fell in love with his pupil and filled him with such an inflated sense of his own importance that his arrogance rivalled that of the Kaiser. Like Willy, too, Carol simultaneously worshipped and resented his mother, one moment gazing adoringly at her, the next going out of his way to wound her.

Missy's eldest daughter, Elizabeth was, like Cousin Charlotte, a difficult and moody child who grew into a cold, unaffectionate woman, intent on stirring up trouble for her family. As was the case with Aunt Vicky, Missy's chief consolation came from her younger children all of whom remained devoted to their mother.

It was characteristic of Missy that, out of a seemingly desperate situation, she had risen and would continue to rise in the estimation of her husband's future subjects. Outwardly she and Ferdinand played the role of a happily married couple and, as Crown Princess, her personal charm endeared her to the Roumanian people in a manner that could never be rivalled by her more puritanical cousin, Sophie, Crown Princess of neighbouring Greece. With her natural flair and verve, Missy compensated for a loveless marriage in the arms a fervent lover – setting an example, which would soon be followed by her younger sister, Ducky.

Chapter 19 – Who Can Guess What His Tastes May Be?

Hessians
Louis: Grand Duke of Hesse, widower of Princess Alice
Ernie: Son of Louis and Alice
Alix: Ernie's youngest sister

Edinburghs
Ducky: Victoria Melita, second daughter of Affie & Marie, Duke and Duchess of Edinburgh and Coburg
Sandra & Baby Bee - Ducky's younger sisters.

One spring morning in 1892, Grand Duke Louis of Hesse-and-By-Rhine sat down to lunch with his son, Ernie, and youngest daughter, Alix. During the meal he suffered a stroke and was carried, paralysed, to his bed.

While Queen Victoria gasped in horror, his daughters hurried from Prussia, Russia and Malta to be at his side but by the time they reached the New Palace, 'the best and kindest of fathers' was barely conscious. He died in the early hours of the morning, 15th March 1892.

Crushed and bewildered as she was, Queen Victoria's heart again went out to her orphaned grandchildren and particularly to the Grand Duke's successor, twenty-three-year-old Ernie.

Until then, Ernie had been living a carefree existence, indulging his passion for art, and enjoying the company of his unmarried sister, Alix. Now, suddenly saddled with the weight of responsibility for the Grand Duchy, all that would have to change; and, fond as she was of her grandson, the Queen had little faith in his ability to cope at such an early age.

She sent him message after message full of sound advice and, above all, recommending that he should find a wife as soon as possible, not only to help him carry out his duties but also to secure the Hessian dynasty.

There might have been another motive in the Queen's persistent pestering. Perhaps she wondered why Ernie seemed disinclined to marry and appeared so content with his artistic friends that he would have been happy to continue his bachelorhood indefinitely. Perhaps, too, she had picked up the hint in Vicky's letter: 'who can guess what [his] tastes may be?'

Whether the observant Queen suspected Ernie's bisexual tendencies and hoped to avoid a scandal, or simply believed that he would be happier with a wife, she would not let the matter drop. She had even selected him a bride from among her own granddaughters: Cousin Maud of Wales. As it quickly became apparent that Ernie had little in common with Maud, Queen Victoria simply switched her attention to another cousin: eighteen-year-old Victoria Melita (Ducky) of Edinburgh.

Whenever the couple met in one of her English palaces, the Queen delighted in seeing them laughing together and became increasingly convinced that they were ideally suited. Both were fun-loving and artistic and, since Ducky was living in neighbouring Coburg, she was familiar with the mores of German Grand Duchies and would, in her grandmother's opinion, make an excellent successor to Princess Alice as Grand Duchess of Hesse.

Throughout the summer of 1892, Queen Victoria cajoled and beleaguered Ernie to propose but neither he nor his sisters were quite so enthusiastic. To his sisters Ducky appeared too frivolous and flippant to take the duties of a Grand Duchess seriously, while Ernie, who had never quite recovered from the death of his haemophiliac brother, Frittie, feared for the health of his children and had doubts about the wisdom of marriage between first cousins. In response, the Queen had her personal physician compile a medical report which assured him that, since both parties were perfectly fit, inter-marriage would 'strengthen' the stock.

As Ernie continued to prevaricate, the Queen became more impatient. If he did not propose soon, she warned, Ducky might slip away; the Duchess of Edinburgh was renowned for marrying off her daughters at an early age and while Ernie dithered there were plenty of other young princes who would be only too happy to step in before him.

In fact Ducky herself, to her grandmother's chagrin, had already fallen in love with another cousin on her mother's side: Grand Duke Kyril of Russia. For the Queen, who still 'grieved as much as ever' over Ella's Russian match, it must have come as a relief to hear that the Orthodox Church forbade marriage between first cousins and consequently nothing could come of Ducky's hopes.

Queen Victoria bombarded Darmstadt with letters but, frustrated by Ernie's tardiness in replying, decided to take more direct action. She simultaneously invited both cousins to visit her at Osborne and there at last in the winter of 1893, Ernie proposed, Ducky accepted and a date was set for a spring wedding.

The following April, the splendid gathering of royalties converging on Coburg gave rise to a premature optimism that the marriage would be a success. The streets were crowded with so many guests that passers-by were delighted to see carriages stopping on the road as princes, empresses, duchesses and grand dukes descended to greet one another. The Kaiser and his mother, Empress Frederick, the Prince of Wales, the Tsarevich Nicholas, the Crown Prince and Crown Princess of Roumania, Grand Duke and Grand Duchess Serge of Russia, the Duke of Connaught and his daughters, Daisy and Patsy, and numerous other relatives from Russia, England and Germany enjoyed a family reunion and settled as comfortably as they could into the overcrowded palaces. The highlight of the gathering was the arrival of Queen Victoria, who, having put so much effort into bringing about the wedding, made a special effort to be present.

Not everyone, however, was delighted to see the Queen. Amid all the rejoicing, the bride's father, Affie, was seething with rage. In his mother's entourage he had spotted the Munshi, Abdul Karim, her pretentious Indian secretary and the latest in her line of favourites. Not since the days of John Brown had any of Queen Victoria's retainers irked the royal family as much as the arrogant Munshi. His constant presence and endless complaints had been unpalatable enough in England but Affie refused to stomach such behaviour in Coburg. Standing on his authority both as Duke of Coburg and as the bride's father, Affie adamantly refused to allow him to join the royal guests in the chapel. For once, despite her tears and displays of distress, the Queen was forced to give way and the Munshi, bristling with indignation, was banished to a stand with lesser members of the household.

The wedding service took place on 19th April in the Lutheran chapel of Schloss Ehrenburg, where the young Tsarevich Nicholas observed that Ernie and Ducky made 'a lovely couple.' In the joyful celebrations that followed there was every reason to believe that Ernie might yet prove the ideal husband for his cousin. They both took pleasure in parties, dancing and entertaining, and Ernie's sensitive nature complimented that of his far more passionate wife. They shared, too, a fervent interest in art for, while Ernie was a connoisseur and collector, Ducky was a very talented designer and artist.

In the company of their numerous cousins, the future seemed rosy but once the merry band had departed and the couple were alone Ducky quickly discovered that her marriage was doomed to failure. Their wedding night was as disastrous as her sister, Missy's, had been and left her 'completely shattered and disillusioned.' If she hoped that matters would improve in time, the proud granddaughter of

Victoria Melita (Ducky) & her daughter, Elizabeth

the Tsar soon realised she had overestimated Ernie. His penchant for young men was unabated and, unlike Cousin Marie Louise, Ducky could not resign herself to life with a homosexual husband.

For his part, Ernie had believed that his wife would gladly adopt the numerous charities his mother had founded but Ducky showed no interest in the affairs of Hesse and thought her husband and his little Grand Duchy so dull that she seized any chance to escape.

A year after the wedding their first and only child was born, causing a good deal of wrangling between the Queen Victoria and Ducky's mother about the choice of an English or German obstetrician. By then, however, the marriage was already rapidly deteriorating. As Ducky complained that her husband was fonder of footmen than he was of her, they were soon living separate lives, held together by two frail bonds: their daughter Elizabeth, whose obvious preference for her father grated on Ducky's nerves, and the knowledge that Queen Victoria would never consent to a divorce.

In April 1896, Ernie and Ducky returned to Coburg for the marriage of the Ducky's younger sister, Alexandra (Sandra), to Ernst of Hohenlohe-Langenburg. The Queen complained that nineteen-year-old Sandra was too young to be married, particularly to a man fifteen years her senior, and with typical family histrionics the bride and her younger sister, Baby Bee, wept throughout the service, but the marriage would prove the happiest and most stable of all the Edinburgh princesses'. The couple settled into a Schloss near Hesse where, between 1897 and 1911, Sandra gave birth to five children: Gottfried, Marie Melita, Alexandra, Irma and Alfred, the youngest of whom died within his first year.

Two months after Sandra's wedding, Ducky found another excuse to escape from Hesse to the glamour of Moscow for the coronation of her cousin, Tsar Nicholas II. The delights of Russia were all the more alluring for Ducky when she came face to face once more with her first love: the dashing, if taciturn, Grand Duke Kyril Vladimirovich. From then on, there was no hope of saving her marriage; her thoughts were only of Kyril.

Trapped and frustrated, Ducky sought escape from Hesse at every opportunity, visiting her relatives across Europe, in the full knowledge that in her absence Ernie was entertaining his male lovers. In 1899 she stayed at Balmoral with Queen Victoria and Cousin Thora of Schleswig-Holstein, where her dissatisfaction was obvious to everyone.

Ducky attempted to make light of her unhappiness but beneath the 'amusing' façade, she was in despair and wept to her grandmother that the only solution was divorce. The Queen had no need of her explanations; she had already made own discreet and thorough enquiries into the goings-on in Hesse and genuinely pitied Ducky's plight but still she remained adamant on the subject of divorce.

Faced with no alternative, Ducky made one final attempt to accommodate her grandmother's wishes and salvage her marriage. Perhaps, she hoped, another child might draw her and Ernie closer together but, after suffering a miscarriage in the spring of 1900, she gave up all hope of a future with Ernie. Leaving Darmstadt, for her mother's villa in the South of France, she sought comfort in the arms of her lover, Kyril.

Intensely disappointed by the outcome of her schemes, Queen Victoria firmly declared she would never again indulge in matchmaking. Not only had the marriage brought nothing but unhappiness for both parties, it had also led indirectly to the marriage she had been most anxious to avoid: that of her favourite granddaughter, Princess Alix of Hesse.

Chapter 20 – She Is Like My Own Child

Russians
Ella: Grand Duchess Serge, second daughter of Princess Alice
Serge: Ella's husband
Alexander III: Tsar of Russia
Marie Feodorovna: Tsarina of Russia; sister of the Princess of Wales
Nicholas (Nicky): Russian Tsarevich; son of Alexander III and Marie Feodorovna

Alix: Princess of Hesse: youngest daughter of Princess Alice; younger sister of Ella

At the time of Ernie's wedding, his younger sister, Alix, wandered through the New Palace in a quandary. For the past two years since her father's death she had lived contentedly with her brother, playing hostess at his Grand Ducal receptions, while he took care of her 'chivalrously,' acting as her 'father, mother and friend.'[106]

After the wedding all that would have to change. The arrival of a new Grand Duchess would leave Alix redundant as a hostess and, fond as she was of Ducky, she did not relish the prospect of playing gooseberry in her own home. Marriage was her only option but, nearing her twenty-second birthday, Alix had already rejected 'the highest position there is' and her chances of finding an eligible suitor were rapidly diminishing. Princes and dukes regularly visited Darmstadt but Alix had too much independence of spirit to settle for a loveless match. There was only one man to whom she had ever been deeply attracted and for almost a decade she had struggled to put him from her mind.

Ten years earlier, when she visited Russia for her sister Ella's wedding, twelve-year-old Alix had been enthralled by the gentle Tsarevich Nicholas (Nicky). He was shy and softly spoken and, even at that early age, had been particularly attentive to her as they scratched their names together in the window of a villa at Peterhof.

In the intervening years Alix had blossomed into a striking young woman who could not fail to win Nicholas' attention when she returned to Russia to visit Ella in January 1889:

> "Tall she was, and delicately, beautifully shaped, with exquisitely white neck and shoulders. Her abundant hair, red gold, was so long that she could easily sit upon it when it was unbound. Her complexion was clear and as rosy as a little child's."[107]

Ella, convinced that the couple were destined for each other, watched their budding romance with a mounting excitement and, when Nicholas told her of his affection for her sister, she promised she would do all she could to help bring together. But the course of true love was not to run smoothly for Hessian princess and the Russian Tsarevich. While Ella was eagerly pressing for the match, Nicholas' mother, Tsarina Marie Feodorovna, was busily preparing lists of suitable brides for her son, and Alix of Hesse did not feature among them. In spite of her affection for Ella, the Tsarina believed that the future Tsar of all the Russias could make a more advantageous match than a lowly Hessian princess, particularly one whose nervous unsociability did not bode well for a future Empress of all the Russias.

Tsar Nicholas II

Nicholas viewed each suggestion with an increasing sense of desperation but to Ella the solution was obvious: he must follow his heart. She would, she promised, 'move heaven and earth' to bring them together and would not rest until her plans came to fruition. In every conversation with her sister, she spoke of the kindly Tsarevich and repeatedly reminded Alix that Nicholas thought of her constantly. She encouraged them to write to one another and invited Alix to her country estate, Ilinskoe, in the hope of furthering the romance.

Nicholas' mother, the Tsarina, was far from pleased and voiced her fears to her sister, the Princess of Wales, knowing that she in turn would pass on the news to the Queen Victoria whose legendary dislike of Russia would surely bring a swift end to Ella's plans. The news both alarmed and angered the Queen. She had never wanted Ella to marry a Russian but the thought of her favourite granddaughter becoming Empress of so violent a country was more than she could bear. Victoria, as the eldest Hessian sister, must tell Ella that Alix would not be allowed to marry a Russian; and Ernie must forbid her from ever visiting Russia again.

Ella, whom the Queen had once 'not credited with so much independence of character', refused to yield. Letters poured into Darmstadt from Russia, filled with flattering descriptions of the lovelorn Tsarevich; how he missed Alix, how he loved her, how he longed to see her again. The letters were painful enough for Alix, but when Ella appeared in person, it was even harder to bear. Alix was ruining Nicky's life, she said, could she not at least send him a kind word, a message, perhaps even a photograph?

Alix was in turmoil. Her grandmother's warnings left her plagued by nightmares and a sense of impending doom. She loved Nicholas deeply and could not deny it but, more than Queen Victoria's admonitions and her own unaccountable fears, her conscience troubled her deeply. According to Russian law, the wife of the Tsar had to be of the Orthodox faith and Alix simply could not abandon Lutheranism.

Year after year, Ella continued her relentless campaign, alternately cajoling and bullying Alix to reconsider. Alix's scruples, she claimed, were unwarranted; the question of religion need not trouble her, after all she herself had converted and found Orthodoxy far more fulfilling than Protestantism. Even the Tsarina had come to realise that her son could only be happy with Alix and was ready to welcome her into the Imperial Family. Still Alix would not give way.

The impasse dragged on until Ernie's wedding in April 1894. Knowing that Nicholas would be present as a first cousin of the bride, Alix panicked and wrote desperately to his sister, begging her to warn him that there was no point in prolonging his misery as she could never consent to be his wife.

Ella refused to give up hope. As soon as she arrived in Coburg, she drew her brother into a conspiracy to bring the couple together by inviting Ernie and Alix to her rooms at a time when she knew Nicholas would be calling, whereupon she and Ernie

---

* see chapter 21

made a subtle exit, leaving them alone. The plan failed. Nicholas proposed but a weeping Alix reiterated that she could not change her religion. Still Ella remained hopeful and, for once, found a willing ally in her own former suitor, Cousin Willy.

For some time the Kaiser had been hoping to forge stronger ties between Russia and Germany to counteract the Russians' alliance with Prussia's archenemy, France. What better way could there be to ingratiate himself with the heir to the Russian throne than to help him gain his heart's desire and at the same time install another German princess in St. Petersburg? Talking with Nicholas late into the night, Willy promised that he would persuade Alix to change her mind. The following morning, with supreme hypocrisy considering his treatment of his own sister, Sophie*, the Kaiser assured his cousin that conversion to Orthodoxy did not entail turning her back on Lutheranism.

The day after Ernie's wedding, Nicholas proposed again and this time Alix yielded. They emerged smiling into an adjoining room where the Kaiser, Ella, and various other royalties were waiting, and made their announcement. The whole company rejoiced, hugging one another in 'an orgy of kissing,' and even Queen Victoria was so touched by the romance, gave the couple her blessing. Only later did the Queen confide her true feelings to her diary:

> "My blood runs cold when I think of her so young...on that unstable throne...She is like my own child."[108]

Tragically, time would justify her fears.

---

* see chapter 21

After Ernie's wedding, Alix returned to England with her sister, Victoria, and the Queen, who advised her to seek a cure for her recurrent sciatica at the spa in Harrogate. There, as Nicholas prepared for a grand wedding in St. Petersburg and Ella scoured her shelves for Orthodox literature to send to her, Alix had the first glimpse of what her future life would entail. Stories of her recent engagement filled the English newspapers and small crowds gathered to gape at the future Empress of all the Russias.

"Her temporary sojourn in our midst," reported the Harrogate Advertiser, "is of a strictly private character and, as a rule, she is allowed to move about freely without being subject to annoyance or undue observance, but in every community will be found some 'black sheep' and there is a class of snobs who possess some wealth but certainly precious few manners. Their sole desire seems to be in dogging the steps of this royal lady, and by their actions they are doing their best to prevent her from obtaining that benefit, repose and pleasure for which she came into our midst."[109]

Confined to a wheelchair and unused to being on show, Alix was annoyed and embarrassed by the intrusion. It did not bode well for a woman who would soon be expected to shine on the most glittering stage in the world.

The following month, at Queen Victoria's invitation, Nicholas arrived in England. For a few days, he and Alix enjoyed the relative seclusion of her sister Victoria's house at Walton-on-Thames before moving on to the more formal atmosphere of Windsor. In spite of the necessary presence of a chaperone – in this case, Alix's Aunt Helen, the

Duchess of Albany – the romance flourished until, by the time the Tsarevich left for Russia at the end of July, he and Alix could hardly bear to be parted. At least they could look forward to a further meeting at Wolfsgarten in the autumn, where they would be joined by the rest of the Hessian sisters.

After a month with her grandmother in Osborne, Alix returned to Darmstadt at the end of August. Now in the excitement of her forthcoming wedding, her nightmares were fewer, her sciatica improved and the future was filled with promise. She was 'longing more than ever' to see the Tsarevich again when suddenly a desperate telegram arrived from the Crimea. Nicholas' father, Tsar Alexander III, had been taken ill on his summer estate, Livadia, and his condition was deteriorating so rapidly that Nicholas dared not leave his side. The plans for a meeting in Wolfsgarten would have to be abandoned; instead, he pleaded, could Alix come to Russia?

Within days, Alix and Victoria had set out for Warsaw from where Ella would travel on with Alix to Livadia. Only when they reached the Russian border did Ella realise that in the panic no one had thought to make to make special arrangements for Alix's arrival. So it was that the future Empress of All the Russias made an unpropitious entry to her new homeland among all the ordinary passengers.

Alix of Hesse

The sudden death of forty-nine-year-old Tsar Alexander III on 1st November 1894 came as a great blow to the whole of Europe. He might not have been the most popular monarch but his firm rule and strength of character had brought relative peace and stability to his country, which few believed his more passive son would be able to maintain. Queen Victoria feared the implications for Alix while the Duchess of York's thoughts turned to her frail sister-in-law, Toria of Wales: 'I do hope precious Toria won't be ill!'

Devastated by his loss, Nicholas sobbed that he was unequal to the task ahead of him and pleaded with Alix to have the wedding brought forwards. With selfless courage, she rose to the occasion, immediately converted to Orthodoxy and agreed to 'seal her fate,' in her grandmother's ominous words, on the Dowager Empress's birthday, a mere three weeks after the death of the Tsar.

Shortly after one-fifteen in the afternoon of 26th November 1894, Alix, leaning on her brother's arm, walked through the imposing corridors and malachite ballrooms of the Winter Palace to the chapel where she and Nicky were married according to the Orthodox rite. In spite of the gathering of royalties, including the Prince and Princess of Wales and the Duke of York, recent events gave the occasion a sombre atmosphere. The new Tsar, it was reported, looked pale, and both his bride and his mother wept throughout the ceremony. Even amid the cheering crowds lining the streets of St. Petersburg, inauspicious whispers were heard: "She has come to us behind a coffin."

Yet, for all the trials that Alix was to suffer in Russia, hers was one of the greatest royal romances of all time. She loved Nicholas with a passion, surpassing even that of her grandmother for beloved Albert; and to the end of their lives his devotion and his longing to 'return to her arms' never wavered. They complimented one another: he, a calming influence on her frequently overstretched nerves;

she, a powerful source of inspiration to override his natural diffidence:

> "It was a real love-match - one of those ideal unions that seem to belong to fairyland, and tales of which are handed down through the ages. Their love grew with their life together, drew them ever closer, and never abated. The Emperor's diaries and the Empress's letters to the Emperor show what they were to each other."[110]

In fact, love alone would sustain them throughout the perils, sorrows and disasters of the tragic reign of Tsar Nicholas II.

Part III
"The Last Link Is Cut Off"
(Changes and Conflicts)

Chapter 21 – One Must Be Tolerant

Sophie: Daughter of Vicky; Crown Princess of Greece
Tino: Crown Prince of Greece; Sophie's husband
Willy: Kaiser Wilhelm II; Sophie's brother
Dona: Willy's wife
Uncle Bertie: Prince of Wales
Ella: Daughter of Alice; Grand Duchess Serge/Elizaveta Feodorovna
Serge: Ella's husband

"My religion and faith," wrote Princess Marie Louise shortly before her death, "have been the anchor to which I have clung through all my life with its many difficulties, joys and sorrow."[111]

It was a sentiment shared by many of her cousins and one which Queen Victoria would have been pleased to echo, for, in spite of her trenchant remarks about over-pious people, lengthy sermons and the dreariness of bishops, her own faith was deep and sincere. Princess Alice had worried the Queen by probing too deeply into theological questions, and she repeatedly urged her granddaughters to resign themselves to the will of God with a simple and unquestioning trust. As she reminded her grandchildren not to neglect their prayers, nor to fail to attend church, Queen Victoria had no idea that one day one of those granddaughters would become a canonized saint.

While the English princesses were naturally raised as Anglicans, their German cousins were confirmed in the Lutheran Church. The Queen, as Head of the Church of England, naturally hoped that her grandchildren would adhere to her faith and yet, as she wrote to Vicky, religion was a matter for the individual's conscience and 'one must be tolerant.' True to her conviction, Queen Victoria repeatedly ordered her viceroys overseas to respect the beliefs and rites of her non-Christian subjects; she surrounded herself with Indian servants, whose religious practices she was eager to defend; and, when four of her granddaughters converted to other faiths·, she proved far more understanding than many other members of her family.

When Sophie of Prussia arrived in Greece, her wedding to Crown Prince Constantine (Tino) was conducted according to both the Lutheran and Orthodox rites. Unlike the Russian Tsarevna (wife of the Tsarevich) there was no obligation for a Crown Princess of the Hellenes to convert to Orthodoxy. The Danish-born King George continued to adhere to Protestantism although he had agreed to raise his children in Orthodoxy – a matter made easier by the fact this his wife, Queen Olga, was a Russian of Orthodox faith.

From the time she arrived in Athens, Sophie was surrounded not only by the brilliant Byzantine basilicas and chapels but also by people who devoutly practised the Greek faith. So impressed was she by their rites and creed that, within a year of her marriage, she decided to convert. Tino and the Greek people were delighted; when he eventually succeeded his father, he would be the first Greek-born and Orthodox king for several centuries and it seemed appropriate that his wife should share his faith. In Athens there was rejoicing but Sophie was not so naïve as to expect the same exultant response from her native Prussia.

· Three during Queen Victoria's life time, the fourth after her death.

Moretta's wedding in 1890 provided the opportunity for her to break the news of her decision to her family. Vicky, who had always advocated religious tolerance, had to confess that she felt 'rather a pang' of grief and would have preferred the 'question never to have arisen,' but she raised no objections. Queen Victoria was equally supportive, since, as she told a lady-in-waiting, she admired the Greek Church. Sophie's sisters, too, received the news with equanimity but Willy and his wife were aghast. Causing a scene and stamping his feet, the Kaiser absolutely forbade his sister to abandon Lutheranism and when Sophie replied that, since Willy had 'no religion whatsoever,' he was hardly in a position to make such a demand, the rigidly Evangelical Kaiserin Dona flew to her husband's defence. The Kaiser, she declared, was the Head of the Church in Germany and if Sophie dared to disobey him, she would suffer eternal damnation!

Astonished by Dona's arrogance, Sophie replied that her salvation rested in God's hands and, reassured by her mother's assertion that she was no longer the Kaiser's subject, she returned to Greece determined to ignore the threat.

Willy, his pride severely wounded, poured out his wrath in a series of letters to his fellow sovereigns. A month after the argument, Dona gave birth to a premature baby, causing Willy to complain to his grandmother that if his child died he would hold Sophie entirely responsible for its murder. Queen Victoria did not bother to reply to his outburst though she did suggest to Vicky that it would have been more prudent for Sophie to keep her decision private.

Having received short shrift from his grandmother, Willy bombarded Sophie's father-in-law with letters, urging him to prevent her conversion and warning that if she should disobey him she would not be permitted to enter Germany again. The King gently replied that he had no right to interfere in what was essentially a matter for the princess and her conscience.

Kaiser Wilhelm II (Willy)

On 2nd May 1891, Sophie was anointed in the Orthodox Church and wrote to tell Willy of the *fait accompli*. Exploding with fury, the Kaiser announced that she was banished from his country and if she dared to set foot on German soil she would be arrested. As the family gaped in astonishment at his high-handedness, Sophie summed up her opinion of her brother in an open telegram to Vicky: 'quite mad.'

Mad his decision might have been, but the pronouncement left Sophie in an awkward position. As Emperor, his word would be obeyed and the prospect of being arrested was both scandalous and humiliating, yet Sophie would not forfeit the right to visit her mother at Friedrichshof. It was left to Uncle Bertie in England to provide a solution. The Prince of Wales had been snubbed several times by his Prussian nephew and, more than willing to offer Sophie his support, he conceived a plan whereby she might flout the Kaiser's orders. She should travel, he suggested, incognito, making no mention of her intended destination but entering Germany by way of Italy or France. It was vital, he said, that her husband should accompany her, since the Kaiser would not dare to arrest the Crown Prince of Greece.

The scheme worked successfully and Sophie continued to make regular unchecked visits to her mother at Friedrichshof but it would be four years before Willy officially lifted the ban.

Word of the Kaiser's reaction to Sophie's conversion must have sent a shudder down Cousin Ella's spine for, at the very moment that Sophie was arguing with Willy, Ella was agonising over how to tell her family that she, too, intended to convert to the Orthodox faith.

After seven years of a fruitless and stultifying marriage, Ella had lost none of her beauty or charm. She was still capable of stunning her guests in the ballroom and continued to win the affection of both the aristocracy and the hundreds of ordinary people who benefited from her charities. Yet for Princess Alice's daughter the pleasure of adulation and abundant riches had quickly lost its allure.

From her earliest years, Ella had been a deeply spiritual child and her faith in the goodness of God had sustained her through the traumas and tragedies of her childhood, including the deaths of her mother, brother and sister. Princess Alice had repeatedly emphasised the briefness of life and the necessity of seeing heaven as an ultimate goal:

> "Life is not endless in this world, God be praised! There is much joy - but oh! so much trial and pain and, as the number of those one loves increases in Heaven, it makes our passage easier - and home is there."[112]

As a child, Ella had been fascinated by her ancestor and namesake, St. Elizabeth of Hungary, the queen who, six centuries earlier, had disbanded her court to spend her life in the service of the sick. Inspired by the example of the saint and by her own mother's commitment to the poor, Ella herself had grown up with 'a longing to help those who suffer.' Now, in the midst of such opulence, her Lutheran faith appeared self-righteous and was becoming as unfulfilling as her marriage. Beneath the priceless jewels, the palaces and exaltation, Ella was slowly suffocating in the superficiality of her life.

Only on the country estate of Ilinskoe could she find peace. There, profoundly impressed by the peasants' sincere and humble devotion, she felt herself increasingly drawn to Orthodoxy. In September 1888, a pilgrimage to Jerusalem for the consecration of a church, made a deep impression on the young Grand Duchess. The spiritual atmosphere of the Holy Places and the mysterious Russian rites convinced her that God was calling her to the religion of her adopted home. By the time she returned to St. Petersburg she had made a decision to learn all she could about Orthodoxy. Her husband, Serge, was overjoyed; he longed for her to convert and, what was more, in a marriage where so much was lacking, shared faith might draw them closer together.

There was, however, a problem. At the age of sixteen, in the presence of her grandmother, Ella had made her confirmation, committing herself to Lutheranism, and she firmly believed that promises made before God were binding for life. Still more poignantly, before leaving Darmstadt she had given her father her word that she would never abandon the faith of her childhood. Torn between her inner conviction and the promises she had made, she entered a spiritual crisis like that which her mother had endured almost thirty years earlier. Privately she studied the lives of Russian saints and the works of contemporary Orthodox writers but for two more years, unable to renege on the promise she had made to her father, she prevaricated.

"...Then again came many months of doubts and worries. I always wished to put it off although 'au fond de mon coeur' I already belonged to [Orthodoxy]. Alas, I am very bad and did not have enough strength, enough faith."[113]

Eventually, in the course of her reading, Ella discovered a loophole. It was not necessary to abjure Lutheranism to embrace Orthodoxy; in effect she could convert without breaking her promise. There could be no more excuses. At Christmas 1890, Serge 'wept with joy' when she told him that she had finally made her decision but with great trepidation she sat down to write an explanatory letter to her father.

"May God forgive you!" he wrote in reply, accusing her of spurning her true faith and turning her back on all she had been brought up to believe.

In Russia, too, her conversion was viewed cynically in some quarters. Her husband, the gossips claimed, had forced her into the decision, since he was about to be made Governor General of Moscow and in such a prestigious position he needed an Orthodox wife. Ella did not argue. In the early morning Saturday 25th April 1891, she quietly slipped into the Chapel where in a private ceremony attended by the Tsar, Tsarina and Serge, she was received into the Orthodox faith.

"No conversion was ever more sincere, thorough or complete," wrote the French Ambassador, Maurice Paléologue, "...All her instinct for dreams and emotion, fervour and tenderness suddenly found its outlet in the mysterious rites and pomp and pageantry of Orthodoxy. Her piety soared to amazing levels. She knew heights and depths whose existence she never suspected."[114]

It would have suited Ella from then on to withdraw into a more ascetic existence but within a month, she and Serge had left St. Petersburg for Moscow. The duties of the wife of the Governor General – a position virtually equivalent to that of a viceroy – were numerous and her days were spent 'receiving, seeing heaps of people, giving receptions, dinners, balls…' Whatever time she could spare she spent praying in one of the Kremlin's many basilicas or involving herself in charitable works. Patronising hospitals and orphanages, 'a certain mixture of idealism and mystery added to her natural charm which made her adored by all with whom she came into contact.'[115]

Ella's benevolence and beauty quickly won the hearts of the Muscovites, and, as her lady-in-waiting wrote:

"People quickly got into the habit of referring to her, of putting her at the head of new organisations, of making her the patroness of charitable institutions."[116]

Her popularity, however, did nothing to improve the reputation of her husband. Word of his reactionary views had preceded him from St. Petersburg and, from the moment he arrived in the city, his actions justified the Muscovites' fears. Convinced that the Jews were at the heart of every revolutionary plot, Serge ordered their expulsion from the city before imposing a series of stern regulations on the universities. Stories and lewd jokes about his alleged perversions circulated through the city while his genuine attempts to improve the lives of the poor passed unnoticed.

In fact, those who knew Serge well, found him approachable and supportive. Countess Tolstoy was one of many who came to him to present a petition and found the Grand Duke 'exceeding courteous and affable.' When she requested a particular position in a specific regiment for her son, Serge listened attentively and within a short time the young man received his commission. The countess was also aware of an occasion when, out of loyalty to his retainers, Serge made the three hundred mile journey from St. Petersburg to Moscow for one day to be present at the wedding of one of his servants.

Unwaveringly loyal, Ella never uttered a single word of criticism of her husband and yet, ironically, rather than bringing them together, her conversion drove her and Serge further apart. He viewed her 'excessive' devotions with anxiety and, fearing that her inspirations were based on superstition, frequently warned her not to trust her own judgement in spiritual matters.

If, in her loneliness, Ella hoped that her sister Alix, as an equally enthusiastic convert, might empathise with her devotion, she was about to discover that the Tsarina's faith was leading in quite a different direction.

Chapter 22 – We Were All So Hoping for A Boy

Russians
Alix: youngest daughter of Alice; Tsarina Alexandra
Feodorovna of Russia
Nicholas (Nicky): Alix's husband; Tsar Nicholas II
Ella: Grand Duchess Serge; Alix's elder sister

Shortly after Alix's engagement, Ella had warned her sister of the dangers of making a poor first impression in her new homeland. Her warning was to prove tragically appropriate. Contrary to Ella's high expectations, Alix had made a very poor initial impression in St. Petersburg and the results would overshadow the rest of her life.

For any of Queen Victoria's granddaughters, the dramatic transformation from the relatively lowly position of a minor German princess to the Empress of so vast an empire would have been daunting, and for Alix of Hesse the sudden elevation to Empress Alexandra Feodorovna was positively traumatic. Thrust from the backwater of a small German Grand Duchy into the gaudy and glittering limelight of the wealthiest court in the world, she stood tongue tied and blushing before the aristocracy who expected her to shine as brilliantly as her predecessor had done. Unable to speak Russian, she might have been grateful that French was the customary language at court, yet even that she spoke with a 'terrible accent' and, according to one observer could barely 'squeeze out a word.'

From the start, the nobility compared her to her ebullient mother-in-law, who delighted in hosting receptions and leading the social life of the capital. The contrast between the Dowager Empress and her successor showed Alix in a most unfavourable light. Shy among strangers, her awkward silences were mistaken for arrogance, and formal gatherings became so tortuous that at the first possible opportunity she made her excuses to escape, firing unjust rumours that she believed the company beneath her.

> "She undoubtedly possessed [a Victorian] strain, as in many ways she was a typical Victorian;" wrote her friend, Lili Dehn. "She shared her grandmother's love of law and order, her faithful adherence to family duty, her dislike of modernity, and she also possessed the 'homeliness' of the Coburgs, which annoyed Society so much."[117]

More familiar with the sedate palaces of Queen Victoria than the decadent world of St. Petersburg high society, she glared with disdain on the loose morals and idleness of the Russian nobles. "Most Russian girls seem to have nothing in their heads but officers," she complained but her attempts to impose her own standards met only with mockery and contempt.

> "The Empress," wrote her close friend Anna Vyrubova, "possessed a heart and a mind utterly incapable of dishonesty or deceit, consequently she could never tolerate it either in other people. This naturally got her heartily disliked by people of society to whom deceit was a matter of long practice."[118]

With Ella's encouragement, Alix tried to interest the aristocracy in charitable works. True to her upbringing, she established nurse training schools based on the ideas instituted by Aunt Lenchen in England and funded from her own private income; she visited hospitals, secretly paid out fortunes to various medical charities and even called on the sick in their own homes, but her efforts to engage the upper classes in more meaningful activities did nothing to increase her popularity:

> "One of her early projects was a society of handwork composed of ladies of the Court and society circles, each one of whom should make with her own hands three garments a year to be given to the poor. The society, I am sorry to say, did not long flourish. The idea was too foreign to the soil."[119]

Nor did her natural and genuine simplicity appeal to the aristocracy, who:

> "...could not understand why on all the earth their Empress knitted scarves and shawls as presents for her friends, or gave them dress-lengths. Their conception of an Imperial gift was totally different, and they were oblivious of the love which had been crocheted into the despised scarf or the useful shawl – but the Empress, with her Victorian ideas as to the value of friendship, would not, or could not, see that she was a failure in this sense."[120]

Unsurprisingly, Alix withdrew ever more frequently from society, seeking solace within the walls of her favourite home, the Alexander Palace, with a few close friends and her beloved Nicky. Content in her husband's company and isolated from the world, Alix was convinced that the opinions of the aristocracy were of no consequence. The 'real' Russians – the peasants, like those whom she had met on Ella's country estate – were devoted to their Tsar. St. Petersburg was, in her view, filled with foreign schemers and, with ever-increasing vehemence, she urged Nicholas to pay no heed to the advisers who sought only to manipulate and trap him.

Unfortunately, Nicholas had neither the desire nor the temperament for power. In the early years of his reign, unprepared for the weight of responsibility, he stood in awe of his giant uncles who towered over him physically. His character contrasted sharply with that of his father, the mighty Alexander III, and his willingness to listen to opposing points of view gave the impression that he vacillated too easily and lacked any firm conviction.

With his mild manner and gentle way of speaking, Nicholas was more suited to the role of country gentleman than the autocratic Tsar of All the Russias, and his reign seemed doomed to disaster. Tragedy even marred the coronation celebrations when thousands of Muscovites were crushed to death as they waited for the customary hand-outs of souvenirs and free meals.

In a non-autocratic country, Alix would surely have prospered since many of her perceived failings were identical to those of her grandmother. Queen Victoria had been much criticised for her failure to appear in public after the Prince Consort's death and, like Alix, she excused herself on account of shyness, ill-health and nerves. Both were devoted to their husbands and both were equally quick to disregard the advice of family and ministers who warned them of too close an association with 'favourites'. Queen Victoria's attachment to John Brown and her refusal to heed the complaints of his critics would be mirrored to a more devastating effect, in Alix's perceived dependence on the peasant, Grigory Rasputin. Neither the Queen nor her granddaughter readily accepted advice but where Queen Victoria was able to rely on the good will of her ministers and the loyalty of the people, there was no such fidelity for Alix. As a constitutional monarch, Queen Victoria was never held directly responsible for the problems of her country; as the foreign wife of an autocrat, Alix took the blame for every disaster that befell the Russian people.

Unsurprisingly, an air of sadness seemed to surround her, as Countess Olsufieff observed:

"...even in the height of her prosperity [she] never quite lost the sad lines of the mouth which gave her beauty a preordained tragedy."[121]

For all her disappointments, Alix had at least the consolation of discovering within months of her wedding that she was pregnant and, if anything could help endear her to the Russian people, it would be the birth of an heir. Since the death of Catherine the Great, the Salic law debarring females from the throne had been operant in Russia and so, as word of her condition spread, the Imperial Family united in prayer that the baby would be a boy.

In autumn 1895, Ella travelled from Moscow to Tsarskoe Selo and remained at Alix's side throughout the twenty-hour labour. At nine o'clock in the evening of 15th November, the baby – a 'huge' daughter – was born. Across St. Petersburg, soldiers fired their hundred-and-one gun salutes while the family participated in a *Te Deum* in thanksgiving for the safe delivery of Grand Duchess Olga Nicolaevna. Though the parents were elated and the family rejoiced, there was a general sense of disappointment that the child was not a boy.

Times had certainly changed since Queen Victoria had named a cow in the royal dairy, 'Alice.' Now, thirty years later, Nicholas was writing confidently to the Queen that he was delighted that

Alix was nursing the baby herself. The Queen's reaction is unrecorded.

Little Olga delighted her parents, neither of whom saw any cause for alarm in her gender. After all, when Queen Victoria's first child, Vicky, was born, the Queen had accurately predicted, 'the next one will be a prince.' Alix had good reason to hope that the same would be true in her case, particularly when the following year she was pregnant again. In May 1897, after a shorter and easier labour, she gave birth to a second daughter, Tatiana. Two years later, when a third daughter, Maria, was born, there was even greater sense of disappointment in the country at large.

The daughters of Tsar Nicholas II

In 1901 Alix, pregnant for a fourth time, was convinced that this time she would bear a son. In June, Anastasia was born. Nicholas recorded that he was pleased that the birth had gone well and without complications, but even he could hardly conceal his disappointment and, on hearing the news, went for a long walk alone.

The desperate longing for a son did not diminish the deep love that both the Tsar and Tsarina had for their daughters. Both of them worshipped their 'precious girlies' and Alix, like her own mother, took far more direct responsibility for them than was common among Queens and Empresses. Breast-feeding them, bathing them, playing with them and attending to their education, her letters and diaries were filled with details of their health, their temperature and even, as her daughters grew older, the dates of their periods; and yet, until she had a son, she had failed in her duty both as a wife and an Empress.

Alix was desolate. She had prayed, she had hoped, she had produced four daughters and, at the age of thirty-two, she was becoming desperate; the only solution she could envisage was a miracle, and Russia, as she was about to discover, was filled with miracle-workers.

Alix, no less than Ella, had taken her conversion to heart. According to Baroness Buxhoeveden, 'she held views that were considered unduly strict by many modern Russians, and zealously studied the intricate works of the old Fathers of the Church.'[122]

But for all her sincere religious devotion, Alix's desperation to bear a son was driving her further and further to the edge of what her detractors would describe as superstition.

"Her occultism has been grossly exaggerated," wrote Lili Dehn. "Her superstitions were of the most trivial description...I will readily admit that she possessed a strong element of mysticism which coloured much of her life; this was akin to the 'dreaming' propensities of her grandfather, the Prince Consort, and environment, and the Faith of her adoption fostered this mystic sense."[123]

All the same, Alix needed a miracle and would go to any lengths to receive one. She prayed before her icons, made pilgrimages and bathed in holy springs, but when her efforts seemed fruitless, she turned instead to mystics and dubious healers.

In attendance at Court were two Montenegrin princesses, Grand Duchesses Stana and Militsa. Though both had a reputation for dabbling in spiritualism, Alix was intrigued by their tales of mystics and agreed to invite several Holy Fools to the palace. Dressed in rags, they rambled incoherently while the Tsarina looked on and waited in vain for her miracle. Still there was no sign of an heir until, at last, the Montenegrins found a new 'healer,' – a Frenchman named Philippe Vachot, who, they claimed, had the power to influence the sex of an unborn child.

In the summer of 1901, Alix invited 'Monsieur Philippe' to the Alexander Palace to pray with her, and was so impressed by his confidence and charm that she felt sufficiently at ease to confide her worries to him. The Tsar was equally convinced of the Frenchman's sanctity and soon he and Alix were making daily visits to Militsa's Znamenka Palace to listen to the bizarre preaching of Monsieur Philippe. Since the meetings took place with the utmost secrecy, outsiders could only speculate about what was going on within the palace walls. The stories became increasingly outlandish: the Tsar was being drugged; they were involved in witchcraft and séances; and the most unlikely tale of all: Philippe slept at the foot of the Imperial bed to influence the conception of a son.

Nonsensical or not, the rumours were sufficiently alarming to provoke the Minister of the Interior into ordering an investigation into the healer's background and the subsequent report confirmed his suspicions. Philippe was a swindler with three previous convictions for practising medicine without a licence.

Alix received the report with ambivalence; holy men, she claimed, were always subject to criticism and one need only read the Bible to see how many prophets had been rejected by their own people. Even when a worried Ella arrived from Moscow to warn her sister not to be taken in by Philippe, Alix refused to listen and, just as her grandmother had ignored her family's pleas to part with John Brown, she refused to discard her healer. Her devotion to Philippe was absolute, particularly when she realised she was pregnant again and 'Our Friend', as he had now become, assured her that this time the child would be a boy. Now, with a heavenly guide, she had no need of worldly assistance and dispensed with the medics who had seen her through previous pregnancies, entrusting herself wholly to the prayers of Doctor Philippe.

The secret meetings continued and the months passed with Alix's mounting excitement at the prospect of giving birth to a Tsarevich. In mid-August 1902, rather later than she had anticipated, she eventually went into labour but when the court doctors were finally permitted to attend her they discovered what several members of the family had suspected from the start. Alix was not and had not been pregnant. The symptoms she had experienced for the whole nine months were the result of anaemia and her longing to bear a son. To lessen her humiliation an official announcement stated that the Empress had suffered a miscarriage.

Notwithstanding the crushing outcome, Alix's confidence in Philippe remained unshaken. Blaming her own lack of faith for the disappointing result, she clung to him more desperately than ever, and yet, in the face of such opposition from the rest of the family, the healer realised that his days in Russia were numbered. In his typically dramatic fashion, he announced that his mission at the court was completed and he must return to France. Before he left he promised that soon another teacher would come to take his place, and with Philippe gone, Alix kept her eyes open for the friend who would follow.

Chapter 23 - The Sun Has Gone Out Of Our Lives

Battenbergs
Beatrice: Princess Henry of Battenberg; youngest daughter of Queen Victoria
Liko (Henry) Battenberg: Beatrice's husband
Ena (Victoria Eugenie): Daughter of Beatrice & Liko

Edinburghs/Coburgs
Affie (Alfred): Queen Victoria's third son; Duke of Edinburgh & Coburg
Marie: Affie's wife; Duchess of Edinburgh and Coburg
Young Affie: Only son of Affie & Marie

Albanys
Helen: Duchess of Albany; Widow of Prince Leopold
Alice of Albany: Daughter of Leopold & Helen
Charles Edward: Son of Leopold & Helen

A decade after her Golden Jubilee, Queen Victoria prepared to celebrate her sixty years on the throne. Older now and frailer, she had no desire to entertain the numerous foreign royalties who had descended upon London ten years earlier, and insisted that this time the jubilee would be less of a family event and more a celebration of the British Empire. Even so, no less than eighteen of her granddaughters attended, preceding the Queen in seven carriages as the stately procession made its way from Buckingham Palace to St. Paul's Cathedral*. No longer able to walk unaided, the tiny monarch remained in her carriage for an open-air service of thanksgiving, before returning to the palace for a grand jubilee dinner at which Ella and her brother, Ernie, and sister-in-law, Ducky, were invited to share the Queen's table.

Neither Ella nor her grandmother could have failed to notice that Ducky and Ernie had arrived separately for the celebrations and would later depart independently, drawing further attention their unhappy marriage.♦

Of the granddaughters who were unable to attend, the Roumanian Crown Princess, Missy, was 'terribly, terribly, disappointed' not to be there but her husband had recently been struck with a near-fatal bout of typhoid; the Tsarina of Russia was pregnant with her third daughter, Tatiana; and it would have been difficult for Sophie of Greece to participate in the celebrations when her country was in the throes of the Turko-Greek War." Noticeable,

---

* The procession comprised sixteen carriages in all. The Queen's granddaughters travelled as follows: eighth carriage: Princess Alice of Albany with Princess Victoria Eugenie (Ena) of Battenberg; ninth carriage: Princess Victoria Patricia (Patsy) of Connaught, Princess Victoria (Thora) of Schleswig-Holstein; tenth carriage: Princess Beatrice (Baby Bee) of Coburg, Princess Margaret (Daisy) of Connaught, Princess Aribert of Anhalt (Marie Louise); eleventh carriage: The Hereditary Princess of Saxe-Meiningen (Charlotte), Princess Frederick Charles of Hesse (Mossy), Princess Adolph of Schaumburg-Lippe (Moretta), The Hereditary Princess of Hohenlohe-Langenburg (Sandra), Princess Louis of Battenberg (Victoria of Hesse); twelfth carriage: Princess Charles of Denmark (Maud); thirteenth carriage: Princess Victoria of Wales (Toria), The Princess Henry of Prussia (Irène); fourteenth carriage: Princess Louise, Duchess of Fife, Grand Duchess Serge of Russia (Ella), The Grand Duchess of Hesse (Ducky).

♦ see chapter 30

251

too, for his absence was the Kaiser, to whom the Queen Victoria had refused an invitation since he was openly supporting the Turks in the conflict. Willy was furious at the snub and incensed that his younger brother, Henry, dared to accept the Queen's invitation.

The celebrations were a great success and the rapturous applause that greeted Queen Victoria demonstrated the extent of her popularity. Marie Louise, sitting beside her grandmother in the carriage recalled that:

> "The crowd was immense, the cheers and acclamations deafening. The Queen had asked me to accompany her back to Windsor and on the way I turned to her and said: 'Oh, Grandmama, does this not make you very proud?' She replied, 'No, dear child, very humble.'"[124]

For the Queen, though moved by the demonstrations of affection, the occasion was tinged with sorrow. She felt deeply the loss of her son-in-law, Beatrice's husband, Liko Battenberg, whose death the previous year had been the first in a series of family tragedies that would cast a dark shadow over the remainder of her reign.

In spite of her initial misgivings about Beatrice's marriage, the Queen had soon come to love Liko. His cheerful sense of humour and commitment to his family, not to mention his striking good looks, greatly appealed to her and she noted with satisfaction that although he and Beatrice were devoted to one another they made none of the tasteless shows of affection that so grated on her nerves. So fond was the Queen of his company that he had even succeeded in persuading her to provide a more comfortable smoking room than the one which she had reluctantly allocated to Prince Christian. In fact, she had come to enjoy his presence so much that she was unwilling to let him out of her sight.

But Liko was straining at the leash; the Queen's affection and the love of his wife and children could not compensate for the extreme dullness of life at court. Unable to renege on the promise made before his marriage, he watched enviously as his brothers went about their exciting adventures while he frittered away his hours attending to his children's education and carrying out minor duties for the Queen. In 1889, Queen Victoria appointed him Governor General of the Isle of Wight and Carisbrooke Castle but still he remained unfulfilled and sought every opportunity to escape abroad.

Henry of Battenberg (Liko)

Beatrice understood his need for excitement and raised no objections when he disappeared for months at a time on various yachting and continental expeditions but in his absence she missed him terribly, wept as he departed and worried that far from home his affections might stray. At the first hint of a possible scandal she dispatched a ship to bring him back.

Holidays and expeditions allowed him some release but could not satisfy his need to find a more useful role. In the autumn of 1895, however, he heard of a mission to end the slave trade in Ashanti in Ghana. The Queen, reluctant to be parted from him and fearful for his health in that notoriously disease-ridden part of Africa, hesitated about granting him permission to participate in so dangerous a venture until Beatrice selflessly prevailed upon her mother to give him leave to go. Queen Victoria could hardly refuse; after all her soldier-grandson, Christian Victor of Schleswig-Holstein, was taking part in the same campaign.

For Beatrice, Liko's departure aboard the *Coramandel* on 8th December was traumatic but, according to one of the Queen's ladies-in-waiting, Liko was 'bursting with excitement.'

Hardly had the ship reached Africa when, on 10th January 1896, Liko contracted malaria. For a while his condition appeared to improve and he wished to continue the expedition but his doctors and fellow officers thought him too ill to carry on and sent him homewards aboard the *Blonde*. Before the ship docked at Madeira, Liko suffered a relapse and, realising that he was dying, sent long and affectionate messages back to his wife and children, grieving at the thought that he would die so far from home. He died on 20th January 1896.

"Our grief and our misery is untold!" the Queen told Vicky, "The sun has gone out of our lives."[125]

When his body, preserved in rum, was eventually brought to the Isle of Wight, the Queen accompanied his family, including his nine-year-old daughter Ena, to receive the coffin. The funeral took place in Whippingham Church near Osborne, where eleven years earlier Liko and Beatrice were married.

For Liko's grieving widow, a minor family squabble brought further grief. While Beatrice mourned the loss of her husband, her elder and more beautiful sister, Louise, announced that her own grief was equally deep since Liko had always preferred her to his wife and had once made amorous advances towards her. As Louise's own marriage was something of a sham and she was renowned for making mischief in the family, Beatrice, though deeply distressed, dismissed her allegations as lies. Whether or not there was any truth in Louise's tale, Beatrice loved Liko deeply and had enjoyed eleven blissful years with a husband she had never hoped to find.

According to all who met her, the heart-broken princess accepted her widowhood with remarkable courage and dignity. For her grieving mother, however, further sorrows were to follow. Within five years of Liko's death, she had lost a son and two grandsons and discovered that her eldest daughter was dying.

In 1898, the royalties returned to Coburg to celebrate Duchess Marie's twenty-five unhappy years of marriage to the increasingly alcoholic Affie. Among the intended guests was their only son, Young Affie, who had been sent away from home at an early age to be groomed in Potsdam for his future role as Duke of Coburg. The training was intended to turn him into an efficient and reliable officer but it had had the opposite effect. Young Affie had developed into a dissolute and unstable young man with his mother's stubborn temperament and his father's addiction to drink. By the age of twenty-five, he had contracted venereal disease and was consequently dismissed from the German army.

His Orthodox mother despaired of his licentiousness, and shortly before her Silver Wedding anniversary an argument flared between them when he allegedly announced his intention of marrying an unsuitable bride. In the course of the argument, according to several erroneous reports, Young Affie shot himself and sustained a serious though not fatal wound. His true illness, which had led to 'paralysis of the larynx, caused by the state of the brain,' was an even greater scandal to his mother who decided that it would be better if he were absent from Coburg when her visitors arrived for the celebrations. His doctors warned that he had very little time to live but the Duchess dismissed the prognosis and, against his and his father's wishes, packed him off to recuperate in Meran in Austria. Just over a week later, on 6th February, he died. The official reports stated that the cause of death was consumption.

Affie, who, according to Queen Victoria, was 'in dreadful state' on seeing his son's remains, never recovered from the loss and within eighteen months he, too, was dead of throat cancer, exacerbated by his excessive drinking.

Young Affie's death was to have unexpected consequences for his seventeen-year-old cousin, Alice of Albany. The Salic law precluded females from inheriting the Dukedom of Coburg and, since Affie had no other son, there was much debate about who would succeed him. The next in line was Affie's younger brother, Prince Arthur, Duke of Connaught, but neither he nor his son had any desire to leave England or to show obeisance to the German Emperor. The Kaiser, too, always in awe of his English uncles, expressed his preference for a younger man and accordingly offered Coburg with its £300,000 a year income to the late Prince Leopold's son, thirteen-year-old Charles Edward, Duke of Albany.

After a great deal of soul-searching, Charles' mother, Helen, accepted the Duchy on his behalf and agreed that Cousin Sandra's husband, Ernst of Hohenlohe-Langenburg, would act as regent until Charles came of age. Notwithstanding the fact that his young cousin spoke very little German, the Kaiser insisted that he should leave Eton at once to enrol in the Lichterfelde Military Cadet School at Potsdam. Aunt Vicky, fearing that Charles might go the same way as Young Affie, was firmly opposed to the scheme and vehemently made her feelings known to her mother. Queen Victoria agreed but the Kaiser had made his decision and, in spite of their reluctance to leave their beloved Claremont House, the Albanys decided to comply.

In August 1899, Alice and her mother moved into the Villa Ingenheim, a relatively small cottage near the cadet academy in Potsdam, where Charles was to spend three miserable years, taunted and bullied by the other boys in the school. For Alice, the contrast between Windsor and the Kaiser's militaristic court, governed by etiquette and tradition, appeared both amusing and bizarre.

The court was, in Alice's opinion, 'very stiff and formal,' compared to that of her grandmother. Serving officers were obliged to appear in uniform at social gatherings, and the numerous ceremonies that littered the German calendar were even more trying for the princesses. The ceremonials, which began in the morning, could last for up to seven hours after which the princesses barely had time to change into the 'full regalia of tiaras and trains' for State Banquets which continued late into the night.

Yet Alice, with a cheerful disposition and an eye for the comic, was delighted by her new surroundings. If Cousin Willy was pompous, he could also be generous, hospitable and amusing. Alice observed that, though he was a stickler for the formalities and public displays, he was very different and 'quite ordinary' within his own home. She and Charles were regular visitors to his palace in Potsdam where they became close friends of his sons. Formal balls were an almost nightly occurrence and for a young princess there was no limit to the number of handsome young officers eager to become her dance partner.

Alice and her mother remained in Germany until Charles had completed his education and was deemed old enough to fend for himself. By the time that she returned to Claremont House in 1903, her grandmother's staid and seemingly changeless court had gone forever; the Victorian era was over, its sobriety replaced briefly by all the gaudy glamour of the new Edwardian age.

Chapter 24 – We Shall Never See Her Anymore

Hohenzollerns (Prussians)
Vicky/Empress Frederick: Queen Victoria's eldest daughter; Dowager German Empress
Vicky's children and their spouses:
>Willy: Kaiser Wilhelm II
>Dona (Augusta Victoria): Willy's wife, German Kaiserin.
>Charlotte: Princess of Saxe-Meiningen
>Henry
>Irène: Henry's wife; daughter of Princess Alice
>Moretta (Victoria Moretta): Princess of Schaumburg-Lippe
>Sophie: Crown Princess of Greece
>Mossy: Princess of Hesse-Kassel

Christians
Lenchen (Helena): Queen Victoria's third daughter; Princess Christian
Christian: Prince Christian of Schleswig-Holstein; Lenchen's husband
Lenchen's children:
>Christle: Prince Christian Victor
>Thora (Helena Victoria)
>Marie Louise

At the beginning of July 1897, Vicky returned from her mother's Diamond Jubilee celebrations to her beloved Friedrichshof. There, between visits from her daughters and frequent trips to Italy, she continued to amass her artistic collections with the same enthusiasm she had shown as a child when collecting fossils to add to her collection in the Swiss

Cottage. Friedrichshof was so full of antiques and treasures that, according to a regular visitor, Marie Louise, the 'wonderful' place became more of a museum than a house.

Vicky's concern for her antiques did not prevent her from welcoming children into her home and one of the chief delights of her widowhood was the pleasure she took in her grandchildren. It saddened her deeply that Willy's wife, Dona, seemed intent on alienating her from their six sons and had acerbically pointed out that the choice of the name Victoria for their only daughter was not made out of deference to her grandmother.

> "I am sorry to say poor Dona is not a help but an obstacle," Vicky sighed to her mother. "...They never ask or consult me on any one subject, great or small; but only invite me to their family dinner, just as they would an aunt or a cousin."[126]

While one daughter-in-law exacerbated the antagonism between Vicky and her son, the second, Irène of Hesse, proved far more accommodating. Since Irène's marriage to Henry in May 1888, the mutual and long-standing affection between aunt and niece had deepened, not least because Irène had done so much to improve relations between Vicky and Henry. Life with the Kaiser's volatile brother was not always easy for the Hessian princess:

> "[He] was a tall and handsome man, but inclined to be – let us say – temperamental. At times he was overbearing and very satirical, and at others friendly and charming. His wife was a small woman, simple in manner and of a kindly, unselfish nature."[127]

Notwithstanding her docility, Irène succeeded in calming his fiery temper, and by the time of the

Diamond Jubilee, Queen Victoria's lady-in-waiting, Marie Mallet thought him 'simple friendly and courteous...the nicest male royalty going.'

The couple had settled in the Königliches Schloss in Kiel from where Henry continued his naval duties and indulged his passion for motor cars and engines, and to where, in March 1889, Vicky and Moretta had hurried to assist Irène through the birth of her first child.

Suffering none of Queen Victoria's revulsion about the unecstatic state of pregnancy, Vicky set to work preparing the nursery and layette for the baby. Though the welcome she received was cordial and her efforts were greatly appreciated, she could not help but feel disappointed to find so few books in the house˙. It seemed incongruous that the well-educated daughter of Princess Alice showed so little interest in world events and was unable to discuss matters of political importance; but if Vicky

Irene of Hesse

wanted reassuring that this truly was Alice's daughter, she needed only to recall how easily her sister had shocked the Queen by breast-feeding her baby. Now it was Vicky's turn to be appalled when Irène made no attempt to hide her pregnancy behind shawls and rugs, but appeared quite openly in public right up to the time of the birth.

˙ Queen Victoria herself was an avid reader, though her taste in books did not always live up to the more intellectual Vicky's expectations. See Appendix IV

Shocked or not, Vicky remained at Irène's side through the 'quick, easy' birth of a son, Waldemar, on 20th March 1889. The baby's healthy appearance belied a terrible truth. It soon became clear that Waldemar was a haemophiliac, which perhaps accounts for the seven-year gap before Irène gave birth to a second child, Sigismund. Four years later the family was completed with the birth of a third son, Henry.

"I wonder that you are pleased at Irène's having a third boy." Queen Victoria wrote to Vicky, "There are far too many princes in Prussia."[128]

There was an unfortunate irony in the remark, for even as Irène was hoping for a daughter, her younger sister, Alix, Tsarina of Russia, was still desperately praying for a son.

Boys or girls, Vicky delighted in her grandchildren and looked forward with pleasure to Sophie's frequent visits to Friedrichshof with her large family or the arrival of Mossy and Fischy with their twins.

Alongside her aesthetic and domestic interests, Vicky continued to enjoy the beautiful scenery of Krönberg, walking and riding daily as she had done since childhood, until an accident forced her to curtail her outings and marked the beginning of her decline.

In September 1898, while out riding with Mossy, Vicky's horse, startled by a steam threshing machine, shied violently, hurling Vicky to the ground. Though bruised and badly shaken, she was able to walk home and wrote to her mother the next day that, apart from a headache, she had quite recovered.

In reality, Vicky was far more ill than anyone realised. Throughout her life, she had been troubled by various rheumatic ailments but following the accident she suffered severe back pain, which intensified with the passing of time. After consulting several doctors who presented conflicting medical opinions, she was eventually diagnosed with breast cancer, which had spread to her spine. Determined to continue living life to the full, she kept the news from her family, referring to her pain simply as lumbago and confiding the truth only to her youngest sister, Beatrice, and their mother.

For several months, she was able to make her regular excursions to Italy and France until, by the end of 1899, the pain left her confined to bed for long periods and she had no alternative but to reveal the truth to her daughters. Charlotte was the last to be told and, although she promised to keep the news to herself, she immediately announced her mother's illness to the world.

Mossy, Moretta, and Irène were on hand to offer what comfort they could, and Sophie hurried from Greece to be at her mother's side. Vicky endured her sufferings with fortitude and a touching concern for others, apologising to her nurses for upsetting them by her screams. Yet, hard as she tried to maintain a positive outlook, the pain, relieved only by minimal amounts of morphine, was excruciating and, at its height, she refused to see anyone for fear of causing them distress. So loud were her cries of agony that even the soldiers guarding her palace requested permission to move out of earshot.

"I have been suffering" she told her mother in October 1900, "to such an extent, but though in no ways alarming, so I trust you will not worry yourself one moment about me. I shall be prevented for some days from leaving my bed, and the attacks of spasms that seize me in the back, limbs and bones are so frequent that it is difficult to find a pause long enough to write in..."[129]

This was her final letter to the Queen.

For Queen Victoria, her eldest daughter's illness was but one in a series of heartaches that marred the end of her reign. In the closing years of the century, she mourned not only for Liko, Young Affie and the Duke of Edinburgh and Coburg, but also, as the mother of her country, she grieved for the young officers dying by the dozen in the South African War. Her concern for the soldiers was genuine and she repeatedly sent telegrams assuring them of her gratitude whether in victory or defeat. Though the Queen never doubted the justice of the British cause, the conflict bore an ominous portent of the division that a future war would wreak in the family.

Vicky and her three younger daughters supported the British and shared the Queen's concern for her troops. From Sophie in Athens, from Vicky in the Friedrichshof, and from Mossy in Hesse-Kassel parcels arrived for the Queen's soldiers while the princesses studied English newspapers for reports of the cruelty of the Boers.

Much of the rest of Europe, however, viewed the situation very differently. In Russia, Alix and Ella read stories of the British atrocities including the claim that their grandmother's troops were using Boer women and children as shields. The Russians were firmly behind the Boers and even the Tsar, who claimed to discuss the matter every day at dinner, agreed that the British were the aggressors, leaving Alix torn between loyalty to her grandmother and her husband.

From Prussia, the Kaiser pompously offered his grandmother advice on how best to proceed but at the same time praised the Boers' successes. The strength of anti-British feeling made life especially difficult for those English princesses, Marie Louise of Schleswig-Holstein and Alice of Albany, who were living in Germany. Alice's brother, as a German officer cadet had no option but to support the Kaiser's view, while for Marie Louise, who had one brother, Albert, in the German army and another, Christle, serving with the English forces, the situation was still more difficult.

Christle, a Captain in the King's Own Rifle Corps, had heroically endured and survived numerous hardships in the campaign until, like his Uncle Liko before him, he contracted malaria and enteric fever. His sisters, anxiously awaiting news at Balmoral, heard that he was being well treated in the military hospital in Pretoria but, within days, pneumonia had set in and he died on 29th October 1900. At his own request his body was buried alongside his fellow officers in Pretoria.

It was left to the heart-broken Thora to take the news of the death of yet another grandson to the Queen.

The series of family bereavements, Marie Louise's divorce, anxieties about Vicky's illness and the stress of the war brought about a rapid deterioration in Queen Victoria's health. Her sight was failing and, scarcely able to walk any distance, she spent much of her time in the company of her granddaughter, Thora, who patiently sat at her side, listening even as her mind began to fail and she rambled occasionally incoherently of events of the past.

On the 18th December 1900, Queen Victoria left Windsor for the last time, setting sail for the Isle of Wight to spend Christmas at her beloved Osborne House. It was a cold, bleak winter and the frail Queen was visibly fading. She complained of feeling weary and tired, and the festivities of the season were marred by the sudden death of her friend and lady-of-the-bedchamber, Lady Jane Churchill, who was found dead in her bed on Christmas morning.

Though few people realised it, Queen Victoria herself was steadily declining. She ate little and slept little and, by mid-January, appeared to be becoming more forgetful and apathetic until eventually she was confined to bed. As the seriousness of her condition began to be realised, telegrams flew across the continent warning of her decline. Princesses hurried to the island to take their turn in approaching Grandmama's bed to whisper a last good-bye.

Racing, too, across the Solent, much to his aunts' distress, was the Queen's eldest grandson, Kaiser Wilhelm II. He had always had the greatest respect and affection for his grandmother, and genuinely wished to see her for one last time.

Throughout the 22nd January the Queen lapsed in and out of consciousness, asking that her little dog, Turi, should be brought to her bed. Shortly before noon she seemed so close to death that the royalties were summoned to her bedside. As her chaplain-in-closet, Dr Randall Davidson, began his prayers the Queen was able to recognise the members of her family: Victoria Battenberg, who was staying on the Royal Yacht *Osborne*; the Dowager Duchess of Coburg and her little grandchild, Ducky's daughter, Elizabeth of Hesse; Daisy and Patsy Connaught who arrived with their parents and joined the Prince of Wales and the Queen's younger daughters, Lenchen, Louise and Beatrice in their vigil. For a few hours she rallied and the family withdrew but by mid-afternoon she had suffered a relapse. At half-past six in the evening of 22nd January 1901, Queen Victoria, died in the Kaiser's arms.

Ten days later, a long procession of royal mourners followed the coffin towards the yacht *Alberta,* which was to take the Queen's body back to England. On 4th February, through flurries of snow, the cortege set out from the Albert Memorial Chapel in Windsor to Queen Victoria's final resting place beside beloved Albert in the mausoleum at Frogmore. For Marie Louise, standing beside the coffin brought a deep sense of 'peace and awe', but, in typical Wales' fashion, her cousin, Maud, confessed that she found the funeral procession to 'rather trying & exhausting.'

"I cannot believe that she is really gone, that we shall never see her anymore. It seems impossible," wept the young Tsarina Alix, whose fourth pregnancy had prevented her from making the journey to England. "How I envy you," she wrote to her sister, Victoria, "being able to see beloved Grandmama being taken to her last rest."[130] A memorial service was held for the Queen in St. Petersburg where, for the first time since her arrival in Russia, the Tsarina wept in public.

While Ducky avoided the funeral, remaining in France with her Russian lover, her elder sister, Missy, was deeply distressed at being prevented from accompanying her husband to the ceremonies.

She sensed the implications of the loss of 'dearest Grandmama' and in a letter to her mother described her longing to return to England:

"To see it all again if only for a day or two…to have a last peep at the old house…without dear old Granny the last link is cut off!...I tell you it is inconceivable sorrow for me."[131]

For Alice of Albany, who had returned from Germany for the funeral it was an equally devastating experience:

"I had come to regard her as permanent and indestructible – like England and Windsor Castle."[132]

But it was the future Queen Mary who, perhaps, most accurately expressed the country's sense of bewilderment:

"The thought of England without the Queen is dreadful even to think of. God help us all."[133]

Grief-stricken at the death of her grandmother, Mossy of Prussia faced the most difficult task of all: breaking the news to her mother. Vicky heartbroken and racked with pain, wept that she wished she were dead, too.

For six more months, she struggled on, her agony increasing by the day. In February 1901, she received a final visit from her brother, the new King Edward VII. In spite of the friction between Willy and Uncle Bertie, the encounter passed off amicably, thanks largely to the tact of Sophie and Mossy who ensured that the conversation did not veer into disagreement. Bertie was horrified by his sister's rapid deterioration; as she sat 'propped up with cushions; she looked as if she had just been taken off the rack after undergoing torture.'[134] Before they left, the King's physician Sir Francis Laking persuaded her doctors to administer larger doses of morphine to combat her pain.

Through the last few months of her life, Vicky's received regular visits from her family. Mossy and Moretta barely left her side and, to the end she continued to take an interest in current events and her daughters' futures. When Sophie arrived from Greece, Vicky urged her to continue to care for the poor of her country. To the last, too, Vicky remained first and foremost an English princess. To her friend Bishop Boyd-Carpenter, she confided that she hoped he would preside at her funeral and read the English Burial Service over her.

In the early evening of August 5th 1901, Vicky, surrounded by her children, died reciting the Lord's Prayer. The funeral service she had requested was carried out at the English Church Homburg, to be followed some days later by a Lutheran funeral at Krönberg, after which she was interred with Fritz at Potsdam. In her will she left her favourite home at Friedrichshof to her youngest daughter, Mossy.

The death of Queen Victoria severed the ties uniting the royal cousins. Without Grandmama as their mainstay, there would be no common bond to keep the family together. With the dawning of the new century, the old world had passed away and the ominous clouds across the Solent portended a future far bleaker for the family than anyone could have predicted.

Chapter 25 – Poor Girl She is Utterly Miserable Now

Bertie: King Edward VII
Alexandra: Bertie's wife
Toria: Unmarried daughter of Bertie & Alexandra
Maud: Princess Carl of Denmark; youngest daughter of Bertie & Alexandra
Daisy: Elder daughter of Arthur, Duke of Connaught
Alice of Albany: Daughter of Prince Leopold
Ducky: Victoria Melita; daughter of the Duke of Edinburgh & Coburg; wife of Ernie of Hesse; Grand Duchess of Hesse
Ernie: Grand Duke Ernst Ludwig of Hesse
Alix: Tsarina of Russia; sister of Ernie of Hesse
Nicholas (Nicky): Tsar Nicholas II of Russia

The summer 1902 saw London bustling with preparations for the coronation of King Edward VII. So many years had passed since Queen Victoria's accession that even the most aged courtiers had no recollection of the protocol of such ceremonies but for Bertie that posed few problems. Unlike his mother, the new King revelled in the limelight and there could be no better way to mark the beginning of a new reign than by the most impressive show of all: a coronation reflecting all the grandeur and pomp of the British Empire. The organisation of the whole event was entrusted to Lord Esher with instructions that this was to be a spectacle to outshine all spectacles.

By mid-June the preparations were complete; Westminster Abbey was prepared and the many visiting royalties who had arrived in London were settling into various palaces. Then suddenly, twelve days before the ceremony, disaster loomed: the King fell seriously ill and, though he determinedly protested that he could not disappoint his guests, his doctors diagnosed appendicitis which required immediate surgery. There was no alternative but to postpone the coronation. Even then, no one could be sure that the King would survive surgery, as one doctor later confessed to Toria, he was sure 'that His Majesty would die during the operation.'

Overweight, addicted to fine wines, gargantuan meals, fat cigars and pretty women, it seemed that the heir who had waited for so long to come to the throne would in the end be denied his inheritance.

For an anxious forty minutes, Queen Alexandra and her daughters, Toria and Maud, waited in an adjoining room while Frederick Treves performed the surgery. Yet somehow, against the odds, Bertie pulled through. Word of his recovery was greeted with rejoicing throughout the country and made the celebration of his coronation, two months later than planned, even more spectacular.

Behind the scenes came the usual family wrangling about the order of precedence. This time it was not the Kaiser but his younger brother, Henry, who was most disgruntled at being placed towards the back during the ceremonies. His temper was soothed when his sister-in-law, Victoria Battenberg, now settled with her family in London, agreed to bring her children to spend Christmas with him and Irène at Kiel, providing him with the ideal opportunity to show off his new steam car and boat.

Paradoxically, Henry's sister, Charlotte, who was so used to making mischief, had no complaints about the coronation. Recently recovered from one of her recurring bouts of illness, she thoroughly enjoyed the celebrations and wrote cheerful letters from Sandringham describing how much she loved England.

The accession of the new King, coinciding with the dawn of a new century, seemed to revitalise the country. The Boer War finally reached its conclusion and a precarious peace reigned in Europe. Queen Victoria's old world had vanished overnight and her successor's court seemed suddenly young, modern and alive.

No two monarchs could have differed more starkly than the perpetually mourning widow of Windsor and the portly *bon viveur*, King Edward VII. From the moment he ascended the throne a great wind of change blew through the English palaces. On the King's instructions, out went the late Queen's numerous mementos of her stalwart John Brown; modern styles replaced the old Victorian décor; and the hushed and smoke-free rooms of Buckingham Palace echoed to the sound of cigar-puffing Sybarites. In Windsor, too, the King implemented alterations, often to the distress of the courtiers who had become so accustomed to Queen Victoria's methods that they were reluctant to welcome change.

More distressing for Bertie's sisters was his decision to donate the Queen's beloved Osborne House to the nation. To the princesses it had always been a beautiful holiday home filled with happy memories and the added attraction of having been personally designed by the Prince Consort. To Bertie it symbolised all the pain of his repressed childhood. What was more, he loved Sandringham and London and had no intention of escaping, as his mother had so often done, from the bustle and noise of the city to the peaceful seclusion of the Isle of Wight, which bored him.

Notwithstanding his love of the pleasures of life, the King had more in mind than redecorating his palaces. Throughout his sixty years of waiting, he had formed clear and incisive ideas about how to govern the realm. His talents might have been overlooked in Queen Victoria's lifetime but now he would bring them to the fore. His charm, tact and diplomacy impressed not only his subjects but foreign ministers, too. As long as Bertie lived, peace in Europe seemed secure.

While the King's cronies revelled in the glamour of court life, and the new Queen Alexandra basked in the affection of her husband's subjects, her father's accession did nothing to ease the burden of unhappy Toria. As her elder sister, Louise (who was created Princess Royal in 1905) continued to enjoy a semi-reclusive life with her small family, and Maud and her sailor prince disappeared to Denmark, Toria was obliged more frequently than ever to follow at her parents' heels on their numerous royal visits. As her illnesses multiplied, her reputation for hypochondria spread; hearing that the princess had slipped and fallen during a ball at the height of the London season in 1903, the Grand Duchess of Mecklenburg-Strelitz commented acerbically, "But oh! Poor...Victoria's fall, truly grievous, she who is already so delicate."[135] Most of the family shared her sentiments.

It did not ease the unhappy princess's burden to watch her younger cousins walking to the altar to be married. In February 1905, she attended the wedding of Uncle Leopold's daughter, Alice of Albany, to Prince Alexander (Alge) of Teck, younger brother of Princess May, the Duchess of York. Although he was almost ten years older than his bride, there was much to commend the Eton-educated Alge. Handsome and dashing in his cavalry officer's uniform, he had seen active service during the South African war and had even been mentioned in dispatches during the siege of Mafeking.

The wedding took place in St. George's Chapel, Windsor, and was a 'most cheerful' occasion. A colourful gathering of royalties attended the ceremony, including Alice's cousin, Queen Wilhelmina of the Netherlands; and among the bridesmaids were two other cousins, Daisy and Patsy Connaught the elder of whom was soon to marry the sober and scholarly, Prince Gustav of Sweden.

Following a honeymoon in Cannes, the newly-weds, at Uncle Bertie's invitation, settled into apartments at Windsor Castle from where the lively Alice had easy access to all the parties and dances of the capital. The couple travelled frequently, visiting Alice's brother, the Duke of Coburg, and representing King Edward in such distant places as South Africa and the Far East.

In spite of the age difference, it was a remarkably happy marriage that produced three children, May, Rupert and Maurice, the youngest of whom died tragically before his first birthday. The sorrow was made all the greater for his parents as they were away in Coburg at the time, visiting Alice's brother.

Four months after Alice's wedding, the royalties returned to Windsor for Daisy Connaught's wedding. The beautiful Daisy had a choice of several eminently suitable candidates, among them the Crown Prince of Portugal and the arrogant King Alfonso XVIII of Spain, but in 1905, during a visit to Egypt, she met and fell in love with Gustav, heir apparent to the Swedish throne. By the end of the holiday, Daisy and Gustav were engaged and the wedding took place at Windsor on June 15th.

Margaret of Connaught (Daisy)

Daisy's gentle nature and striking beauty soon won the hearts of the Swedish people.

"Daisy was unique:" wrote her cousin Marie Louise, "she possessed the most beautiful character and I can truthfully say was beloved by all who had the privilege of knowing her."[136]

Two years after her marriage, King Oskar died and she rose to the rank of Crown Princess. Hers, too, was a happy marriage, resulting in a daughter, Ingrid, and five sons: Gustav, Adolph, Sigvard, Bertil and Carl Johann.

While Alice and Daisy were celebrating their weddings, their cousin, Ducky, was living down the scandal of her recent divorce. For years she had known that her unhappy union with Ernie was irreparable and only respect for her grandmother had prevented her from making the final break. The whole family was aware that the couple were living apart – Ernie remaining in Darmstadt, while Ducky occupied her mother's villa in Nice where she frequently entertained her lover, Grand Duke Kyril of Russia. Now that Queen Victoria was gone, there was no reason to prolong the intolerable situation and at last on 21st December 1901 the divorce was officially announced on the grounds of 'invincible mutual apathy.'

The not unexpected news might have come as a relief to the Edinburgh family but to Ernie's sisters it struck as a double blow. Not only had they been relying on Ducky to provide an heir for their native Grand Duchy but they also dreaded the scandal if, in the course of the divorce proceedings, the allegations of Ernie's homosexuality should be made public. In an earnest attempt to limit the damage, Alix wrote a carefully worded letter to Nicholas' sister, professing to pass no judgement on her cousin, while insinuating that she, not Ernie was to blame, and urging her sister-in-law to pay no heed to gossip.

Following the divorce, Ernie remained in regular contact with his little daughter, Elizabeth, who stayed with him for several months each year. In autumn of 1903, the Tsar invited them to join the Imperial Family at his hunting lodge in Poland where, within days of their arrival, eight-year-old Elizabeth fell seriously ill with typhoid. Her aunt, the Tsarina, believing that there was no cause for alarm, delayed sending for her mother so that by the time Ducky heard of the illness at the beginning of November, the little girl was already dead. Ernie's sisters, Victoria and Ella rushed to Darmstadt for the funeral where Ernie and Ducky were briefly reconciled in grief.

Two years later, Ernie found a far more compatible wife in Princess Eleonore (Onor) of Lich. Unlike her predecessor, Onor was happy to take over many of Princess Alice's charities and proved a very popular Grand Duchess of Hesse. In spite of Ernie's alleged homosexuality, he found happiness with Onor, who bore him two sons: George Donatus and Ludwig.

For Ducky, life was far less serene. The Orthodox Church maintained its stance on marriage between first cousins, and, even if Kyril was prepared to defy that ruling, as a member of the Imperial Family he could not marry without the Tsar's permission – permission which Nicholas felt unable to give.

While Ducky, morose and despairing, mooched around Nice, the eccentric Queen Elizabeth of Roumania suggested that she should resign herself to a single life and concentrate on serving others by founding a religious order!

Such was Ducky's unhappiness that even her staunchly Orthodox mother pleaded with the Tsar to allow her to marry Kyril in secret but, with Alix vehemently opposed to the scheme, Nicholas stood firm.

From Nice, Ducky watched anxiously as Kyril saw active service with the Russian fleet during the Japanese War of 1904-5˙ escaping death by a whisker when his ship, *Petropavlovsk*, was sunk by an enemy mine. Surely, she hoped, his heroic return would persuade the Tsar to lift the ban but Nicholas remained intransigent. Worn out with pleading and waiting, Kyril decided to take matters into his own hands. In autumn 1905, he arranged to meet Ducky at her mother's home in Tergensee in Bavaria where on Sunday October 8th they were secretly married.

When the news reached Russia, Alix was incensed, and Kyril's arrival at the Tsar's home in Tsarskoe Selo a few days later did nothing to appease her anger. Denying the Grand Duke access to the Alexander Palace, she ensured that Nicholas

---

˙ see chapter 26

imposed on him the full penalty for disobedience. Kyril was stripped of his titles and banished from the country. Only two years later, when Ducky gave birth to a daughter and converted to Orthodoxy, did Nicholas agree to endorse the marriage and restore the Grand Duke's titles. Still, relations with the Imperial Family were so taut that Kyril and Ducky opted to remain in Paris until after the birth of a second daughter in 1909.

It was, perhaps, as well that they remained away from St. Petersburg, for their exile coincided with one of the most horrifying and tumultuous periods in the reign of Tsar Nicholas II.

Chapter 26 – Revolution Is Banging On the Door

Nicholas (Nicky): Tsar Nicholas II of Russia
Alix: Tsarina Alexandra of Russia; daughter of Princess Alice
Ella: Grand Duchess Serge; Alix's elder sister
Serge: Grand Duke Serge Alexandrovich; Ella's husband
Marie: Duchess of Edinburgh and Coburg, Serge's sister
Victoria: Princess Louis of Battenberg; eldest sister of Alix & Ella

Grand Duke Kyril's flouting of the Tsar's authority was but one of a series of misdemeanours committed by members of the Tsar's extended family throughout the reign of Nicholas II. Each seemingly minor transgression, each affair, each morganatic marriage, and each breach of Nicholas' authority, might have been insignificant in itself but together they amounted to a severe undermining of the autocracy.

As Russia struggled from medieval feudalism to industrialisation, the country was clamouring for reform. For centuries peasants in remote rural communities had accepted the distant Tsar as God's anointed ruler but now, as they flocked into the overcrowded cities, attitudes were changing. Workers toiling in appalling conditions were easy prey for radicals who were demanding an end to the 'tyranny' of Tsardom. Even the most conservative thinkers were forced to accept the inevitability of a shift to a more democratic form of government.

While domestic conditions were changing, international relations, too, brought their share of challenges. If Russia were to compete with the rest of the industrialised world, she needed access to the Pacific but even the major port of Vladivostok was ice-bound for several months each year. The ideal solution would be to extend the Trans-Siberian railway eastwards through Korea but the neighbouring Japanese were totally opposed to such a plan.

It occurred to some of the Tsar's advisors that it might be possible to take advantage of the situation in the east, not only to secure Korea and Manchuria, but also to improve the Tsar's standing in the eyes of his people. The vast Russian ranks easily outnumbered the small Japanese army and an early victory would restore a sense of national pride and reunite the people behind their Emperor. Heedless of the warnings of the Finance Minister, Count de Witte, the ministers and Nicholas' uncles painted an image of a glorious Tsar leading his army through a blaze of glory behind the Romanov double-headed eagle.

The dull reality was quite different from that heroic fantasy. The Japanese had no desire for war and would willingly have settled the matter through negotiation but, as Russian troops continued to move through the region, they had no alternative but to take up arms.

In January 1904, the Japanese struck the first blow, attacking the Russian fleet at Port Arthur, provoking Russia to declare war. A tide of patriotic fervour swept the country as crowds gathered to cheer the troops setting out on their long journey east.

Although already in the later stages of her final pregnancy, Alix threw herself wholeheartedly into the war effort. She opened a hospital at Tsarskoe Selo where she paid daily visits to the wounded and arranged for the men to learn various crafts during their recuperation.

> "The great salons of the Winter Palace were turned into workrooms and there every day society flocked to sew and knit for our soldiers and sailors fighting such incredible distances away, as well as for the wounded in hospitals at home and abroad...Every day the Empress came to inspect the work, often sitting down at a table and sewing diligently with the others."[137]

In the Kremlin, her sister, Ella, also threw herself wholeheartedly into the war effort, organising well-equipped ambulance trains and arranging packages of icons and gifts to be sent to the Front. As the wounded returned to the city, she made daily visits to the military hospitals, taking the time to talk to each patient and learn more about his background and circumstances.

> "But the most remarkable achievement which was due to her, and to her alone," wrote her lady-in-waiting, "was the organisation of women workers, drawn together from all stations of life, from the highest to the lowest, whom she united in the Kremlin Palace, where workrooms were arranged. From morning till evening all through the war, this busy hive worked for the army, and the Grand Duchess saw with joy that the immense gilded salons hardly sufficed to contain the workers...all her days were spent in this work, which assumed gigantic proportions."[138]

In spite of the tireless efforts of the Imperial Family, the list of Russian casualties grew. Far from being a weak little enemy, the Japanese were well-disciplined, efficient soldiers capable of inflicting terrible losses on the massive Russian army. The proposed 'short' war was rapidly turning into a prolonged fiasco and patriotism was replaced by anger and resentment.

By autumn, after nine months of fighting, the disillusioned Russians had grown weary of sacrificing their sons in the hopeless campaign. Disturbances broke out in the streets of Moscow and St. Petersburg and the reactionary Minister of the Interior was assassinated. Strikes threatened to bring St. Petersburg to a standstill and the unrest was in danger of spilling into greater violence.

"Revolution is banging on the door," wrote the Tsar's cousin, Konstantin Konstantinovich.[139]

Ministers asserted that the only means of placating the revolutionaries was to create a constitution. For Nicholas and Alix, the suggestion that Tsar should hand over his authority to an elected council (the Duma) was unthinkable. At his coronation, Nicholas had taken an oath to uphold the autocracy and consequently felt duty-bound to adhere to the promise made before God. Alix urged her husband to be strong, dismissing the ministers' reports of imminent revolution as scare-mongering and assuring him that the ordinary Russians loved their Emperor.

It was true that many thousands of his subjects still revered their Tsar. He was their Little Father who loved his people and only permitted the injustices they endured because he was unaware of their sufferings. If they could only reach him and tell him of their plight, he would surely deal kindly with their grievances. Encouraging such thoughts was a socialist priest, Father Gapon, who, in an attempt to prevent bloodshed, offered to lead a peaceful procession to the Winter Palace so that the people could petition the Emperor.

On Saturday 21st January 1905, Gapon, unaware that the Tsar was several miles away in Tsarskoe Selo, informed the Minister of the Interior, Prince Mirsky, that the following day he would lead over one hundred thousand people to the palace. At the thought of so vast a crowd, Mirsky panicked. He warned the Tsar that violence might erupt and advised him to stay out of the city, before summoning mounted troops to guard the bridges of the frozen River Neva to prevent the crowds from reaching the palace.

The next day, Sunday 22nd January, thousands of men, women and children walked peacefully through the streets of St. Petersburg with the sole intention of presenting Nicholas with their petitions. As the orderly procession neared the Neva bridges, many of the marchers held aloft icons and portraits of the Tsar and Tsarina to demonstrate their fidelity and trust.

With absolute faith in their anointed Emperor, the crowds ignored the soldiers' warnings to turn back and, as the vast horde continued to advance, the terrified generals ordered the troops to open fire. Within minutes over a thousand of the Tsar's devoted subjects were gunned down, dropping their blood-stained icons beside the corpses of little children.

As news of the massacre spread through the country, Moscow exploded into violence. The city had long been a hot bed of sedition and now, as revolutionaries incited the citizens to take up arms against 'bloody Nicholas the Butcher,' barricades rose in the streets. The entire Romanov family became a symbol of oppression and tyranny and the most obvious target for the revolutionaries' anger was Ella's much-maligned husband, Grand Duke Serge.

One member of the Imperial Family to escape the revolutionary wrath was Ella. Before the outbreak of war, her charitable works had earned her a saintly reputation and once the hostilities began her popularity soared.

> "Moscow worshipped its Grand Duchess, and showed its appreciation by the quantities of gifts brought to her for her soldiers...Her personality was so inspiring that the coldest people took fire from contact with her ardent soul."[140]

Even as the barricades rose in the streets, Ella ignored the police warnings to remain out of sight, and continued to make her daily round of the hospital wards. But Ella was not blind to the dangers. Serge had received several death threats while she herself was sent anonymous letters warning her not to appear with her husband in public.

The strain of such an existence was enormous, and a final blow to reactionary Serge was the realisation that the Tsar was planning to grant limited reforms. Unable to accept the changes and worn down by the stress of his position, Serge finally decided to tender his resignation as Governor General of Moscow.

In the early afternoon, February 17th 1905, as her husband left the Kremlin for the Governor General's residence to clear his papers, Ella was working on her Red Cross projects when an explosion shattered the silence.

"It's Serge!" Ella cried, rushing from the palace and summoning a sleigh to speed her to the scene. As she approached Senate Square, the gathering crowd tried to hold her back but it was too late. Before her in the snow lay a tangled mess of flesh and bone – all that was left of her husband. His head, his leg and his arm had been blown off by a terrorist's bomb. The blast was so great that, days later, his fingers were found on the roof of the Kremlin.

Scrambling through the gore for Serge's medals and icons, Ella called to the soldiers for a stretcher from one of her Red Cross ambulances, then, with her own hands, placed what was left of her husband on the palette, which she ordered to be covered with soldiers' coats and taken to a neighbouring monastery. A silent crowd followed her into the chapel where the stretcher was placed on the altar steps while she knelt and prayed.

"The horror left a deep trace on her countenance, which only passed away when, having learnt the futility of earthly existence, she received the experience of divine beauty, and after this time her eyes seemed to be gazing at a vision of the other world."[141]

That evening, though obviously still in shock, Ella summoned a carriage to take her to the hospital where Serge's coachman lay fatally wounded. To avoid causing him further distress, the doctors had told him that his master was only slightly injured and, as Ella neared his bed, he asked for news of the Grand Duke.

She smiled gently, "It was he who sent me to you."

285

That night the coachman, passed away in his sleep.

Fearful of further assassinations, the Tsar was prevailed upon to issue an order forbidding the Imperial Family to travel to Moscow for the funeral. Ella's sister, Victoria, hurried to Russia, and Serge's sister, Marie, arrived from Coburg with Ella's young cousin, Beatrice. Constrained in Tsarskoe Selo, Alix could only take comfort from the news that Ella was 'bearing her terrible grief like a saint.'

Ella of Hesse

Two days later, Ella revealed the depths of her sanctity. Carrying a Bible and an icon of Christ, she set out for the prison where her husband's killer, Ivan Kalyaev, was being held. In a private meeting, she wept as she told him that she had forgiven him and, without least hint of malice or anger, asked what had driven him to commit such a crime.

Touched as he was by her sorrow and evident sincerity, Kalyaev told her that he felt no remorse as he believed his actions had been entirely justified. As she rose to leave, she told him, "I will pray for you," and handed him the icon and Bible.

Newspapers later reported that she had petitioned the Tsar for a pardon but, since the assassin failed to repent, her request was refused.

Kalyaev's execution did nothing to still the tide of unrest sweeping through Russia, and by August it was clear that there was nothing to be gained from prolonging the disastrous Japanese War. In the humiliation of defeat, Alix continued her work for the wounded soldiers, organising schemes to teach the disabled men new trades and providing them and their families with new cottages, but again her efforts passed largely unnoticed and the violence continued unabated. In the Caucasus, rebels attacked and murdered officials, and in Moscow, angry mobs manned barricades in the streets until Nicholas realised he had no alternative but to call a Duma, effectively signing away the three-hundred-year-old autocracy.

With the opening of the Duma in October 1905, a semblance of peace was restored. The barricades were dismantled, the strikers returned to work and the future Russian leader, Lenin, living in some luxury in Switzerland, gloomily observed that the opportunity for revolution had passed. Nonetheless, the Tsar's reputation had suffered a blow from which it would never fully recover. While Alix was disgusted at the manner in which he had been forced to accept the Duma, anarchists were disappointed that the reforms had not gone far enough. Ella, meanwhile, mourning the loss of a husband she had loved, was about to make a more radical change in her life than even the most extreme Bolsheviks could have imagined.

Chapter 27 – A Sensible Girl Full of Good Intentions

Maud: Princess Carl of Denmark; Youngest daughter of Edward VII
Carl: Maud's husband; younger son of King Frederick VIII of Denmark
Patsy (Patricia): Younger daughter of Arthur, Duke of Connaught
Ena (Victoria Eugenie): Daughter of Princess Beatrice

In the early months of 1905, while Ella was coming to terms with the horrific murder of her husband, Cousin Maud of Wales was enjoying a peaceful existence in relative obscurity in Denmark. Though she had never lost her nostalgia for England, she was happy with her sailor prince and delighted to spend several months of each year in the haven of Appleton Lodge. It would have suited Maud to remain forever in untroubled anonymity with her husband and their three-year-old son, Alexander, but life was about to take a strange turn for the shy Princess Carl of Denmark.

For ninety years the Kings of Sweden had ruled neighbouring Norway but by the turn of century, following a series of political upheavals, the Norwegians were pressing for independence with a separate monarchy. Since there was no ruling House in their country, they asked King Oskar of Sweden to appoint them a sovereign from his own family but, unwilling to yield to such a revolutionary proposal, he refused. The Norwegians then turned to the Danish King Frederick VIII who had no such qualms and recognised that his second son, Carl, was the most obvious candidate.

Neither Carl nor Maud had any desire to reign in a foreign country, particularly when they were told that large groups of Norwegians favoured a republic. For several months, in spite of pressure from his father in Denmark and his father-in-law in England, the prince refused the throne until at length, in November 1905, the Norwegians succeeded in convincing him that he truly was the people's choice.

A warm reception greeted the new King and Queen on their arrival in the capital, Christiania (now Oslo). Carl's decision to adopt the ancient Norwegian name of Haakon VII and to change the name of his son from Alexander to Olaf proved popular with his new subjects. Maud, too, made a good impression. She had already begun to master the language, and her regal yet unassuming manner, and determination to take her responsibilities seriously soon earned the Norwegians' respect and affection.

Maud of Wales

In wider Europe, however, Carl's decision to accept the throne did not win universal acclaim. The Kaiser, opposed to any scheme promoted by 'Uncle Bertie' – the British King Edward VII – had preferred a Swedish contender, though in a typical about-turn he later assured Carl of his support. Other royalties were not so easily appeased and several complained about the idea of an elected monarch which, they felt, undermined the whole concept of monarchy.

Maud herself had not entirely succeeded in overcoming her shyness and, as the day of the coronation drew nearer, all her old insecurities returned. Nonetheless, she managed to overcome her nerves to rise to the occasion. Even though a recurrence of neuralgia prevented her from walking in the coronation procession, her manner and bearing impressed the enthusiastic crowds lining the route to Trondheim Cathedral. Throughout the ceremony she played her part with the finesse that would characterise all her undertakings in Norway.

In spite of her delicate health, Queen Maud, like many of her cousins, involved herself in numerous charitable causes including, to the horror of the more prudish, a refuge for unmarried mothers. Whatever the critics may have thought of her 'revolutionary throne', she and Carl proved popular monarchs who endured few of the upheavals that were soon to beset their cousins and other European dynasties.

While Maud was accustoming herself to the idea of a foreign throne, her cousin, nineteen-year-old Patsy Connaught – 'tall beautiful, gifted and a brilliant artist'[142] – had journeyed to Spain with her parents. Travelling through Madrid, she was horrified to hear the enthusiastic crowds acclaiming her as their future Queen. The shy young princess had no ambition to become the Queen of anywhere and still less to be the wife of the arrogant philanderer King Alfonso XIII, who only a few months previously had been equally taken with her elder sister, Daisy.

Undaunted by Patsy's obvious lack of interest, the King was so convinced of his own magnetism that he decided to pursue the match and journeyed to

England later that year with a view to making Patsy his bride. His efforts were in vain. Patsy resisted his advances and would remain unmarried for over a decade.

In 1911, she and her parents set sail for Ottawa where her father, Prince Arthur, was to take over as Governor of Canada. As her mother's health declined, Patsy assumed the responsibility for hosting her father's receptions and carried out her duties with such graciousness that she was rewarded by having several regiments and a mountain range named in her honour.

Patsy's refusal did not trouble the fickle Spanish King. As soon as he realised that Patsy was unmoved by his approaches, he quickly switched his attention to her eighteen-year-old cousin, Ena Battenberg.

Since the death of Queen Victoria, Ena and her mother had been living peacefully in Kensington Palace from where Princess Beatrice kept her eyes open for suitable candidates for Ena's hand. Unlike her own mother, Princess Beatrice had no qualms about permitting her daughter to marry, and had encouraged the suit of the Russian Grand Duke Boris Vladimirovich, (brother of Ducky's husband, Kyril) whose name had once been scandalously linked to Cousin Marie of Roumania. The arrival of the Spanish King put paid to the notion of a Russian match and was about to change the young princess's life forever.

What attracted Ena to the pompous Spaniard, eleven years her senior, remains unclear. Having acceded to the throne before his first birthday, Alfonso was a self-centred, lecherous chauvinist and, if the Russian throne appeared insecure, Spain's was positively rocking. During the lifetime of

Alfonso's father, the country had briefly been a republic and, even after the restoration of the monarchy, separatist groups were demanding independence. Several attempts had been made on Alfonso's life and he was so used to anarchists' attacks that when a car backfired in London his guards assumed it was an assassination attempt and almost shot an innocent bystander. Moreover, Alfonso was a Roman Catholic and, by order of the Spanish parliament, his wife had to be of the same faith.

Perhaps Alfonso's seductive manner and suave appearance eventually won the heart of the English princess. Throughout the summer he courted her in the fashionable haunt of royalties, Biarritz, and before the onset of autumn, Ena had agreed to convert to Catholicism (after all, her godmother had been the Roman Catholic French Empress Eugenie).

The Bishop of Nottingham, Robert Brindle, instructed Ena in the Catholic faith and, on 7th March 1906, she was received into the Church at San Sebastian. Though the Archbishop of Canterbury was troubled by Ena's conversion, few members of her family raised any objections but, to Ena's surprise, the British public was outraged. So great was the general disapproval that Ena's cousin, George, the Duke of York, felt obliged to warn her mother to keep Ena away from London until the resentment died down.

Nor was the news of the engagement greeted with great rejoicing in Spain. Alfonso's mother revived the old complaint that the Battenbergs were not 'of the blood' and considered Ena unworthy of the Spanish King. In response, King Edward VII elevated his niece from a mere Highness to a Royal Highness and, a month later, in May 1906, amid many tears Ena – 'a sensible girl...full of good intentions' – and her mother set sail for Madrid.

On 31st May, royalties from Russia, Germany and England mingled in the sweltering Spanish sunlight for the wedding. The dusty roads and squalid conditions of the capital gave rise to a good deal of muttering among the foreign guests but their complaints might have taken on more significance if they had realised how close they were to death. As the company gathered for the Nuptial Mass, celebrated by the Archbishop of Toledo, the Archbishop of Westminster, and Bishop Brindle, an uninvited guest armed with a bomb was desperately trying to enter the impressive Church of St. Hieronimo, which the couple had selected instead of the expected larger Cathedral of San Franciso. An anarchist, Mateo Morral, almost succeeded in obtaining a ticket when, at the last minute, access was denied him and the three-hour long Mass proceeded

Victoria Eugenie of Battenberg (Ena)

without incident. But Morral was not to be deterred.

Amid cheering crowds, the newly-married couple left the cathedral and set off in procession for the short drive to the Royal Palace. As their coach wound its way through the streets, Morral, watching from an upstairs balcony, hurled a bomb concealed in a bouquet of flowers onto the street below. Miraculously, at that very moment, the royal coach paused and the bomb missed the carriage, leaving Ena and her husband unharmed. The King climbed out of the coach only to discover the extent of the horror. One of Alfonso's equerries and several footmen, soldiers and bystanders had been blown to pieces. Alfonso immediately sent word to Ena's mother that her daughter was unharmed, and her cousin, Toria of Wales, helped her from the carriage.

Gazing on the terrible scene, Ena, her white wedding-dress splattered with blood, remained rigid in shock until she was led to another carriage and hurriedly returned to the palace. There she threw herself into her mother's arms, weeping in horror while her unperturbed Aunt Marie, Dowager Duchess of Coburg, and sister of the recently assassinated Grand Duke Serge of Russia, drifted around telling anyone who would listen, "I'm so used to this sort of thing!"

That afternoon, which should have been spent in joyful celebrations, the new Queen toured the hospitals to visit the injured. Later that day, she and Alfonso courageously rode again in an open carriage through the streets of Madrid. In the days that followed, Alfonso attended the funerals of the victims while Ena recovered from the ordeal. Ironically, it later emerged that the bomb had been thrown from the only house in the city owned by the Queen Mother.

After such a horrific reception, it came as relief for Ena to escape from Spain in August to spend part of her honeymoon in the remote tranquillity of Scotland in the company of Uncle Arthur, Duke of Connaught. The Scots were delighted to welcome the Scottish-born Queen and the news reports were effusive in their praise. She was, they said:

> 'So fair and placid and majestic, such a solemn contrast to her boyish, nervous-looking, energetic husband.'[143]

Sadly, the differences between Ena and Alfonso would become more apparent once they returned to Madrid.

The death of more than thirty people on her wedding day marked only the beginning of the Queen's unhappiness in Spain. Her plans 'to do good there' were thwarted time after time and, like Cousin Sophie of Greece, she soon found herself an outsider in her husband's country. In the family tradition, she worked hard to improve the medical services but, rather than appreciating her efforts on their behalf, the Spaniards, believed it demeaning for a woman, and still more a princess, to take an interest in nursing. Even the Church objected to her interference, accusing her of usurping the work of established Religious Orders. On a personal level too, her temperament proved ill-suited to the Spanish culture; her English reserve earning her 'a reputation of frigidity.'

Most wounding of all for Ena was the treatment she received from her blatantly unfaithful husband. When their eldest son was diagnosed with haemophilia˙, Alfonso cruelly blamed his wife for the boy's condition and carelessly returned to his mistresses.

Three years after her wedding there came a glimmer of hope. One of Ena's cousins was about to marry into the Spanish Royal Family and her arrival in Madrid might have eased the young Queen's loneliness. As it turned out, the appearance of Baby Bee (Beatrice) of Edinburgh, merely added to Ena's woes.

Described by Queen Victoria, as 'a pretty girl with a very pretty figure' Baby Bee had, like her

---

˙ see chapter 28

elder sister, Ducky, made the unfortunate mistake of falling in love with a Russian Orthodox first cousin. As histrionic as her sisters when it came to romance, Baby Bee was in her late teens when she began a correspondence with the Tsar's younger brother, the attractive and charming Grand Duke Mikhail (Misha). For several months, she and Misha poured out their feelings for each other with adolescent fervour, but Misha knew that there could be no future in their relationship. He need only look at Ducky and Kyril to realise how unbending the Orthodox Church would be when it came to marriage between first cousins. He knew, too, that in his case there was even less chance of obtaining a dispensation than there had been for Kyril, since he was, at the time, the heir to the Russian throne. Baby Bee, however, blinded by love, remained optimistic.

When the Dowager Empress Marie of Russia realised that her son was on the verge of creating a scandal, she desperately tried to arrange a more suitable marriage and dropped several strong hints that he intended to marry Patsy Connaught. London newspapers went so far as to print announcements of the forthcoming wedding until the distraught and much-courted Patsy, who hardly knew the Grand Duke, insisted on an immediate correction.

By the end of 1903, under sustained pressure from his family, Misha conceded defeat and wrote to Baby Bee from Denmark, urging her to break off their correspondence. Beatrice was devastated and, as she cried constantly and refused to eat, her mother packed her off to Egypt to recover. In her absence, Ducky attempted to save face by announcing that her sister had never entertained any thoughts of marrying the Grand Duke and her reaction was due to the shock she had received at being so misunderstood. No one believed the excuse, particularly when Beatrice returned from Egypt appearing sicklier and more lovelorn than ever. To further her recuperation, her mother took her to the villa in Nice where Ducky was staying and from where in January 1904, the Tsar's sister, Xenia, reported that she looked so unwell that her family feared she would lose her mind.

Two years' later, as Misha formed an equally dangerous attachment to his sister's lady-in-waiting, Beatrice, her sanity intact, accompanied her mother to Madrid for Ena's wedding. All thoughts of the Grand Duke now banished, she met and fell in love with the Spanish King's cousin, Infante Alfonso of Bourbon-Lyons, Duke of Galliera.

Beatrice of Edinburgh (Baby Bee)

Baby Bee was eager to marry but again religion threatened to scupper her plans. Those who married into the Spanish ruling family were expected to convert to Catholicism but the Coburg princess was far less obliging in the matter than Cousin Ena had been. When it was clear that Baby Bee could not be persuaded to convert, the Spanish King urged the couple to marry in secret, which they did in 1909. What the King had failed to consider, however, was that he was a constitutional monarch who had no right to make such decisions. When the news came out, parliament took a dim view of the Infante's misdemeanour, stripped him of his commission and banished him from the country.

The couple settled for three years in Switzerland where two sons, Alvaro and Alonzo, were born. In 1912, the Spanish parliament relented and permitted the couple to return to Spain where, the following year, a third son, Ataulfo, was born.

If Queen Ena was initially pleased to welcome her cousin back to court, she soon discovered that Baby Bee would prove neither an asset nor a friend. Rather than attempting to ease the lonely Queen's burden, she went out of her way to humiliate her, openly flirting with the King and even procuring new mistresses for him. Her bizarre behaviour became so unpleasant that eventually the King's mother intervened and persuaded him to order her to leave the country again.

Baby Bee's departure, however, did nothing to heal the rift between Ena and Alfonso. It was too late. The King could never forgive his wife for introducing 'the terrible disease of the English family' into his dynasty.

Chapter 28 - The Terrible Illness of the English Family

Charlotte: Princess of Saxe-Meiningen; Vicky's eldest daughter
Alix: Tsarina of Russia
Nicholas: Tsar Nicholas II of Russia
Ella: Alix's elder sister
Irène: Princess Henry of Prussia; Alix's elder sister
Louise, Toria & Maud: Daughters of Edward VII
Ena: Queen of Spain; daughter of Princess Beatrice
Alice: Princess of Teck; daughter of Prince Leopold

Queen Victoria had left a rich legacy to her granddaughters. To her they owed many happy memories, their status, their innate nobility and their stoical sense of duty. But there was another more tragic legacy: a legacy of ill-health which would not only affect the princesses themselves but would also have far-reaching consequences for several European dynasties.

Perhaps if the Prince Consort's warnings of the need to bring 'strong dark blood' into the family had been heeded, the cousins might have been spared some of their suffering, for, in spite of Sir William Jenner's assurances that inter-breeding among such healthy stock would produce strong children, a variety of medical problems were prevalent in the family, several of which were inherited from their grandmother. Letters to and from the princesses and their mothers were filled with references to their ailments, not all of which can be explained away by the tight-fitting corsets and the fashionable delicacy of aristocratic Victorian women.

Following extensive research, Rohl, Warren and Hunt[144], discovered strong evidence to suggest that several generations of Queen Victoria's family suffered from the hereditary malady, porphyria. Characterised by a variety of symptoms including aversion to heat, rashes, severe abdominal pain, weakening of the legs and irrational behaviour, the illness had been in the family for several generations, manifesting itself most clearly in the 'madness' of Queen Victoria's grandfather, King George III.

Though certainly more sane than her grandfather, Queen Victoria, unable to bear stuffy rooms, constantly longing for fresh air and displaying illogical mood-swings, *might* have suffered from the illness. At the time of her mother's death in March 1861, Queen Victoria was on the verge of a nervous breakdown and the death of Prince Albert nine months later, left her prostrate with grief. During her extended period of excessive mourning many of her ministers seriously believed she was on the brink of insanity and were convinced that she would abdicate in favour of her eldest son.

Though more rational in her behaviour, Vicky had certainly inherited many of her mother's physical symptoms. Her aversion to heat left her constantly exhausted and desperate to escape from balls and social functions in the early years of her marriage. On several occasions she suffered from such terrible rashes that she was obliged to cover her face when appearing in public. Charlotte, in turn, inherited Vicky's symptoms to a greater degree and she would pass them on to her tragic daughter, Feo.˙

Even in childhood, Charlotte's health had been poor, plagued as she was by continual nasal and throat complaints. Her delayed adolescence gave

---

˙ In 1945, after years of ill-health, Feo committed suicide by putting her head into a gas oven.

way to an abnormal growth spurt resulting in her 'top-heavy' appearance, and after her marriage her symptoms multiplied. She fainted three times during her extended wedding celebrations and her behaviour was often unaccountable not only to her family but even to Charlotte herself:

> "She has the wish to be amicable and make herself pleasant," Vicky had told the Queen, "but the poor dear Child never can be a helpmate or resource to anyone...Nature has made her so..."[145]

Frequently affected by numerous physical complaints, towards the end of the century Charlotte was virtually spending half the year in bed, tormented by rheumatic pains, sciatica, dental abscesses, abdominal swellings, paralysis of the legs and a myriad of other symptoms – which, incidentally bear a strong resemblance the symptoms Prince Albert endured in the weeks before his death˙. As her condition remained undiagnosed, several of her doctors considered her ailments hysterical in origin, though both Charlotte and her mother seemed to recognise a similarity in their sufferings, caused by an underlying problem in their metabolism.

Though there is insufficient evidence to suggest that any of her cousins also suffered from porphyria, several of Charlotte's symptoms were common to other members of the family. As children, the Wales girls were constantly ailing with neuralgia, rheumatic pains, dental problems, sciatica, and ear infections. At the time of her divorce, Marie Louise was advised to travel for the sake of her health which had been severely affected by 'a series of never-ending bad colds'; in his boyhood, the Kaiser endured months of trouble from ear

---

˙ See Appendix I

infections, which recurred throughout his life; Victoria of Hesse's eldest daughter was deaf; and so intense was the pain in Alix of Hesse's ears that she had to take a cure after Mossy's wedding. Like Maud and Charlotte, Alix suffered too from facial neuralgia and pains in her jaw. Alix's sister, Ella, who was, in her grandmother's opinion 'not very strong,' was also particularly prone to colds and bronchial complaints:

> "Ella has again had one of her bad attacks in her throat," Princess Alice wrote to the Queen when Ella was four years old, "...Two nights ago she could not speak - barely breathe - and was so uncomfortable, poor child."[146]

Though in Ella's case the symptoms were exacerbated by the icy Russian winters, she herself considered them simply as family complaints. Following surgery to remove a benign tumour in 1908, she wrote the Tsar that she was 'astonishingly well' except:

> "A wee cold or rheumatic twinges or gout can't be prevented as our family all suffers from the latter...There is hardly a person who has not that."[147]

In their correspondence, the cousins make numerous references to their sciatica, rheumatic pains and weakness in their legs. The heat of Athens, often left Sophie 'very ill', particularly during her pregnancies; Maud was so blighted by neuralgia that she was unable to walk in her coronation procession; Marie Louise of Schleswig-Holstein, later consulted spiritual healers in search of a cure for arthritis; and shortly before her wedding, Alix of Hesse was so troubled by sciatica that her grandmother had sent her to the spa at Harrogate.

Alix's problems increased after her marriage, and were exacerbated by pregnancy. The sciatic pain was often so severe that she was unable to walk and was reduced to being pushed around in a wheelchair. In early 1897, she was confined to bed for seven weeks and, by the end of the following year, her doctors recommended complete rest.

"Unluckily I cannot get about at all," she wrote in 1904, "and spend my days on the sofa ... walking and standing causes me great pain.... I know I must lie, it is the only remedy."[148]

Alix's complaints were not confined to her legs; headaches, exhaustion, and eventually 'an enlarged heart' added to her woes:

"The Empress certainly had bad luck where her health was concerned," wrote Baroness Buxhoeveden. "In the years when she was neither expecting nor nursing a baby, she invariably fell ill. One winter she had influenza three times; another year she had measles..."[149]

Alongside their physical ailments, several of the princesses had inherited another unwelcome legacy from their grandmother: nerves. Queen Victoria wholeheartedly empathised with nervous complaints for throughout her life she suffered terribly, particularly when under stress.

'Nerves' and 'neurasthenia' were to feature regularly in the family correspondence. Vicky informed her mother that her daughter, Mossy's nerves were 'not of the strongest'; and doctors were amazed by Charlotte's 'broken down nerves'. In the midst of a dispute with Sophie of Greece, Victoria Battenberg's daughter came to the conclusion that her Prussian cousin was 'a bit mad.' Even the stoical Marie of Roumania was liable to periods of depression during which she took to her bed, while her younger sister Baby Bee had 'almost lost her mind' over the affair with Misha. The slightest stress could stretch Toria of Wales's nerves to their limit, and, during the First World War, the Tsarina was so stressed that courtiers suspected that she was insane.

The tensions of life in Russia were not solely responsible for Alix's sensitivity; even before her marriage she had, according to Baroness Buxhoeveden, been 'nearing a breakdown' because:

"The shock of her father's death and the fatigues that followed it were too much for her. She...had to be taken for a cure to Schwalbach by her brother."[150]

As if porphyria, rheumatism, sciatica and nervous instability were not enough, there was a still more devastating legacy in Queen Victoria's family. Through one defective gene, the Grandmother of Europe had 'infected' four European Houses with the terrible bleeding disease, haemophilia.

The blood of the haemophiliac fails to clot, which in the 19th Century, before the discovery of Factor VIII, meant that the slightest knock could cause bleeding into the joints, resulting in excruciating swellings, deformity or paralysis. A blow to the head could cause a fatal brain haemorrhage and even a minor cut could prove fatal.

Since the condition is carried in the dominant X gene, girls rarely suffer from haemophilia, but they can be carriers, transmitting the condition to their sons. In the Victorian era, there was insufficient knowledge of genetics to predict which of members of a family might have inherited the disease and the randomness of its occurrence made it all the more difficult to bear. Within one family group, some brothers might be haemophiliac, others perfectly healthy; some sisters carriers, others not, but there was no method of knowing which girls had inherited the gene until their sons were born. Prince Leopold was the only one of Queen Victoria's four sons to have been haemophiliac, but two of his five sisters, Alice and Beatrice were carriers.

Since the age of seven, Irène of Hesse had been familiar with the devastating effects of the illness. In 1873, she had seen her three-year-old brother, Frittie, die as a result of a brain haemorrhage following a fall, and she was equally aware of the terrible agonies suffered by Uncle Leopold. Yet in 1888, when Irène married Cousin Henry, she had no idea that she had inherited the defective gene and would introduce the 'English disease' into the Prussian royal family with the birth of her first son, Waldemar. Mercifully, Irène's second son, Sigismund escaped the illness, but her third and youngest child, Henry, was also a haemophiliac. In February 1904, in an almost identical replay of Frittie's tragic death, three-year-old Henry fell and bumped his head, dying shortly afterwards. When the tragic news reached St. Petersburg, Irène's sister, Alix, was devastated but, as she wept for her nephew, she had no idea that at that very moment the unborn baby she was carrying had also inherited the disease.

On 12th August 1904, only half an hour after going into labour, the Tsarina gave birth to a son. The years of prayers, pilgrimages and consultations with healers and quacks suddenly seemed worthwhile. The Tsar, 'mad with joy', gave orders for the canon of the Peter and Paul Fortress to fire the 301-gun salute to welcome the new Tsarevich Alexei. Even in the midst of the horrors of the

Russo-Japanese War, the country rejoiced that the dynasty seemed secure.

The beautiful golden-haired baby with his father's striking blue eyes, was christened twelve days later and in a show of gratitude to the troops fighting against Japan, every soldier in the army was proclaimed his godfather.

"No heir to the crown had been born in Russia, as heir, since the seventeenth century, and the ceremony was surrounded with splendour that matched the importance of the event. It took place in the Chapel of the big Peterhof Palace on August 24th, 1904. King George V of England (then Duke of York) and the German Emperor were among the baby's godfathers. The Empress Marie Feodorovna was his godmother. The baby Tsarevich was appointed Colonel of many regiments and decorations were showered on him. Imperial bounty in every form, amnesties, remittances of sentences, gifts of money were among the signs of the Emperor's joy at the birth of an heir."[151]

The delight of his parents was ineffable. Every letter and every diary entry contained references to 'Baby' and there was no reason for Alix to suspect that there was anything wrong with her son. After all, her elder sister, Victoria, had given birth to four children, none of whom was a haemophiliac, and Alexei appeared too healthy to have inherited the terrible disease. Within a month, his mother was to be cruelly disillusioned.

In September 1904, Alexei began bleeding from his navel and when the doctors' efforts to staunch the flow failed, Alix was left in little doubt as to its cause. The longed-for Tsarevich was a haemophiliac. For his mother the news was overwhelming. 'She hardly knew a day's happiness after she knew her boy's fate,' wrote her friend, Anna Vyrubova. From that moment, the rest of her life would be devoted to the care of her son. Every bump, every knock and every graze caused her indescribable

Tsarevich Alexei

anguish as night after night she sat by his bedside, helplessly listening to his cries. Tormented by fear for his safety, and guilt for having passed on the disease, she spent hours on her knees, desperately praying for a cure.

> "Everything possible, everything known to medical science, was done for the child Alexei. The Empress nursed him herself, as indeed, with the assistance of professional women, she had nursed all her children. Three trained Russian nurses were in attendance, with the Empress always superintending. She bathed the babe herself, and was with him so much that the Court, ever censorious of her, complained that she was more of a nurse than an Empress."[152]

To add to her anguish, the Tsarina knew that it was imperative to keep the truth from the public. By the time that Alexei's diagnosis was confirmed, Russia was in the throes of the Japanese war. If it were known that the heir was a sickly child who could die at any moment, revolutionaries might well seize the chance of overthrowing the monarchy. Moreover, it would hardly improve the reputation of the Empress were it known that she had introduced haemophilia into the three-hundred-year-old Romanov dynasty. Nicholas consequently decided that Alexei's haemophilia should be kept a state secret. No one outside their immediate circle – not even Nicholas' sisters – should be told the true nature of his illness.

Living under such stress, Alix's already taut nerves were stretched to the limit. One minute she was kneeling by her son's bed, trying to soothe his pain and desperately trying to control her tears; the next she must appear before her guests, struggling to appear unperturbed. The Tsarevich's tutor, Pierre Gilliard, recalled an occasion when Alix's daughters were presenting a play before a number of guests:

> "I could see the Tsarina in the front row of the audience smiling and talking gaily to her neighbours. When the play was over I...found myself in the corridor opposite Alexei's room, from which a moaning sound came distinctly to my ears. I suddenly noticed the Tsarina running up, holding her long and awkward train in her two hands. I shrank back against the wall, and she passed me without observing my presence. There was a distracted and terror-stricken look on her face...A few minutes later the Tsarina came back. She had resumed her mask and forced herself to smile pleasantly at the guests who crowded around her."[153]

Only among her sisters could Alix unburden herself. Ella had been informed of the truth; and Irène, who knew better than anyone the stress of such an existence, came as often as possible to offer what support she could; but no amount of sympathy could ease Alix's suffering. The strain was unbearable. Her own health rapidly deteriorated so that for the greater part of a decade she was a semi-invalid, as her friend Anna Vyrubova recalled:

"In the autumn of 1910 the Emperor and Empress went to Nauheim, hoping that the waters would have a beneficial effect on her failing health. They left on a cold and rainy day and both were in a melancholy state, partly because of separation from the beloved home, and partly because of the quite apparent weakness of the Empress. On her account the Emperor showed himself deeply disturbed. "I would do anything," he said to me, "even to going to prison, if she could only be well again.""[154]

The spas were of no avail and, when earthly help failed, the Tsarina turned with increasing desperation to her icons, praying fervently for a miracle to save her son.

In spite of her unutterable anguish, Alix at least had the unfailing support of her husband. Nicholas never blamed her or so much as hinted that Alix was responsible for their son's affliction. On the contrary, their shared suffering and anxiety drew the Tsar and Tsarina even closer together. For Queen Ena in Spain, there was no such comfort.

Like her cousins, Ena was familiar with haemophilia. Two of her three brothers were afflicted by the illness and before her engagement her family believed it imperative to inform Alfonso of the risk. The King, with no direct experience of the condition, ignored the warning and it was only after the birth of their first son, Alfonso, Prince of the Astorias, that he understood the effects of the 'terrible illness of the English family.'

Since the Spanish throne was no safer than that of Russia, King Alfonso had as much need of a healthy heir as the Tsar had but, unlike Nicholas, he was quick to deny all responsibility for the boy's poor health and laid the blame entirely at Ena's feet. Since only healthy sons could inherit the throne, young Alfonso was struck from the succession.

Although Ena had grown up with haemophiliac brothers, her husband's reaction made it difficult for her to cope with her sickly son. Unlike Alix, who could not bear to be separated from the Tsarevich, Ena was unable to face little Alfonso and, sending him away from Madrid, avoided seeing him for long periods. If she hoped that subsequent healthy children might restore her husband's affection and assuage his insatiable appetite for mistresses, she was quickly disappointed. Her second son, Jaime born in 1908, escaped haemophilia but, following an infection while still a baby, became deaf and unable to speak. He, too, was struck from the succession.

Ena's third child, Beatriz, was a haemophiliac carrier; her fourth, a haemophiliac son, died soon after his birth. Her fifth and sixth children, Maria Cristina and Juan, were healthy but her seventh and last child, Gonzalo, was another haemophiliac who died before his twenty-first birthday.

For Empresses and Queens, the tragedy of haemophilia would have far reaching consequences, but the anxiety was equally traumatic for cousins in less elevated positions. Irène's first-born haemophiliac son, Waldemar, survived to the age of fifty-six, outliving many of his hardier cousins, despite frequent bouts of bleeding from the crippling illness. The sons of Alice of Albany were not so fortunate. As the daughter of the haemophiliac Prince Leopold, Alice was certain to have inherited the defective gene. While there is a possibility that her baby son, Maurice, had died of the illness before his first birthday, her elder son Rupert might have avoided the condition. He survived until 1928 when, at the age of twenty-one, he died of 'repeated haemorrhaging' following a road accident in Paris in 1928.

Chapter 29 – A Saintly Heroine & A Lascivious Satyr

Louise: Duchess of Fife; Princess Royal; eldest
daughter of King Edward VII
Macduff: Louise's husband; Alexander, Duke of Fife
Maud and Alexandra: Louise's daughters
Ella: Daughter of Princess Alice; widow of Grand
Duke Serge of Russia
Alix: Ella's sister; Tsarina of Russia

Ever conscious of her health, Louise of Wales,
Duchess of Fife, escaped each summer from the cold
British winters to warmer climes. In November
1911, accompanied by her husband, Macduff, and
their two daughters, Alexandra and Maud, she
boarded the P&O liner, *Delhi,* bound for Egypt by
way of the Bay of Biscay. In spite of her delicate
constitution, the rough seas and strong winds did not
unduly bother her and, on the night of 12th
December, she retired to her cabin untroubled by the
rising storm. While the royal party slept, gales
forced the ship off course towards Morocco where it
ran aground, throwing several crew members
overboard and destroying many of the lifeboats.

Awoken by the chaos, Louise and Macduff
made their way to the deck where officers urged the
princess and her family to hurry into the remaining
lifeboats. With remarkable calm, Louise displayed
her true nobility and insisted on remaining on board
until all the other passengers were safe.

When word of the danger reached the British
fleet, boats were immediately dispatched to assist in
the rescue and eventually Louise, Macduff and their
daughters, dressed only in their nightclothes covered

by coats and lifejackets, were able to climb into a rescue vessel. Their ordeal was only just beginning. Waves lashed at the boat, filling it with water and ultimately throwing the family overboard, kept afloat only by their lifejackets.

Drenched and exhausted, the family and sailors found themselves washed up in a forlorn spot and trudged shivering for miles through the darkness of the continuing storm. Eventually they reached Tangier where they finally found warmth and rest.

Although it took several weeks for Louise to regain her strength, she had come through the disaster unscathed and her courage earned the admiration of her rescuers. A month later, the family embarked on a recuperative cruise along the Nile, where it was soon apparent to Louise that the shipwreck had affected her husband more deeply than she had first realised. He contracted a series of chills, which developed into pleurisy and pneumonia. He died on the 19th January 1912.

In England, the Royal Family awaited the return of his coffin and, for a second time in three months, the reputedly weak Louise impressed everyone by her composure and strength of character.

> "What a saintly heroine our poor darling
> Louise has become!" wrote a proud Queen
> Alexandra, "a changed being who can bear
> every cross now!"[155]

Resigning herself to the will of God, Louise calmly accepted her widowhood and assumed full responsibility for her daughters and the running of Macduff's estates. Her eldest daughter, Alexandra, inherited her father's title and became the first Duchess of Fife in her own right. Two years later she married her mother's first cousin, Arthur, the brother of Daisy and Patsy Connaught.

Louise was not the only one of Queen Victoria's granddaughters to be regarded as a saintly heroine that year. Just as Macduff's death brought out Louise's finest qualities, the shock of her husband's assassination had led to a far more dramatic transformation in the life of her Hessian cousin, Ella. Though heartbroken at Serge's horrific murder, the forty-year-old Grand Duchess refused to give way to despair. For twenty years, she had been seen as little more than a beautiful appendage to the Grand Duke – a bejewelled ornament who, for all her numerous charitable causes, remained entirely under Serge's overbearing command.

Beneath her passive exterior, however, Ella had lost none of the intelligence or strength of character she had inherited from her mother. Her decision to convert to Orthodoxy had not been taken lightly and with each passing year she had absorbed herself more deeply in her faith. She may have endured Serge's accusations of 'immoderate devotion' in silence but throughout her difficult marriage she had 'kept her ears open' to what was going on around her and had nurtured a secret dream.

Now, relieved of her duties as the wife of the Governor General, she withdrew from aristocratic society to adopt a more ascetic existence. Dispensing with the trappings of royalty, she stripped her Kremlin apartments of their expensive furnishings and, adopting a vegetarian diet, divided her time between prayer and charitable works, venturing ever deeper into the heart of Moscow's slums. The ignorance, poverty and debauchery she encountered revived her childhood longing 'to help those who suffer.'

It was no longer enough for her to patronise charities from a distance. Like her mother before her, Ella felt drawn to take a more direct approach. After many months of careful planning and consultations with Church elders, she gradually disposed of her possessions, dividing her jewels into three parts: those which belonged to, and were returned to, the Crown; those which she gave to her relatives; and those which she sold to purchase a piece of land in the poorest part of Moscow. There, she built a convent, orphanage, church and hospital where the poor could be treated free of charge. She undertook a course of nurse training and, after two years of wrangling, the Orthodox Church agreed to grant her foundation official recognition as a convent. The foundation was named The House of Martha and Mary, as it was intended to combine the contemplative approach of the biblical Mary, who sat at Jesus' feet, with the more active approach of her sister, Martha, who served the guests. On April 2nd 1910, Ella donned a pearl grey habit and pronounced the vows of poverty, chastity and obedience, and was then created the Abbess of her Order.

> "It was a beautiful ceremony, which those who took part in it can never forget. She left the world where she had played a brilliant part, to go, as she said herself, 'into the greater world, the world of the poor and the afflicted.'"[156]

In her desire to create a beautiful haven for the poor, Ella had the white buildings of her foundation surrounded with flowers and trees. She employed the finest artists in Russia to decorate the walls of her church with frescos and paintings, and funded a permanent chaplain for her sisters:

> "It is a very gentle and delicate experience to stand on the stone flags of the wide church," wrote a visiting Englishman. "[The sisters'] religion is a religion of good deeds. They visit, clothe, comfort, heal the poor, and all but work miracles, flowers springing in their footsteps where they go."[157]

Far from the gaudy world of the ballrooms, Ella dedicated herself wholeheartedly to her new life. Sleeping for only a few hours on a plain wooden bed, she spent the nights trailing through the back streets of Moscow in search of child prostitutes and abandoned children. She personally attended the most abject patients in her hospital, often receiving those whom other hospitals were unable or unwilling to treat. Countess Olsufieff recalled one such case of a cook who had been burned so badly by an overturned oil stove that death seemed inevitable.

> "She was brought, already suffering from gangrene, from one of the hospitals of the town. The Grand Duchess herself did the dressings, which were so painful that she had to pause each moment to comfort and reassure the patient. It took two hours and a half twice a day to do the dressings, and the Grand Duchess's gown had to be aired afterwards to get rid of the terrible smell of gangrene, yet she persevered in the treatment till the woman was cured to the astonishment of the doctors, who had given her up."[158]

As the foundation flourished, Ella extended the work to establish hostels for students and young workers, and a scheme for employing messenger boys, providing them with accommodation and fair wages. Thousands of requests poured in each week, and Ella, employing the administrative talents she had learned in childhood, attempted to deal with them all.

Her saintly reputation soon spread through the country and wherever she went, crowds gathered to kiss the hem of her garments as she passed, but if the poor were convinced that a saint lived among them, the aristocracy were aghast. Many of her former friends considered her lifestyle demeaning to the Imperial Family and rumours spread that she had suffered a nervous breakdown and intended to shut herself off from the world. Only with the staunch support of her sister, Victoria Battenberg, did Ella manage to convince her relatives in Darmstadt and England that this was no sudden adventure but a dream she had nurtured since childhood which 'grew in me more and more.'

Unfortunately, no one was less convinced of Ella's sanctity than her younger sister, the Tsarina. With more than a hint of animosity Alix poured scorn on her endeavours, accusing her of self-seeking and a desire to be called a saint.

"Oh, I wish you knew me better," Ella wrote in exasperation to the Tsar, "I know Alix imagines I allow people to call me a saint...I - good gracious! - What am I, no better and probably worse than others. If people have said foolish exaggerated things is it my fault, but they don't say it to my face."[159]

But the fact that the Muscovites did revere her as a saint must have been galling for Alix, who had seen all her own attempts at charitable works backfire. What was more, Ella's spirituality was respected and admired, while Alix's equally sincere devotions were criticised as superstitious and bizarre. The growing tension between the sisters was becoming more pronounced, particularly since Alix had now fallen under the pernicious influence of one man to whom Ella's way of life was abhorrent: a debauched Siberian peasant named Grigory Elfimovich Rasputin.

Around the time of the birth of the Tsarevich, Rasputin arrived in St. Petersburg claiming that the Virgin Mary had appeared to him in a vision and sent him on a mission to serve the Imperial Family. By his evident simplicity and powers of healing he soon succeeded in ingratiating himself with some of the most powerful clerics in the capital and it was not long before accounts of his miraculous cures reached the Tsarina.

Intrigued by the stories and desperate to find some means of healing her son's haemophilia, Alix invited him to the Alexander Palace where the little Tsarevich Alexei lay desperately ill after another bout of bleeding. Rasputin leaned over the boy, whispered softly to him then left, assuring his mother that there was no cause for alarm. Alexei's pain vanished and within hours the swelling in his leg had subsided. Alix had received her miracle. This 'Man of God' was the Friend whom Philippe had promised.

> "'Why should humanity nowadays,' she said, 'be deprived of the comfort and support given to former generations?' St. Seraphim of Sarov had not lived so very long- ago and the Church had canonised him. Thus she reasoned, in her conviction that to her, too, had been vouchsafed the blessing of seeing a wonder-working saint walk upon this earth."[160]

To Ella and other members of the Imperial Family, Rasputin was nothing of the sort. Described by one observer as a 'lascivious satyr', his theology was distorted and bizarre. Sin, he claimed, was beneficial, since only the sinner could repent and, by receiving forgiveness, draw closer to God. The harder and more often a man sinned, the greater would be his humility and hence his sanctity. The doctrine suited the lascivious moujik, who took great delight in stripping young and beautiful women of their pride, and 'testing his flesh' in the brothels of the capital.

Rasputin

Stories of his licentious behaviour and the number of innocent young women he had seduced were alarming enough, but for Ella it was still more disconcerting to hear the gossip surrounding his relationship with the Tsarina. Since the Tsarevich's illness remained a state secret, few people outside the Tsar's immediate circle were aware of the reason for the peasant's frequent visits to the Alexander Palace, and, as he bragged of his proximity to the Imperial Family, rumours soon spread that he and the Empress were lovers.

Ella's attempts to warn Alix that the peasant was compromising her reputation met with a swift rebuttal. Prophets, Alix said citing biblical examples, were never accepted by their own people and were always the victims of slander. For his part, Rasputin

319

was happy to encourage the growing rift between the sisters. In his opinion, Ella's chastity was evidence of nothing but hypocrisy and conceit. A beautiful woman had a duty to use her God-given gifts to give and receive pleasure but Ella had remained faithful in an apparently loveless marriage and, still worse, she had adopted the celibate lifestyle of a nun.

"There is a lack of warmth in the relations between the Grand Duchess Elizabeth and the Empress Alexandra," the French Ambassador, Maurice Paléologue, observed. "The original cause, or at any rate the principal reason, for their estrangement is Rasputin. In Elizabeth Feodorovna's eyes Grigory is nothing but a sacrilegious impostor, an emissary of Satan. The two sisters have often had disputes about him which have several times led to an open quarrel. They never mention him now."[161]

Ella was not alone in voicing her concerns about the peasant's rising influence. Nicholas' mother and several Grand Dukes and Grand Duchesses were becoming increasingly perturbed by the stories of his debauchery. Nor were the tales confined to Russia; Alix's sisters in Germany and England were equally anxious. Prince Felix Youssoupov recalled dining with Victoria Battenberg in England where she asked him about Rasputin's influence and was alarmed by his response.

No amount of persuasion, however, could undermine Alix's faith in Our Friend. Even when government reports detailed his unholy activities, she refused to listen. All she saw was the young Tsarevich, one moment crying in agony, the next, sleeping peacefully soothed by the peasant's hypnotic words. Rasputin was her saviour sent from

God and anyone who opposed him no longer merited her affection.

As loyal and obstinate as her grandmother and blinded by the desperation to save her son, Alix could not see that his sinister presence would cause greater devastation to her family and the whole of Russia than the disease he claimed to cure.

Part IV – Marching to Their Deaths
(War & Tragedy)

Chapter 30 – The Bulgarians Have Gone Off Their Heads

Bertie: King Edward VII
Toria: Bertie's unmarried daughter
Sophie: Vicky's daughter; Crown Princess of Greece
Tino: Sophie's husband; Crown Prince of Greece
George: Tino's father; King of Greece
Alice: daughter of Victoria & Louis of Battenberg; Princess of Greece.
Marie (Missy): daughter of Affie, Duke of Edinburgh; Crown Princess of Roumania
Ferdinand (Nando): Marie's husband; Crown Prince of Roumania
Carol: German-born King of Roumania.

In the spring of 1910, King Edward VII, portly and bronchitic, arranged to meet his mistress, Alice Keppel, in Biarritz. Though inured to her husband's infidelities, this most blatant display of affection for the ubiquitous Mrs Keppel greatly irked Queen Alexandra, who decided to embark on a separate holiday of her own with her daughter, long-suffering Toria, in tow. At least on this occasion Toria was spared the boredom of 'that vile' Danish Court to which her mother so frequently repaired, as the Queen opted instead for a Mediterranean cruise, including a visit to her brother, King George of the Hellenes, in Corfu.

Her husband, meanwhile, en route to Biarritz, spent an evening in an ill-ventilated theatre in Paris where he caught a cold, which exacerbated his chronic bronchitis. By the time he reached his destination he was far from well and spent much of the holiday confined to his rooms. Returning to England at the end of April, he insisted on continuing with his duties but it was obvious that his illness was no mere chill, and his friends thought it prudent to send word of his condition to his wife.

When the news reached Queen Alexandra, she implored the King to join her and Toria on the cruise but by then, engrossed in pressing government business, he declined the invitation. Within a week, further telegrams reached the Queen's yacht, urging her to return at once as his condition had seriously deteriorated.

Toria and her mother arrived at Buckingham Palace on 5th May to discover the grey-faced king gasping for breath and requiring oxygen. That night bulletins were issued warning that he was gravely ill and, by the following morning, it was clear he had not long left to live.

While his wife and daughter hovered at his side, Bertie asked to see his mistress. Swallowing her pride, Queen Alexandra dutifully summoned Mrs Keppel to the bedside, and there suffered the ultimate indignity. The King asked his wife to kiss his mistress. The Queen complied, though, as she insisted later, only because 'I would have done anything he asked of me.'

Shortly afterwards, the King collapsed and it was left to Toria to lead a wailing Mrs Keppel from the room. At eleven forty-five that night King Edward VII died. He had waited for sixty years to ascend the throne and had reigned for only nine.

By the time of King Edward VII's death, his daughters and nieces were aligned to no less than nine dynasties, spanning Europe in every direction from Scandinavia to Spain and from England to Russia. On the 20th May 1910, nine European monarchs followed the king's coffin in the funeral procession, among them the King's nephew, Wilhelm, the Kaiser of Germany; the new King George V of Great Britain; Ena's husband, King Alfonso of Spain; Sophie's father-in-law, King George of the Hellenes; Maud's husband, King Haakon of Norway, and her father-in-law, King Frederick of Denmark; and Alix's brother-in-law, Grand Duke Mikhail representing the Tsar. With so many brothers, uncles and cousins demonstrating their good will, it seemed at that moment that Prince Albert's dream of a peaceful Europe cemented by family ties, had become reality.

Nine Kings at the Funeral of Edward VII

The death of King Edward VII marked the end of an era. His uncle's demise brought Kaiser Wilhelm a new sense of his own authority, and rivalries that had long been held in check by the older generation were gradually coming to the fore. The dream that Bismarck had once inspired in him of a mighty German outclassing every other country in Europe took shape in Willy's mind. His army had to be stronger, his navy more powerful than those of his neighbours. Everything German had to surpass anything that Britain could offer. Even his younger

325

brother, Henry, caught the spirit of competition; in 1911, he instituted a motor race from Hamburg to London to pit the German cars against English models.

Meanwhile, the arms race had turned Europe into a powder keg, and the continent was rapidly sliding into the spiral of disaster that would culminate in a greater horror than any of those princely mourners could have imagined. Throughout the late 19th and early 20th centuries, naval expansion, the arms race, and conflicts in both the Balkans and South Africa led the Great Powers into mutual suspicion and mistrust. Princesses who had married into foreign courts found themselves increasingly drawn into the political intrigues of the time. Their presumed divided loyalties led the people of their adopted countries to view them with distrust and even within the family their position became at times quite untenable.

"When I think of my father and of all his friends and of our friends," Vicky had once written, "it appears to me almost ludicrous that Germany and England should be enemies."

Yet the cousins were already beginning to discover the difficult situation in which their cosmopolitan upbringing had placed them.

As long as Queen Victoria lived, she bound the family together but her death in 1901 symbolised the beginning of a changing world and, with the death of Edward VII, the bond uniting the cousins was no longer strong enough to maintain peace in the face of the hidden forces which were actively creating conflict and secretly preparing the destruction of the European autocracies. Already sparks were flying in the Balkans and soon they would explode in the terrible conflagration of the First World War.

For over thirty years, the crumbling Ottoman Empire had provided easy pickings for the neighbouring Balkan states as they vied with one another to expand their territories. Like Bulgaria and Greece, the Russians had long entertained the dream of extending their frontiers into Turkish occupied Macedonia and Thrace to gain the ultimate prize: Constantinople. Fifty years earlier it was the Russians' intention of capturing that city, the ancient Byzantium, which had led to the Crimean War and inspired Queen Victoria's deep mistrust of the country.

In 1897, an unsuccessful Greek campaign had prevented Crown Princess Sophie from attending her grandmother's Diamond Jubilee celebrations and led to yet another dispute between Sophie and her brother, the Kaiser. At that time the Kaiser had openly declared Germany's support for the Turks, infuriating his mother by visiting Constantinople and accepting a gift of captured Greek guns from the Turkish sultan. Now, fifteen years later, as the Greeks prepared to take up arms again, Willy was more willing to lend his support to the League of Balkan Kings.

The League, comprising Greece, Montenegro, Serbia and Bulgaria was more a marriage of convenience than a love match. Following the Sandro Battenberg debacle, another German prince, 'Foxy' Ferdinand, had become the self-styled Tsar of Bulgaria and he was every bit as ambitious as the Greeks and Russians when it came to possessing Constantinople. The Serbs, meanwhile, resentful of Bulgaria's alliance with their archenemy Austria-Hungary, distrusted their neighbours from the start.

Even as they united against Turkey, each of the Balkan kings viewed his allies with suspicion.

On 18th October 1912, the League declared war on Turkey and within a month had virtually brought 'the sick man of Europe' to his knees. Before the end of November, Crown Prince Constantine (Tino) rode at the head of a triumphant Greek army into Salonika where shortly afterwards his father, King George of the Hellenes, received an heroic reception, to the chagrin of Ferdinand of Bulgaria, who was hoping for that honour himself.

The tense dealings between the allies at the Front were reflected in the relations between the Greek princesses at home. Since the outbreak of war, Crown Princess Sophie and her sisters-in-law had been preparing hospitals for the wounded, dividing the work between them. Sophie, then three months pregnant, arranged medical supplies from Athens, while her sister-in-law, Princess Alice (the daughter of Sophie's cousin, Victoria Battenberg) travelled to the Front to organise base camps.

In spite of the League's successes, the Balkan Kings left a trail of injured and dying in their wake. Lacking sufficient supplies and overwhelmed by the number of casualties, Alice found conditions at the base camps so inadequate that she began organising groups of nurses to move from one hospital to the next. Crown Princess Sophie, incensed by this usurping of her authority, exploded with rage. Sophie's sensitivity was understandable since she was certainly under a great deal of stress. Not only was she being unjustly vilified for her German origins but, at four months pregnant, she had also discovered that her husband, Tino, was openly

---

* Princess Alice of Battenberg had married Andrew, the brother of the Crown Prince in 1906. She was the mother of the present Duke of Edinburgh.

conducting an affair with one of the nurses at her sister-in-law's hospital.

In spite of his patent infidelity, the Crown Prince was rapidly earning the admiration and respect of his future subjects. Leaving his father to bask in glory in Salonika, he continued his affair and his triumphant march towards Constantinople.

For King George, life in Salonika differed little from life in Athens. Fraternising with his subjects and appearing more like a country gentleman than a conquering hero, each afternoon he enjoyed a stroll through the town. On 18th March 1913, as he walked along the street, he caught sight of a suspicious character staring at him from the entrance to a café. Only slightly perturbed, the King returned along the same route some hours later whereupon the man pulled out a pistol and fired a single bullet. The King died almost instantly, assassinated not by an enemy or a disgruntled ally but by one of his own Greek subjects, who was subsequently declared insane.

As Sophie consoled her mother-in-law, Queen Olga, Tino hurried to Salonika to accompany his father's body back to Athens for a state funeral. A month later, Sophie gave birth to her last child, Katherine.

Shocked as she was by events, the ill wind of the assassination blew some consolation to the new Queen Sophie of the Hellenes. Tino's sudden change of status brought an abrupt end to his affair with the nurse and, as he and Sophie drove in an open carriage through the streets of Athens, the enthusiasm of the crowds was almost tangible. Tino's conquests had won the hearts of his people and softened their attitude to his wife. For a short while, peace descended upon Greece but the Balkan Wars were by no means over.

No sooner had the League begun to rejoice in its victories than Ferdinand of Bulgaria switched tack. Unwilling to relinquish his dream of a coronation in Constantinople, he turned against Greece and Serbia.

> "The Bulgarians have gone off their heads because of their successes, and want to be the only power in the Balkans," [162] wrote Sophie's cousin, Missy of Roumania.

The Serbs and Greeks responded by allying themselves with their recent enemy, Turkey; and the Roumanians, fearing that Bulgaria threatened their own Balkan interests, found themselves drawn in to the seemingly irresolvable conflict.

For Roumania there were further complications. The German born King Carol had already agreed a secret treaty with Austria-Hungary and consequently had no desire to attack Austria's ally, Bulgaria. While he prevaricated, the Greeks and their allies trounced the Bulgarian forces so that by the time the Roumanian king was prevailed upon to send out his troops, the war was all but won. Nonetheless, in a show of support, the Roumanian army marched south and straight into a cholera epidemic.

According to her own effusive account, Missy's experiences among the disease-ridden troops marked a turning point in her life. Hurrying to the hospitals in her idiosyncratic fashion, she immediately recognised her duty:

> "Looking about me I felt that what was wanted was a leader, an encourager, and one high enough placed to have authority, and who, by remaining calm and steady could become a rallying point for those who were beginning to lose their heads..."[163]

330

Ever conscious of her own beauty and charisma, Missy never doubted that her very presence among the soldiers could raise their drooping spirits and in this, as in most of her enterprises, she proved remarkably successful. Relishing the role of a brilliant heroine illuminating their darkness, she need not work as a nurse as several of her cousins had done. It was enough for her to wander among the wounded, sick and dying, casting her own inimitable radiance over the stark hospital wards and there was no doubt at all that her natural magnetism played a major role in maintaining morale. On a larger scale, she worked tirelessly, travelling from one place to another and employing her natural gifts of administration and persuasion to ensure that the hospitals received the necessary staff and equipment to respond to the needs of their patients.

By the summer of 1913, Ferdinand of Bulgaria had finally accepted defeat and the Greeks and Roumanians were satisfied with their spoils. Their territories were enlarged, their borders extended and the Queen of the Hellenes and her cousin the Crown Princess of Roumania had both had an early taste of the horrors of war. For now, they were content to rest in a fragile peace, unaware that in a little over a year an even greater conflict would engulf the whole continent.

Chapter 31 – This Is The End Of Everything

The long hot summer of 1914 brought the annual migration of royalties from the heat of the capitals to cooler climes. While Charlotte (neé of Prussia), whose husband had recently inherited the Dukedom of Saxe-Meiningen, rotated between Cannes and clinics, Ducky of Edinburgh, now Grand Duchess Victoria of Russia, took a holiday in the South of France. Alice of Albany and her husband, Alge of Teck were preparing to leave for Canada to take over the governorship from her uncle, the Duke of Connaught. Several of their royal cousins paid visits to their families; Marie Louise was preparing to visit Aunt Beatrice on the Isle of Wight; and Queen Maud of Norway returned as usual to Appleton Lodge to find her sister, Toria, more enslaved than ever to their mother. That summer, her cousins Sophie of Greece and Irène of Prussia were also in England, taking advantage of the sea air in Eastbourne.

For Irène's husband, the holiday served a dual purpose. While visiting Cousin George, Henry could sound out the English King's stance in the event of war: if a conflict should erupt in the Balkans and Germany were to come to aid of her allies, would Britain intervene? Though George's reply was vague and non-committal, Henry felt sufficiently confident to inform his brother, the Kaiser, that should Germany become embroiled in the Balkans, Britain would remain neutral.

Irène's sister, Alix, the Russian Tsarina, was also travelling purposefully that summer. In June, she arrived with her family in the Black Sea port of Constantza as a guest of her cousin, Crown Princess

Marie of Roumania. Earlier that year the Roumanians had visited St. Petersburg with a view to promoting a match between Missy's eldest son, Carol, and Alix's eldest daughter, Olga. Neither the Prince nor the Grand Duchess had shown the least interest in one another, and their mothers were such different characters with little in common that the meetings could hardly be viewed as a success. Nonetheless, etiquette demanded a return visit and there was always the possibility that a second encounter might prove more fruitful.

In spite of the balmy summer weather and the romantic setting, the trip was not a success. The worldly-wise playboy Carol was not in the least enamoured of Olga, whose sheltered upbringing made her appear younger than her nineteen years. Nor had Olga, raised in her close-knit family, any desire to leave her Russian home. Although Missy herself had been contemplating the dynastic benefits of the match for several years, even she began to have doubts about the Grand Duchess, not least because she feared that Olga might introduce haemophilia into the Roumanian dynasty.

If relations between Carol and Olga were cool, their mothers were finding each other's company positively chilling. Stories of Missy's affairs could not have endeared her to the 'ultra-moral' Alix, while, for her part, the Roumanian Crown Princess had always found the Russian Empress aloof and disdainful:

> "She managed to put an insuperable distance between her world and yours, her experiences and yours, her thoughts, her opinions, her principles, rights & privileges. She made you in fact feel an intruding outsider, which is of

all sensations the most chilling and uncomfortable."[164]

The unsuccessful mission accomplished, the Russian Imperial Family returned to their Crimean estate, Livadia. Occasionally Ella visited, but relations between Alix and her sister were becoming increasingly fraught due to the influence of Rasputin. Many of Alix's former friends, who had been equally quick to condemn his rising influence, had also been side-lined, with the result that, by the summer of 1914, the Imperial Family were virtually isolated in the private havens of Livadia or Tsarskoe Selo. There, alone with Nicholas, her children and her friend, Anna Vyrubova, Alix was able to snatch occasional moments of relief from the stresses of her position.

"Monotonous though it may have been," wrote Anna Vyrubova, "the private life of the Emperor and his family was one of cloudless happiness. Never, in all the twelve years of my association with them, did I hear an impatient word or surprise an angry look between the Emperor and the Empress. To him she was always 'Sunny' or 'Sweetheart,' and he came into her quiet room...as into a haven of rest and peace. Politics and cares of state were left outside...The Imperial Family was absolutely united in love and sympathy."[165]

This idyllic description, however, omitted to mention the numerous hours that Nicholas sat at his desk, working on the pressing business of ruling the country and trying to maintain the delicately balanced peace throughout Europe.

Towards the end of June 1914, Victoria Battenberg attended the birth of her grandchild in

Greece before joining her sisters in Russia. Despite their different lifestyles, Victoria and Ella remained very close. Victoria had nothing but admiration for Ella and her work with the poor, and was only too happy to accept her invitation to participate in one of Ella's many pilgrimages.

In early July 1914, they journeyed to the Siberian town of Alapaevsk where, despite Ella's attempts to remain incognito, the crowds gathered as usual to welcome her, kneeling to kiss her shadow, blessing themselves and reaching to touch the hem of her garments.

The sisters arrived at a monastery where Ella had made the acquaintance of a young monk named Seraphim. While they were speaking, a telegram addressed to the Grand Duchess arrived from St. Petersburg. According to Seraphim, the moment that Ella opened it, her face became deathly pale and her eyes filled with tears. The Tsarina was asking for her prayers; the heir to the Austrian throne, Archduke Franz Ferdinand, who had shared Ella's table at Queen Victoria's Diamond Jubilee dinner, had been assassinated in Sarajevo, the Austrians were preparing reprisals and war seemed almost inevitable.

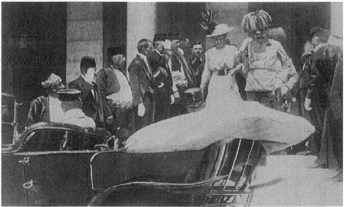

Archduke Franz Ferdinand & His wife, Sophie, in Sarajevo

In Vienna, the aged Emperor Franz Josef struggled to maintain order among the many different nationalities that peopled his Austro-Hungarian empire. The Hungarian Magyars viewed themselves as Roumanian, while the Serbs sought complete independence from Austria and dreamed of creating a separate South Slav (Yugoslav) kingdom. Serbian radicals had already perpetrated several terrorist attacks and so when the Emperor's nephew and heir, Archduke Franz Ferdinand, declared his intention of visiting Sarajevo during a routine inspection of Austrian troops, he was strongly advised not to do so. The Archduke, determined to keep the Empire intact even if it meant sharing government with the unruly Slavs, ignored the warnings.

On 28th June 1914, as Franz Ferdinand and his morganatic wife, Sophie, drove slowly through the streets of the Bosnian capital, Gavrilo Princip, *allegedly* a member of the notorious Serbian terrorist group, 'Black Hand', stepped out from the crowd and fired a pistol at the passengers. The Archduke's wife died instantly, Franz Ferdinand a short time later*.

The catastrophic impact of the assassination was not immediately apparent. According to the usual courtesies, fellow sovereigns and foreign courts dispatched condolence telegrams to Emperor Franz Joseph and mourning was declared throughout most European countries.

Marie Louise, on reading of the murder in the newspaper, 'wondered what would be the outcome of this, but little did I think that it would really mean

---

* The usual explanation for Archduke Franz Ferdinand's murder appears somewhat suspect. Please see Appendix V

war.'[166] The Russian ambassador in Vienna was equally complacent, writing to the Tsar that the Austrian response would be calm and restrained.

Several Austrian ministers, however, had long been waiting for an excuse to crush the disorderly Serbs and, refused to be placated by sympathetic words. The assassination, they claimed, was tantamount to a declaration of war and in response they issued an ultimatum which was so extreme in its demands that the Serbs were at a loss as to how to respond. In desperation, the Serbian Prince Regent turned for protection to his long-time ally, Russia.

Desperate to avoid war, the Tsar persuaded the Serbs to accept the treaty virtually in its entirety. This was not what the Austrians had been expecting or hoping to hear, and on July 19th they declared war on Serbia. The Tsar, duty-bound to defend his little neighbour, saw no alternative but to mobilise his troops along the Austrian border.

As Europe teetered on the brink of a precipice, Kaiser Wilhelm, aghast at the speed with which events had spiralled out of control, telegraphed his Russian cousin, asking him, cajoling him and ordering him to halt the Russian mobilisation. Nicholas, obliged to protect his smaller ally, replied that he could not do that unless the Austrians withdrew from Serbia. The Kaiser's ministers urged him to issue his own ultimatum: unless the Tsar halted the mobilisation Germany, honouring her treaty with Austria, would have no option but to declare war on Russia.

Still, the Tsar remained optimistic and still the Kaiser frantically sought a solution but it was too late. Against the will of both the Kaiser and the Tsar, on 1st August, Germany declared war on Russia. At the same time, the Germans, intent on subduing the

French before they had time to come to Russia's aid, invaded neutral Belgium causing Britain to issue an ultimatum of her own. On August 4th, having received no response from the Kaiser, the British entered the conflict. War had begun on a scale the world had never seen before.

Patriotic fervour swept the continent. In London, vast crowds stood beneath the balcony of Buckingham Palace to cheer King George and Queen Mary. In Berlin, the Kaiser received great applause and the streets were filled with people rejoicing at the impending slaughter. Similar scenes greeted the Tsar and Tsarina outside the Winter Palace in St. Petersburg. When the Russian Imperial family arrived in Moscow for a service of dedication, devoted crowds gathered outside the cathedral. The French Ambassador, Maurice Paléologue, turned to the Tsarina, commenting on what relief she must feel to witness such a display of loyal affection:

"[Ella] joined in our conversation. Her face in the frame of her long white woollen veil was alive with spirituality. Her delicate features and white skin, the deep faraway look in her eyes, the low soft tone of her voice and the luminous glow round her brow all betrayed a being in close contact with the ineffable and divine."[167]

But Ella's calm faith could no more protect her from the tragedy befalling her family than the cheering crowds could console her sister, Alix.

"This is the end of everything," the Tsarina was heard to murmur, knowing that her family would be literally ripped apart. While she, Victoria and Ella were committed to the Entente (Britain,

France, Russia and Belgium), Irène and Ernie were on the side of the Central Powers (Germany and Austro-Hungary).

Though quick to affirm her allegiance to Russia, the broken-hearted Tsarina recalled her childhood in peace-loving Hesse and was eager to assure anyone who would listen that this evil was the fault of the proud Prussians. Her brother, she rightly insisted, had dreaded this war as much as she had, and her sentiments were echoed by Ernie in Darmstadt but, disheartened as he was, the Grand Duke of Hesse knew his duty and, like his father before him, prepared to lead the Hessian troops to the Front.

The declarations of war brought a sudden end to the royal cousins' pleasant holidays and they began a frantic rush to return to their own countries before the outbreak of hostilities. Victoria Battenberg, leaving her jewels for safekeeping in St. Petersburg, returned to England. Irène, after exchanging her English maid for Victoria's German maid, departed for Kiel, where her husband had command of the German Baltic Fleet. Sophie, entrusting her sons to the care of her cousin, King George of Britain, returned to neutral Greece to suffer criticism from both sides of her family. While her brother, the Kaiser, urged the Anglophile Queen to persuade the Greeks to aid the Central Powers, her English cousins were pressing her to do the same for the Entente. Sophie's sisters faced no such dilemma; all four were settled in Germany from where Mossy's sons and Charlotte's husband were immediately called into service in the army.

In neutral Roumania, Missy found herself in a similar situation to Sophie's. The proudly English

Crown Princess favoured an alliance with the Entente but her German-born husband, Ferdinand, and his uncle, King Carol, could not renounce their Hohenzollern blood and were torn between the overwhelming Roumanian support for Russia, and their own familial connections to the Central Powers. For Missy matters were further complicated. Her mother, the Dowager Duchess of Coburg, renounced her Russian origins and adhered to the German side, as did Missy's sister Sandra. Ducky, now settled with her husband in St. Petersburg, pledged her allegiance to Russia.

The strain proved too much for King Carol of Roumania and, within three months of the outbreak of war, he was dead. Missy rose with her usual aplomb to the role of Queen Consort but it would be two years before she could persuade her husband to abandon his neutral stance and join the Allies.

For Alice of Albany and the Christians, too, war came at a terrible personal cost. Alice's English brother, Charles, now Duke of Coburg was forced to support the Kaiser, while she, a sister-in-law of the English Queen Mary, was bound to Britain. Like so many of his cousins, Charles, whose immediate impulse had been to hurry back to England, was vilified by both sides. The English considered him a traitor; the Germans, an Englishman. The same heart-rending situation faced Thora and Marie Louise. They had already lost one brother, Christle, fighting for Britain in the Boer War, and now saw a second brother, Albert, heir to an estate in Silesia, in the uniform of their German enemies. Out of consideration for his family ties, however, the Kaiser ensured that Albert would serve in a non-combatant role.

For those princesses whose countries remained neutral – Daisy Connaught, Crown Princess of Sweden, Queen Ena of Spain and Queen Maud of Norway – life was marginally less complicated. Daisy became the focal point through which siblings and cousins on opposing sides could keep in contact. Through her, it was possible for Thora and Marie Louise to follow the exploits of their brother, Albert, and through her too, Mossy would eventually be able to regain the mementos that the British had found on the body of her dying son. Even so, it was difficult for an English princess to remain entirely impartial in a court which, though officially unbiased, tended to favour the Central Powers.

The battle lines had been drawn up. The divisions were clear and yet, for all their allegiance to their adoptive countries, the princesses could neither deny their origins nor disown their own kindred. In a time of such heartfelt patriotism, foreign princesses would soon find themselves distrusted and even hated by the people they struggled to serve.

Chapter 32 – Hessian Witches and Foreign Spies

Following royal tradition, the queens and princesses of all combatant nations put family feeling aside to dedicate themselves to the war effort. Visiting troops, patronising hospitals and arranging transport for the wounded, each played her part. Even in those countries not directly affected by the war, Queen Victoria's granddaughters played an active role.

In Canada, Patsy Connaught, who as patron of her own Princess Patricia's Light Infantry Regiment had personally embroidered the regimental banner, sold signed photographs of herself to raise money for the allies. In neutral Norway, Queen Maud, no longer able to make her regular excursions to England, established relief committees to fund medical and food supplies; and in Spain, Queen Ena renovated the Red Cross Hospital of Madrid.

In England, the princesses visited the wounded and made improvements to hospital wards. Alice of Albany patronised the Soldiers' and Sailors' Families Association, and, with her husband, made several visits to La Panne in Belgium where the heroic King Albert was struggling to defend what was left of his ravaged country. Thora of Schleswig-Holstein frequently travelled to France to examine the conditions at the base camps and, back in England she founded the Women's Auxiliary Force. Her sister, Marie Louise, settling into a bed-sit in London, converted the girls' club that she had established into a 'perfect hospital with 100 beds.'

"I ran this completely self-sufficient unit myself from 1914 to 1920. It was directly under the War Office, with no well-meaning interference from the Red Cross or other bodies. I suppose I have the strange distinction of being one of the few women who never donned a uniform, not even an overall, during [the] war...I took especial care when visiting my wounded friends to put on my smartest dress and hat, and the men thoroughly appreciated the compliment paid them."[168]

Across the continent, royal women were similarly occupied. For frequently ailing Charlotte, there came the added responsibility of briefly managing the affairs of Saxe-Meiningen in the absence of her husband, who had left with his army to the Front. Her cousin, Sandra (of Edinburgh, now Princess of Hohenlohe Langenburg) enrolled as a nurse to tend the wounded Germans, while her sister, Ducky, organised ambulances for the Russian troops on the Polish front. In Russia, too:

"The Empress [Alix] sat till late in her small dressing-room, the room she generally used, discussing war charities with the Grand Duchess Elizabeth Feodorovna [Ella], who had at once begun to take an active part in everything as well as doing her usual work at the 'Obitel.'"[169]

Alix devoted herself wholeheartedly to the Russian cause. Regardless of her own numerous ailments, she and her elder daughters enrolled for a course of nurse training and were soon busily employed in the military hospitals, dressed in the ordinary uniform of the Red Cross 'Sisters of Mercy.' Confounding those critics who had always viewed their Tsarina as haughty and aloof, Alix dedicated herself to her work with a gentleness and strength of character that amazed her patients.

"It was generally believed that the Empress was difficult to approach," wrote Anna Vyrubova, "but this was never true of sincere and disinterested souls. Suffering always made a strong appeal to the Empress, and whenever she knew of anyone sad or in trouble her heart was instantly touched. Few people, even in Russia, ever knew how much the Empress did for the poor, the sick, and the helpless."[170]

Unflinchingly, she assisted the surgeons, holding amputated limbs and dressing the most horrific wounds. Nursing came as naturally to her as it had to her sister and mother and, for the first time in her life, she found a role in which she was totally at ease.

"Looking after the wounded is my consolation...To lessen their suffering even in a small way helps the aching heart."[171]

Alongside nursing, Alix also employed all her administrative skills to arrange for mobile baths and temporary churches to be taken to the soldiers at the Front. At home, she exhausted herself arranging for numerous smaller hospitals to be established throughout the country.

Travelling to and from the Front, her sister, Ella, already proficient in nursing the most abject patients, visited the base camps and arranged ambulance trains to transferral the wounded back to Moscow.

"The Empress and the Grand Duchess drew into their organisation all ranks of society, officials small and great, government employees, and all the hierarchy of feminine society from the highest to the lowest."[172]

As the stark brutality of slaughter became apparent, the wild rejoicing of August 1914 gave way to disenchantment. While the Kaiser bemoaned the treachery of his cousins, stories of German atrocities in Belgium stoked the hatred of his enemies. The sight of the wounded soldiers returning on hospital trains fired the imaginations of the propagandists, portraying the 'evil Hun' as butchers and murderers.

The royal families were no more immune to the dangers than the least of their subjects. Only two months after the outbreak of war, Mossy of Prussia lost one son, Prince Max of Hesse-Kassel, in Belgium; and two years later a second son, Friedrich met the same fate in Roumania. That same year, Mossy's grief was compounded by the death of her brother-in-law, Moretta's husband, Adolph of Schaumburg-Lippe.

In Russia, the Tsar's cousin, Konstantin Konstantinovich, lost a son-in-law; and, on the British side, Maurice, brother of Queen Ena of Spain, was killed at Ypres on 27th October 1914. For the royal cousins there could be no pleasure in victory wrought at such a cost.

As the war continued relentlessly, the fear of foreign spies became universal and, no matter how firmly the princesses declared and demonstrated their loyalty to their troops, the multi-national nature of their families left them wide open to suspicion and mistrust. When the lonely Toria of Wales befriended a maid servant belonging to an unorthodox church, the maid was unjustly accused of spying for the Germans and summarily dismissed. In October 1914, Victoria Battenberg's husband, Louis, who had served in the British Navy for almost half a century, was pressurised to resign as First

Lord of the Admiralty on account of his German birth. Victoria was aghast and angry with her cousin, King George V, but her sufferings were minimal compared with those endured by her sisters in Russia.

The Tsarina's popularity plummeted as the Russian losses mounted. Though her mother had been English and she had spent the greater part of her childhood and youth with her grandmother in England, the Russians were quick to draw attention to her German origins. Totally unfounded rumours gained momentum, accusing her not only of favouring the enemy, but also of actively forewarning the Kaiser of the Russians' military plans via her 'lover', Rasputin.

Alix was not the only victim of such slanders. The Muscovites, who had so recently been revering Ella as a saint, observed that a large number of the casualties arriving at her hospitals were not Russian soldiers but German prisoners-of-war. Though acutely embarrassed by the fact, Ella was powerless to decide which patients she received, and believed it her Christian duty to treat them all with equal respect. Being naturally fluent in German, she was able to speak with the prisoners and initially encouraged her committee to care for them with compassion, "but," as she wrote to the Tsar, "their kindness was so badly interpreted and everything was put on my back."

By April 1915, the complaints were so violent that, fearing both for the future of her foundation and the reputation of the Imperial Family, Ella pleaded with Nicholas to stop sending prisoners to Moscow:

"These rumours about me are not the chief reason I want to tell you but Moscow is a capital [and] having prisoners in the finest buildings…makes such very bad blood. Couldn't the prisoners no longer be sent to Moscow? The people are furious to see their beautiful buildings for military hospitals – all 18 hospitals for prisoners except three. Forgive me mentioning this but perhaps you don't know of the problem – if you come now and want to see the military hospitals, you will find one or two Russians or none, but hundreds of prisoners."[173]

Still the death toll rose and, as spy-mania seized the country, the chief suspects were the 'German bitches' or 'Hessian witches' in the Imperial Family. Rumours that the Kaiser was planning to use the Grand Duke of Hesse to make a separate peace with Russia led to speculation that Ella was hiding her brother in her convent. Desperate to avoid giving rise to any hint of collaboration, Ella refused to receive a lady-in-waiting recently arrived in Moscow with a letter from her brother, Ernie, but public opinion remained unchanged. While the Tsarina was unreachable in Tsarskoe Selo, the Grand Duchess, walking openly through the streets, was greeted with a barrage of accusations, spat upon, or even stoned. On one occasion a hostile mob gathered outside the House of Martha and Mary demanding to see the German spy who was hiding her brother in the convent. When Ella stepped out to meet them she was pelted with stones and only the timely arrival of a company of soldiers prevented further violence. The crowd dispersed baying for the blood of the Tsarina, Rasputin's 'German whore.'

In Greece, Queen Sophie was the victim of similar slanders. King Constantine (Tino), reluctant to embroil his people in another conflict so soon after the Balkan Wars, was determined to maintain his country's neutrality. His stand brought him into opposition with his powerful and persuasive Prime Minister, Venizelos, who firmly advocated forming an alliance with the Entente. In spite of growing pressure from both sides, Tino stood his ground until autumn 1915 when the British fleet, with Venizelos' encouragement, landed at Salonika. The outraged King dismissed his Prime Minister who responded by establishing a rival government, which divided the country into those who remained loyal to Tino and those who backed Venizelos' demands to enter the war.

In an effort to force Tino to take a stand, Allied propaganda attempted to discredit Queen Sophie by circulating increasingly bizarre stories of her pro-German sympathies. Like her cousin, the Tsarina, she was accused of sending information to her brother, the Kaiser, via a secret telephone line linking her Tatoi home with Berlin. In the summer of 1916, an arsonist set fire to the palace while the Queen and her children were in residence and, though the family escape unharmed, several members of the household were killed.

To increase the pressure on Greece, the Kaiser began wooing the neighbouring states of Bulgaria and Roumania. Ferdinand of Bulgaria wavered until October 1915 when, convinced by a delegation of handsome young officers that the Germans were in the ascendancy, he threw in his lot with the Central Powers. Assuming that the same tactics would prove effective with Missy of Roumania, Cousin Willy dispatched another group, including her brother-in-law, Ernst of Hohenlohe-Langenburg, to Bucharest. Missy, however, was not to be swayed:

"I should die of grief," she said, "if Roumania were to go to war against England."

The Kaiser's reaction in describing her as the 'English harlot' was as nothing compared to the criticism Missy suffered from her own family. While one sister, Sandra, was nursing wounded Germans, another, the fiercely anti-German Ducky, was writing from Russia to urge Missy to join the Entente. At the same time, Missy's mother, the Russian-born Dowager Duchess Marie of Coburg, bitterly criticised the Roumanian Queen for failing to persuade her husband to join the Central Powers. As King Ferdinand's natural sympathies were more German than British, Missy might well have succeeded in so doing, but she adamantly refused to contemplate going to war against Britain. It was with a sense of relief rather than fear that she greeted the news in August 1916 that her husband had finally allied Roumania to the Entente.

Chapter 33 – Poor Nicky! Poor Russia!

In August 1915, weary of following his soldiers' progress from the side-lines and aware that his cousin, the Commander-in-Chief, was close to a nervous breakdown, Tsar Nicholas made a fateful decision to take over supreme command of his army. Loath as Alix was to part with him, she supported the plan, certain that he would win the respect and admiration of his troops. Our Friend, Rasputin, gave the scheme his blessing and assured the Tsarina that this was God's will.

The rest of the family was far less confident. Nicholas had no direct experience of warfare and lacked the physical presence of his predecessor, the giant Grand Nikolai Nikolaevich, to inspire confidence in his troops. Moreover, the blame for every Russia defeat could now be laid squarely at the feet of the Tsar, leaving him more vulnerable than ever to revolutionary attacks. What was more, Nicholas could not have chosen a worse time to take on the task. Ammunition was in such short supply that soldiers were left waiting for their comrades to die so that they could take their guns. Morale in the army had sunk so low that officers frequently abandoned their positions to snatch a few moments pleasure in the nightclubs and theatres of the capital. More disastrous still in the eyes of his critics, was the fact that Nicholas left the reins of government in the hands of his wife, which, in their opinion, meant leaving control of all internal affairs to the peasant, Rasputin.

In spite of the widely held view to the contrary, Rasputin's influence in affairs of state was minimal. Though Alix relied on the peasant's advice, he had, according to Nicholas's sister, 'not a particle of influence' over the Tsar. Nicholas' departure for the Front, however, allowed Rasputin greater access to the Tsarina.

Exhausted by stress and her work among the wounded, Alix's illnesses multiplied:

"The heart trouble that at first had been only a nervous affection then became really serious. She had constant pain and a feeling of suffocation, while almost chronic facial neuralgia had taken the place of the sciatica from which she used to suffer so badly. On account of her heart trouble she had to submit reluctantly to be carried upstairs in the hospitals she visited, though she loathed making a spectacle of herself."[174]

In Nicholas' absence, her dependence on Rasputin appeared to increase. Under his insidious influence, able ministers were relieved of office and replaced by Rasputin's ineffectual and often corrupt cronies. At the same time, 'intriguers' and agent provocateurs from abroad were busily working to create chaos and mistrust until Russia was rapidly spiralling into chaos. The transport system broke down, fuel shortages hit the cities, and the dissatisfaction was spreading from the workers through to the aristocracy.

As newspapers openly reported that the Tsarina and Rasputin were working for the enemy, scurrilous leaflets appeared on the streets depicting Alix and her peasant lover in pornographic poses. Even Nicholas was alarmed and urged Alix to be cautious but his warnings had come too late.

With the onset of winter came further fuel and food shortages and rumours spread that the 'Hessian witches' in the Imperial Family were deliberately starving the masses. Maurice Paléologue reported that:

> "Countess R -, who has just spent three days in Moscow…confirms what I have recently heard about the rage of the Muscovites against the Imperial family: 'I dined in different circles each evening,' she said. 'Everywhere one hears the same indignant outcry. If the Emperor appeared on Red Square today, he would be booed. The Empress would be torn to pieces. The kind, warm-hearted, pure-minded Grand Duchess Elizabeth dare not leave her convent now. The workmen accuse her of starving the people. There seems to be a stir of revolution among all classes.'"[175]

For the Imperial Family the solution was obvious: Rasputin had to go, Alix must stop interfering in politics, and loyal and trustworthy ministers should be immediately appointed. One after another, Grand Dukes and Grand Duchesses arrived at Tsarskoe Selo with desperate warnings but the Tsarina dismissed them and added their names to the ever-growing list of enemies of Our Friend.

> "[Ducky] spoke to the Empress of the unpopularity of the Government. The Grand Duchess was restrained in her language, and the Empress did not believe that her cousin's apprehensions were well founded. She always thought that she and the Emperor must know the situation better than anyone; she had the assurance, backed with the authority of the Minister of the Interior, that it was only the desire to frighten the Emperor into granting hasty reforms that caused the spread of these rumours."[176]

Alix responded to Ducky's advice by telling her not to meddle in affairs that were not her concern. Exasperated by her refusal to listen, several members of the family believed the Tsarina was insane and called for her to be removed to a convent or asylum, or at least to be banished to her Crimean estate, Livadia, until the end of the war. With some justification, Alix responded by accusing her detractors of treason.

By the winter of 1916, Ella, 'frightened at the hostility displayed towards her sister,' determined to make one final effort to remove Rasputin's influence. Arriving at the Alexander Palace on the 14th December, the thirty-eighth anniversary of the death of her mother on whose prayers she had always relied, Ella broached the subject of the peasant. Alix, standing on her dignity as Empress refused to listen. Infuriated by her blindness, Ella lost her temper, prophetically reminding her of the fate of Marie-Antoinette, but Alix simply dismissed her and drove her away 'like a dog.'

"Perhaps," said the heart-broken Ella, "it would have been better if I had not come."

"Yes," the Tsarina replied.

They would never see each other again.

Ella left Tsarskoe Selo for the last time and made her way to the Youssoupov Palace where her young friend Prince Felix was waiting.

"Poor Nicky!" she wept, "Poor Russia!"

Within a fortnight of Ella's meeting with Alix, Rasputin had been murdered. Although intrigue and mystery surround the event and various alternative culprits have been suggested, the fanciful Prince Felix Youssoupov claimed to have carried out the killing. In a last desperate attempt to save the tottering dynasty, he claimed to have enticed Rasputin to his St. Petersburg palace under the pretext that his beautiful wife was unwell and would appreciate a visit from the healer. There, with the support of the Tsar's cousin, Grand Duke Dmitri Pavlovich, he plied the peasant with poisoned wine and cakes before shooting him several times and hurling his body into the frozen Malaya Nevka River. It was three days before the corpse was dragged from the water and the autopsy revealed that neither the poison nor the bullets had killed him. His hands were stretched upwards as though he had been struggling to untie his fetters and scratch his way out of the ice.

For the Tsarina, the death of Rasputin was more than a tragedy; it was a symbol of treachery, a disaster and a portent of doom. Some months earlier, afraid for his life, Rasputin was said to have made an ominous prediction: if he were killed by peasants, the Empress had nothing to fear, but if members of her own family were responsible for his death then neither she, nor the Tsar nor any of the children would outlive him by more than two years. The realisation that Nicholas' cousin, Dmitri, and his nephew by marriage, Felix, were to blame made the horror of his murder all the harder to bear. Still more distressing for Alix was her suspicion that her sister, Ella, had participated in the conspiracy – a suspicion which appeared to be confirmed when an intercepted telegram from Ella to Felix's mother revealed the Grand Duchess's praise for Felix's 'act of patriotism'.

"When the Empress...realised that her nearest and dearest connections were in the ranks of her enemies," wrote her friend, Anna Vyrubova, "her head sank on her breast, her eyes grew dark with sorrow and her whole countenance seemed to wither and grow old."[177]

Prince Youssoupov's 'act of patriotism' had none of its desired effects. Isolated even from her own family, Alix withdrew deeper into her seclusion to rely on the peasant's prayers from heaven.

The country continued to slide deeper towards anarchy and, in the freezing cold winter 1916-17, hungry crowds gathered in the streets burning effigies of the Tsar and Tsarina and demanding an end to the monarchy. Frantic ministers and cousins beseeched Nicholas to implement immediate reforms and grant a constitution but Nicholas, absorbed in the military campaigns, was unable to realise the seriousness of the situation until it was too late.

In early 1917, while her husband was away at the military headquarters in Mogilev, Alix was preoccupied with nursing her children, all of whom had succumbed to an outbreak of measles. Flitting from bed to bed, she paid little heed to reports of mounting dissention in nearby St. Petersburg. As a lack of coal had virtually paralysed the railways, supplies could barely reach the soldiers at the Front let alone the famished civilians. Bread shortages in the capital led to rioting and, when troops were ordered to disperse the mob, they refused to shoot the starving civilians and turned their guns instead on their officers.* In rapid succession, other regiments followed suit, seizing government buildings and even the Winter Palace.

On 13th March, prompted by urgent telegrams from the capital, the Tsar set out for Petrograd but his train was stopped en route; revolutionaries had

---

* There is evidence to suggest that many of the regiments were actually bribed by foreign agents to mutiny. (See Shattered Crowns: The Betrayal by Christina Croft)

blocked the track ahead. Diverted to Pskov, Nicholas received a petition from the Duma and several telegrams from his generals, warning him that his only hope of saving the dynasty was to abdicate in favour of his son. Seeing that the only alternative was to lead his loyal troops into the capital and spark a civil war, the Tsar signed the declaration of abdication handing over his authority to the twelve-year-old Tsarevich Alexei. Within hours, however, Nicholas reconsidered the situation. Bearing in mind Alexei's fragile health and realising that the boy would be separated from his parents, Nicholas amended the abdication manifesto to include his son, and appointed his brother, Misha, as his successor. The following day, without ever having accepted the crown, Misha, too, abdicated and the three-hundred-year rule of the mighty Romanovs came to a pitiful end.

Unaware of events in Pskov and oblivious of the hostile crowd marching towards Tsarskoe Selo demanding her blood, Alix nursed her children and entrusted her safety to the Imperial guard. Calmly she carried out trays of cocoa to the freezing soldiers, most of whom she had known personally for many years, but within a few hours they had vanished. Fearing for his own safety, their Commander-in-Chief, Ducky's husband, Grand Duke Kyril, pledged his allegiance to the Duma and, hoisting a red flag over his palace, ordered his troops to withdraw from Tsarskoe Selo, leaving Alix and her children defenceless.

Fortunately, the crowd stopped short of entering the Alexander Palace. Instead, Nicholas' uncle, Grand Duke Pavel, arrived to break the news of the abdication.

"Abdiqué!" Alix murmured in horror, convinced that had she been at her husband's side he would never have yielded to the pressure. Yet, her love for Nicholas remained unshaken and, without a hint of reproach, she wrote to him at once, addressing him as 'beloved of my soul' and assuring him of her support.

When Nicholas was eventually permitted to return to Tsarskoe Selo under house arrest, Alix met him with dignity and unconcealed devotion, regardless of the scoffing revolutionaries lounging around the state rooms of the Alexander Palace. Only when they were alone did Alix and Nicholas weep in each other's arms.

On 16th March, as news of events in Petrograd filtered through the country, a group of angry mutineers and released prisoners arrived at the gates of Ella's House of Martha and Mary, demanding to see the German spy who was hiding weapons in her hospital.

Ella ordered her terrified nuns to retreat to the back of the convent before going out to meet the aggressors at the gates. When told that they had come to arrest her, she calmly requested permission to finish her prayers. An armed posse followed her into the chapel where, surrounded by weeping nuns, she knelt to kiss the crucifix before inviting the soldiers to do the same.

"Under the spell of her calm, they followed her and kissed the cross, too. 'Now go and seek for whatever you think you will find.' The priest Mitrophanes accompanied them, and they soon came back to the howling mob outside, saying, 'It was a convent, nothing more.'"[178]

Shortly afterwards a second convoy arrived and, having searched the convent, the soldiers were so moved by the care shown to the patients that they promised there would be no further disturbances. According to a telegram sent from the American Consulate to the U.S. Secretary of State the following day:

> "Colonel Gruzinoff has detailed a guard of cadets to guard the nunnery against future intrusion. Nobody but representatives of the Staff of the Moscow Military Circuit is allowed to approach the Grand Duchess...
>
> When informed of the abdication of Nicholas II, the Grand Duchess said, "It is the will of God.""[179]

She would need the same firm faith to sustain her through the unimaginable horrors of the coming months.

Chapter 34 – Have I Not English Blood in my Veins?

News of events in Russia sent shock waves through every palace in Europe. Not only did the Entente powers fear the loss of a vital ally but, as socialist and republican ideas threatened to take hold of war-weary peoples, kings and princes feared for their thrones. If mighty Tsardom could be toppled so easily, there was a strong possibility that other nations would follow suit and depose their monarchs. In a hasty effort to prevent such an outcome, King Ferdinand of Roumania immediately promised reforms as soon as the war was won.

Even in faraway England, King George V sensed that his throne was not quite as stable as it had once appeared. After all, one of the chief charges levelled against half-English Tsarina was that she was German; and the British royal family came from the same Coburg stock. Queen Victoria's letters had been filled with German expressions and, although they had been raised in England, both Edward VII and Princess Beatrice spoke with a slight German accent. English palaces echoed to the sound of Germanic names: Battenberg, Schleswig-Holstein, Saxe-Coburg and Teck. Even the King, the son of the fiercely anti-Prussian Queen Alexandra, could not shake off the fact that he was the grandson of Prince Albert of Saxe-Coburg-Gotha.

For King George V there was a simple solution. He reduced the number of royal personages entitled to the style 'prince' and insisted that his kinsfolk must change their names to demonstrate their Englishness. The Russians had set a precedent, renaming the Germanic sounding St. Petersburg, *Petrograd* at the outbreak of war. After much consideration, the King adopted the very English-sounding name 'Windsor.' His brother-in-law, until now Prince Alexander of Teck, husband of the King's cousin, Alice of Albany, was created Earl of Athlone. Much to his chagrin, Princess Beatrice's son, Alexander, was no longer a Prince of Battenberg but the Marquis of Carisbrooke, while the rest of the Battenbergs anglicised their name to Mountbatten. Louis and Victoria Battenberg were now styled the Marquis and Marchioness of Milford Haven. As for Lenchen's daughters, Thora and Marie Louise of Schleswig-Holstein, the King declared that henceforth the name would be dropped and they would simply be known as Princesses Helena Victoria and Marie Louise.

The Christians lost more than their name in 1917. A year after celebrating his Golden Wedding Anniversary, their German-born father died in London at the age of eighty-four. Kaiser Wilhelm sent sincere messages of condolence to his aunt and cousins, via neutral Sweden.

The spring of 1917 brought sorrow too, to the Connaughts. Shortly before the outbreak of war, the Duke and Duchess had been due to return to England, handing over the governorship to Prince Alexander of Teck. The opening of hostilities thwarted the plan and the Connaughts remained in Canada until 1916. By the time they returned to England, the Potsdam-born Duchess was seriously ill and died at Clarence House on 14th March 1917. Her body was cremated at Golder's Green crematorium and her ashes were buried at Frogmore on the Windsor estate.

While other kings feared for their crowns, the Russian Revolution brought a brief but dramatic rise in status for Vicky's daughter, Mossy, and her husband Fischy of Hesse-Kassel. The Finns declared their independence from Russia and elected Fischy as their king. His reign was short-lived. Within two months of his accepting the crown, communism took hold of Eastern Europe, sweeping monarchies aside.

That summer the Russian question lay heavily on the mind of King George V. He had received a request from the Provisional Government in Petrograd asking him to grant safe haven to his Romanov cousins.

In the early days of the revolution, a lawyer, Alexander Kerensky, was appointed Minister of Justice and he prevented the mob from tearing the hated Tsarina limb from limb. Having discovered the truth of the Tsarevich's haemophilia and having satisfied himself that the stories of Alix's collaboration with the Germans were pure fabrication, he began negotiations with the British Ambassador, Sir George Buchanan, with a view to arranging for the transferral of his Imperial prisoners to the safety of England. For Alix, who recalled so many happy days in her grandmother's court, the prospect was agreeable and both she and Nicholas felt sure they could count on the support of their English cousin, 'Georgie.'

George, however, was about to deal them a terrible blow. Initially the British King acquiesced to the Provisional Government's request but hardly had he consent to the invitation than he began to have serious doubts. Reflecting on the strong anti-German sentiments and the hatred with which he supposed the British public would view the 'tyrannical' Tsar, he dared not risk his own position.

Despite the desperate pleading of Alix's sister, Victoria Battenberg, George refused to receive them. Even when his government urged him to adhere to his original invitation, he remained intransigent and sent word that the Ambassador, should ask the Russians 'to make some other plans for [their] future residences.'

With tears in his eyes Buchanan broke the news to Kerensky who, by August 1917, feared that he could no longer guarantee the safety of his Imperial prisoners in Petrograd. The radical revolutionary Lenin had returned to Russia from a prolonged exile in Switzerland and he and his extreme Bolsheviks had no intention of permitting the Tsar to escape to a foreign haven. For their own protection, Kerensky arranged for Alix, Nicholas and their family to be taken to the safety of Tobolsk in Siberia.

Ironically, while their trusted friend and cousin, George V, refused the Russians asylum in Britain, 'horrid' Cousin Willy was more than ready to welcome his relatives to Germany. Assuring them of a friendly reception in Berlin, he ordered his brother, Henry, Commander of the Baltic Fleet, to allow any ships bearing the Tsar's standard to pass unimpeded. His well-intentioned offers were not so well received. Neither Alix nor Nicholas could contemplate accepting such a gesture from their enemy in wartime.

Even if the Tsar and Tsarina refused his invitation, the Kaiser had not lost hope of rescuing another German princess. Never having quite fallen out of love with Cousin Ella, the Kaiser repeatedly sent messages via Daisy Connaught and the Swedish Embassy to the House of Martha and Mary, pleading with the Abbess to leave Russia while there was still time. Ella, unwilling to abandon her work among the poor, thanked them but refused. She would not even consider leaving her convent to take refuge in the relative safety of the Kremlin.

"Twelve years ago I left the Kremlin," she said, "and I do not wish to return there."[180]

Ultimately, she would pay with her life for that decision.

Barely had the Tsar signed his abdication manifesto than a second sovereign, Tino of Greece, was temporarily removed from his throne. In the summer of 1917, the dismissed Prime Minister, Venizelos, declared war on the Central Powers. When Tino refused to accept the declaration, the French imposed a blockade around Athens with the intention of starving him into submission. In December, as Queen Sophie busied herself in soup kitchens and hospitals, the Allies bombarded the city, aiming their shells towards the palace and driving the Queen and her children into hiding.

Like Nicholas before him, Tino watched his country escalate towards civil war and saw that his only means of avoiding the catastrophe was to abdicate in favour of his son, Alexander, for the duration of the hostilities. The Allies rejoiced but the loyal citizens of Athens were loath to see their king leave and surrounded the front gates of the palace, forcing the Royal Family to sneak quietly away through the back, to the peaceful haven of Switzerland.

As other monarchies foundered and kings feared for their thrones, the war elevated Missy of Roumania to the pinnacle of popularity. With all the ebullience of her charismatic personality, she threw herself into the Allied campaign, inspiring her soldiers with a conviction of the righteousness of their cause.

Her efforts were not without great personal cost. Less than two months after her country entered the war, her youngest son, Mircea, died of typhoid. Though devastated by grief, Missy refused to allow personal sorrow to impede her efforts on behalf of the troops. Within days of the little boy's death, she was touring hospitals, offering her ungloved hand to the wounded and doling out cigarettes and signed photographs of herself to the adoring soldiers.

Missy not only concerned herself with the immediate needs of the soldiers, but also made use of her family connections to urge both George V and the Tsar (prior to his abdication) to support her husband's ill-equipped army. Nicholas did his utmost to assist but help was slow in coming and the disorderly Russian troops, thrown into disarray by events in Petrograd, became increasingly reluctant to sacrifice their lives in defence of a monarchist regime. As German planes bombed Bucharest, enemy armies steadily marched across the country forcing Ferdinand, Missy and their children to escape from the capital to Jassy on the Russian border.

On 6th December 1916, the Kaiser's soldiers took possession of Bucharest, seizing the Roumanians' provisions and leaving the people to starve. Typhoid and smallpox swept the country and Marie's visits to the unsanitary hospitals became even more frequent and distasteful.

"'The retreat from Wallachia,' her Majesty said, 'the sorrow and depression of a vanquished Army is a story filled with tragic grief; the winter was one of darkest horror, thousands of our soldiers died of sheer want.

We could neither feed, clothe, warm, nor house them. Disease in its worst form fell upon us; and being cut off from all aid, we struggled against odds we had no means of overcoming. Row upon row of graves and uncounted numbers of rough wooden crosses throughout the land stand as mute witness of a tale too sad to relate. Thousands of little children, left without father or mother, died before help could reach them, and I, the Queen, heard each cry of anguish, shared each terror, and divided each fear.'"[181]

The fall of the Tsar was a disaster for Roumania in general, and for Missy in particular. Not only had she lost a powerful ally whom, she was sure, could be prevailed upon to send troops to her support, but also she felt very deeply for Nicholas' humiliation, and feared for the safety of her sister, Ducky.

Despite Kyril's ungallant desertion of the Tsarina and his declaration of allegiance to the Provisional Government, the Bolsheviks were determined to root out and destroy every Romanov on Russian soil. Only three months after hoisting the red flag above his palace, Kyril and his pregnant wife were forced to flee to Finland, where at the age of forty-one Ducky gave birth to a son, Vladimir. Even in Finland, as the Bolshevik armies approached, they could not feel safe. Food was in such short supply that Ducky was dependent on her cousin, Daisy, Crown Princess of Sweden (who herself had recently given birth to her youngest child Carl Johann) to send her provisions for the baby. With Daisy's help, the Swedish Embassy was desperately trying to help the family to escape to England.

In the early months of 1917, the Roumanians and their allies clung to the hope that the new Russian regime would honour the Tsar's promise to fight on until victory. For seven months after Nicholas' abdication, the increasingly disheartened Russian troops continued the war but, in November 1917, Lenin and his Bolsheviks seized power with a promise of taking Russia out of the conflict. Officers who refused to abandon their positions were ignored or even murdered by their mutinous subordinates whose sole desire was to return home and reap the rewards of revolution.

In January 1918, Roumania, too, was in danger of falling prey to revolutionaries when the Bolsheviks declared war on the country, ransacked the royal palaces and removed the Crown Jewels to Russia. It was, in part, the Queen's personal popularity that prevented the Roumanian throne from toppling alongside that of Cousin Nicholas.

The departure of their Russian allies left the Roumanians outnumbered and by March 1918 King Ferdinand was bound to admit defeat. Helpless and frustrated, Missy could only gape in horror at her husband's willingness to surrender, declaring to her cousin, George V of Britain, that she would have preferred to die with the army than see the country surrender.

In response, King George offered her asylum but, like her Russian cousins, she was too devoted to her people to abandon them in their hour of need. Besides, even when the outcome seemed inevitable, she was determined to expend all her energies in persuading Ferdinand to reject the Kaiser's terms, advising him to abdicate rather than accept such humiliation.

For all her pleading and cajoling, King Ferdinand agreed to the German demands in their entirety. On hearing what he had done, Missy exploded with rage and even entertained the idea of leading the troops into Russia in the hope of finding refuge in the Crimea and inspiring the Russians to restore the Tsar, but this time even the headstrong Queen was powerless. Ferdinand had signed the treaty and there was nothing she could do about it. Nevertheless, heroic and theatrical to the end, Missy insisted that she had not accepted the treaty and refused to acknowledge defeat.

For now she was forced to live 'under the yoke' but she never doubted that, in spite of present hardships, the Entente would eventually win the war and she waited optimistically for future glory.

Chapter 35 – I Would Rather Die In Russia

Captive in Siberia, the former Tsar and Tsarina kept abreast of world events through the newspapers and faithfully followed the course of the war. Still praying for a Russian victory and optimistic about the possibility of a restoration of the monarchy or at least a comfortable exile in a friendly country, the Tsarina and her daughters prepared for the future. The guards had confiscated most of their belongings but Alix and the girls sewed many of their precious jewels into their undergarments so that when freedom eventually came, they would have some means of supporting themselves. Keeping up their spirits with such hopes, Alix and Nicholas read and prayed and continued the children's lessons, finding comfort in their faith in God's goodness and a fatalistic resignation to his will.

Were it not for the shame of abdication and incarceration and his fears for the future of his people, Nicholas would probably have been happier in Tobolsk than at any time since his marriage. Walking in the grounds with his daughters, chopping wood as he had done when a child, it was almost a relief to be free from the burden of office. But the respite was short-lived.

The first blow came in March 1918 when Lenin signed the Treaty of Brest-Litovsk taking Russia out of the war.

"And they call me a traitor!" Nicholas gasped in horror on reading of the humiliating terms.

When it was rumoured that Cousin Willy had included a secret clause in the treaty, guaranteeing the safety of the Imperial Family, Alix was still more disgusted, declaring: "I would rather die in Russia than be saved by Germans."

A depressed Nicholas agreed and prophetically sighed that no good could come to the Kaiser and his ministers who had stooped to shake hands with the Bolshevik traitors.

Even if Nicholas and Alix had been prepared to accept the Kaiser's offers of asylum, the Bolsheviks (Reds) had no intention of allowing their former rulers to escape from their grasp. Lenin resolved to destroy every trace of the Romanovs and all they had stood for, while his comrade, Trotsky favoured a show trial in Moscow followed by Nicholas' execution. As long as the Tsar was alive, they argued, he would provide the focus for counter-revolution. The Mensheviks' White Army might settle for a constitutional monarchy, while Tsarist supporters, backed, it was said, by Nicholas' foreign cousins, were planning to return the Tsar to his throne. Fearing a successful rescue attempt, the Bolsheviks felt it was imperative to move the prisoners to a more secure location.

On 23rd April 1918, Commissar Yakovlev arrived in Tobolsk from Moscow and ordered Nicholas to prepare to leave for an unknown destination. There were no specific orders concerning Alix or the children but, if they wished to travel with him, they would be permitted to do so. The news brought further heartache to Alix. The young Tsarevich had fallen some days earlier and, suffering another haemorrhage, was too ill to travel. His mother hardly dared leave his side and yet the thought of abandoning Nicholas to face an uncertain future alone was more than she could bear. Both she and Nicholas believed that he would be taken to Moscow and forced to sign the humiliating Treaty of

Brest-Litovsk. Convinced that had she been with him, Nicholas would never have signed the abdication manifesto, Alix could not allow him to be manipulated a second time. After much soul-searching and weeping, she decided to travel with her husband. Their third daughter, Maria, accompanied them, leaving Alexei in the care of his sisters, Olga, Tatiana and Anastasia, until he was well enough to follow.

The Russian Imperial Family

The arduous journey was torture for the ailing Tsarina. Having been hurled about in a cart over the icy tracks and flooded roads, it came as a relief to board a train bound for Moscow. Yurovsky, intending to deliver his 'baggage' safely, arranged for the train to avoid the fiercely anti-Romanov Urals but an ambush thwarted his plans. As they neared Ekaterinburg, armed members of the local soviet stopped the train and insisted at gunpoint that the family be taken into the town, where a house had been requisitioned from a merchant named Ipatiev and ominously renamed 'The House of Special Purpose.'

The hostility of the crowds who gathered to jeer and hiss was as nothing compared to the humiliations that the family endured once they reached the house. Unlike the guards in Tobolsk, the Red Guards had no sympathy whatsoever with their former rulers and went out of their way to debase them. When Alexei and his sisters were eventually able to join the rest of the family, the soldiers ensured that they suffered every possible indignity, even loitering outside the one toilet and refusing to allow the young Grand Duchesses to close the door. On the bathroom walls they had scrawled lewd verses about Nicholas and drawn obscene pictures of Alix and Rasputin. Yet the family remained as devout and devoted to one another as ever and found consolation in each other's company and their prayers; and, while accepting the possibility of imminent death, Alix still dreamed of a future in the Crimea or in England.

Freed from the constraints of war, Lenin turned his attention to his own position in Russia. Now that the Imperial Family were safely in the Reds' custody, he was able to tighten his grip on the new regime by rounding up all the rest of the Romanovs who had remained in Russia. Nicholas' brother, Misha, was placed under house arrest in Perm. His uncle, Pavel, and several other Grand Dukes were imprisoned in the Peter and Paul Fortress in Petrograd, while Nicholas' cousin, Prince Vladimir Paley, and a further four Grand Dukes were transported east to Siberia.

At Easter, soldiers arrived at the House of Martha and Mary and ordered the Abbess to prepare to leave at once. Ella, anticipating her fate, requested two hours to say goodbye to her sisters but was curtly told she had half an hour. Accompanied by two nuns she was placed on a train and informed that she was needed to assist in a hospital in Siberia.

The train eventually reached Ekaterinburg where Ella, granted a limited amount of freedom, was housed in a convent and permitted to join her cousins, the Grand Dukes, for church services. When she heard that her sister was also captive in the town, she pleaded to be allowed to visit her but permission was refused and she had to content herself with sending a letter containing gifts of chocolates and coffee for the inmates of the Ipatiev house.

In early June, Ella and the Grand Dukes were moved again. Fearing that such a concentration of Romanovs would make the town a target for counter-revolutionaries, the Bolsheviks ordered the prisoners to be taken seventy-five miles north to Alapaevsk, where they were accommodated in a disused school. The place was filthy when they arrived but Ella and the two nuns who had travelled with her, set about clearing the rooms and planting vegetables in the gardens.

A cook came daily to prepare meals and later gave evidence that Ella spent her time drawing and praying. Local people, recalling Ella's previous pilgrimages to their town, were saddened by the news of her arrest and secretly passed gifts and messages of support through the fence. The Mensheviks, they said, were gaining ground and it was only a matter of time before the Imperial prisoners would be liberated.

By mid-summer the White Army was rapidly nearing Ekaterinburg and the echo of their guns could be heard through the shuttered windows of the Ipatiev House. Realising that if they delayed any longer the Imperial prisoners could be snatched away to freedom, the Bolsheviks decided to act. One night in June two soldiers arrived at the hotel in Perm where Nicholas' brother, Misha, and his secretary, Brian Johnson, were under house arrest. Forcing them at gun point into a car, the Bolsheviks drove to a remote spot in the woods and there, out of the hearing of the townspeople, shot them dead and hastily buried the bodies in the unknown location. Their remains have never been found.

Until then, the guards in Alapaevsk had been on relatively friendly terms with their prisoners but, following Misha's disappearance, their attitude changed dramatically. No longer would they permit the Grand Dukes to wander in the gardens, and the two nuns who had accompanied Ella from Moscow were ordered to leave the town. Convinced that this could only mean that their beloved Abbess was about to be killed, they begged to be allowed to stay but, despite their tears when all three 'cried like little children,' they were forced into a truck and driven away. They reached Ekaterinburg where they earnestly pleaded with the leader of local Soviet to permit them to return. Their petition was greeted with contempt; soldiers mocked their loyalty and warned them that if they returned they would share the same fate as the Grand Duchess: torture and execution. Undeterred, they continued to plead until the soviet agreed that one of them could return. Barbara Yakovleva, a thirty-two year old nun who had been with Ella since the foundation of her Order, had virtually signed her own death warrant. The other nun, Catherine Yanisheva, was never heard of again.

On a sweltering afternoon in July 1918, a new official appeared at the House of Special Purpose. Jacob Yurovsky, a member of the Bolshevik secret police, had arrived from Moscow to replace the former commandant, the drunken and incompetent Avdeev. More efficient than his predecessor, Yurovsky immediately replaced the old guard with more reliable men from the newly formed Commission for Struggle against Counter-revolution or Sabotage – the Cheka. Though he treated the prisoners with a polite, if abrasive, respect, his insistence on covering the windows with grilles and his apparent fear of an imminent rescue attempt heightened the sense of tension in the house.

Yurovsky had come to Ekaterinburg with only one purpose in mind: the murder of the Imperial family. It was a task that must be carried out in secrecy. Lenin needed international recognition for his new regime, and regicide without trial would place the Bolsheviks in a very bad light. Moreover, as long as he was alive, or believed to be alive, the Tsar might prove a useful bargaining tool with foreign governments. To maintain secrecy, Yurovsky believed that it was vital that all his prisoners should die so none would be left to tell the world of what had happened.

Only those soldiers in whom Yurovsky had absolute trust were informed of his plans as he set about preparing for the murder and the subsequent disposal of the bodies. The cellar of the Ipatiev house was selected as the ideal location for the killing: below ground level, it could not be seen from the road, and the plastered walls would, he thought, dampen the sound of shooting and prevent the bullets from ricocheting across the room. In the days leading up to the massacre, he hand-picked his firing squad and selected a burial site. The Koptiaka woods outside the town were filled with disused mine shafts where the corpses could be easily disposed of and, as a precaution, a separate squad under the command of the Commissar Pyotr Ermakov would be stationed around the site to prevent the intrusion of any unwelcome witnesses.

Oblivious of the plot, the Romanovs continued their dull routine of reading and prayer, and on the evening 16th July, after playing bezique, Nicholas and Alix retired to bed at ten-thirty.

While the family slept, Yurovsky organised his firing squad. Each man was given a specific target and told to aim at the heart so that the operation would be carried out quickly with the minimum blood loss. Throughout the evening, the soldiers drank heavily. Even the most hardened revolutionaries would not find it easy to murder four innocent girls and a thirteen-year-old boy in cold blood.

Shortly after midnight, Yurovsky woke the Tsar's physician, Dr Botkin, and ordered him to rouse the family. There had been shooting in the town, he said, and for their own protection they must come down to the cellar. Half an hour later, the Romanovs calmly descended the twenty-three steps, Nicholas carrying his son, who was unable to walk following a recent haemorrhage. The daughters and their maid, Anna Demidova, carried pillows with them and Anastasia's little dog, Jimmy, followed them down the stairs.

Ushered into the empty room, Alix asked for chairs. Two were brought and she sat down on one of them, as Nicholas placed the Tsarevich on the other. Yurovsky informed the family that, since there were rumours that they had escaped, it was necessary to take a photograph to send back to Moscow, and asked them to assemble accordingly. The girls, their father, Dr Botkin, Demidova, the valet and the cook gathered around Alexei and the Tsarina, awaiting the entrance of the photographer.

The door burst open and Yurovsky hurriedly read from a paper informing the prisoners that, in view of an imminent rescue attempt, the prisoners must be shot.

"What? What?" murmured the Tsar, as Alix and her daughters blessed themselves and the soldiers opened fire. The Tsar, Tsarina and Dr Botkin died instantly with bullets through the head but, for all Yurovsky's careful planning, the massacre descended into savage butchery. The drunken soldiers missed their targets and bullets bounced off the jewels sewn into the girls underclothing, ricocheting across the room and filling the cellar with smoke. The maid, Anna Demidova, screamed and covered her face with the pillow; and ironically, Alexei, who had come close to death so many times, was also still alive and moaning on the floor until Yurovsky put a bullet through his head.

When the bullets proved useless, the soldiers stabbed at the girls with bayonets but still the jewels deflected the blades. In anger and panic the firing squad struck them with rifle butts before shooting them through their heads in an orgy of killing.

As the smoke gradually cleared, Yurovsky ordered the soldiers to take the bodies to a lorry that was waiting in the courtyard, its engine already running to muffle the sound of the guns. Even then, one of the girls cried out; she was not yet dead. The lorry set out through the darkness but the plans were to go further awry. There were no proper roads through the woods, and the wheels stuck in the mud. Yurovsky, desperate to complete his mission before the light of dawn, hastily order the corpses to be transferred to carts and wheeled towards the chosen spot, known as The Four Brothers. By then, Ermakov's men had arrived hoping to take part in the killing and were disappointed to discover than the prisoners were already dead. In their frustration they set about taking rings and medals from the bodies until Yurovsky threatened execution for any man caught stealing. Some semblance of order returned and, as the dawn began to break, they reached the planned burial site.

By morning, news of events in Ekaterinburg reached the ears of the soviet in Alapaevsk. Now it was their turn to massacre their prisoners. At midday on 17th July, a Cheka detachment arrived at the old schoolroom to replace the guards. Throughout the afternoon they searched the prisoners' belongings and warned of an imminent move but by evening nothing seemed to be happening and the Grand Dukes retired to bed.

Suddenly in the middle of the night, Ella and her companion, Barbara, were awoken by two soldiers who whispered that their lives were in danger so they must dress quickly as they were to be taken away to a place of safety. Meekly and silently, they obeyed and as soon as they were dressed the soldiers blindfolded them and led them out to a waiting cart, which immediately set off along the Sinyachikhenskaya road. The Grand Dukes followed in other carts.

For twelve miles the convoy continued through the semi-darkness until it reached a wooded area littered with disused mines. Alighting from the cart, the soldiers ordered Ella to walk forwards and, as she neared the opening of a flooded mine, struck her head with rifle butts plunging her down the nineteen metres into the water. In spite of serious head wound, she succeeded in scrambling onto a ledge as the soldiers forced the other prisoners one after another into the shaft. As in the fiasco of Ekaterinburg, the soldiers soon realised their plans were going terribly wrong. The prisoners had not drowned as they had anticipated, and even after they had hurled hand grenades into the shaft it was clear that at least some of the victims were still alive. From the ledge below they heard the sound of singing: "Lord save your people."

At a loss as to what to do, the soldiers gathered brushwood and set it alight before hurling it into the pit and returning to Alapaevsk, where they spread the story that the Grand Dukes had escaped during a raid by the White Army. Few of the townspeople believed the tale, particularly when peasants reported hearing voices from the mine days later, but they dared not offer assistance or contradict the official line.

The prisoners were left to die of infected wounds and starvation, yet even then, Ella continued her life of service. Beside her on the ledge lay a young Grand Duke, the son of Serge's cousin, Konstantin Konstantinovich. His head was bleeding and he was probably coughing up blood. Tearing strips from her veil, Ella carefully bandaged his wounds. There was nothing else to do then, but pray and endure the slow and painful wait for death.

Chapter 36 – Victors and Vanquished

Days after the massacre in Ekaterinburg, Victoria Battenberg, unaware of her sisters' fate, was desperately trying to secure them a safe haven, if not in England then perhaps in Spain. Queen Ena and King Alfonso were willing to help and negotiations were still underway when the news reached England on 24th July, that the Tsar had been assassinated.

There was still, as yet, no news of the Empress and her children or of Ella but rumours were rife. Alix was in captivity with her daughters in Perm; Ella had been rescued by plane and taken to Czechoslovakia; she was still in Alapaevsk; they were ill; they were well; no one could be sure. For almost a month Victoria, Irène and Ernie remained optimistic until the first blow came before the end of August. Though the bodies had not been found – and would remain hidden for almost seventy years – intelligence reports seemed to confirm that the entire family had been murdered.

King George V was the first to hear of the massacre and immediately ordered the newspapers to refrain from printing the story until Victoria had been informed. He wrote a letter which Alix's close friend and cousin, Marie Louise, volunteered to take to her on the Isle of Wight.

"I have often had to face difficult situations that have needed tact as well as courage," she wrote, "but never anything so terrible as to inform someone that her much-loved sister, brother-in-law, and their five children had all been murdered."[182]

The letter from George V could hardly have brought great consolation, considering his refusal to grant them safe haven.

According to Marie Louise, Victoria's devastating grief was 'too overwhelming for mere words' and her immediate response was to work in the garden 'all day and every day for three weeks.'

Distressing as the news was, Victoria gleaned some comfort from the hope that at least Ella had been spared. Throughout the early autumn, disjointed stories from war-torn Russia continued to suggest that the Grand Duchess had been rescued. It was not until early November that the awful truth was revealed.

Six weeks after Ella had been thrown down the mine, the White Army marched triumphantly into Alapaevsk, where the locals, freed from the fear of the Bolsheviks, reported what they knew of the Grand Dukes' disappearance. The White Army commander, Admiral Kolchak, ordered an immediate investigation and, after following several conflicting leads, the investigator, Malshikov succeeded in locating the mine. Stones and charred wood blocked the entrance to the shaft, which was found to be flooded and so badly damaged by the fire and grenades that it took several weeks before the search for bodies could begin in earnest.

Gradually, in various states of decomposition the corpses of the Grand Dukes were brought to the surface until at last, on 11th October 1918, Ella's body too was recovered.

Though horrified by their find, the investigators were amazed to discover that Ella's body remained intact; by her side was an unexploded grenade, on her breast a cedar wood crucifix and an icon of Christ. Local people, outraged by the murder of the gentle Grand Duchess, flocked in their hundreds to the church in Alapaevsk where Ella and her companions were given an official funeral.

Even then, a further month would pass before Victoria received confirmation of all that had happened. Having so recently heard of the fate of Nicholas, Alix and their children, the death of her closest sister came as a terrible, if not unexpected, blow.

"Victoria's splendid courage remained unshaken," wrote Marie Louise, "She faced [many grievous trials] with calmness and strength and never allowed her sorrows to dim the happiness or joys of those around her."[183]

Victoria, herself found comfort in the knowledge that Ella's faith would have sustained her to the end: 'If ever anyone has met death without fear she will have...'

By the time the news reached her younger sister in Germany, Irène was living in fear for her own life.

The vicissitudes of war continued relentlessly throughout the spring and early summer of 1918. In March the Germans staged a final grand offensive on the Western Front and broke through the Allied lines to regain the Marne. For four months the slaughter continued along the Somme and defeat seemed a real possibility for the combined British and French armies but, by the beginning of July, with American support, they were prepared to mount a counter-attack. On 8th August, the British under Field Marshal Haig broke through the enemy lines and in the weeks that followed the Allied troops made further inroads through the Germans' defences.

In September, a combined force of Serb, Greek, French and British troops launched an attack in the Balkans and by the beginning of October Foxy Ferdinand of Bulgaria had been forced to abdicate.

Within weeks Turkey, too, had yielded and the Austro-Hungarian Empire splintered into separatist groups forcing Emperor Karl to agree to an Armistice on 3rd November.

Of the Central Powers, only the Kaiser was prepared to fight to the end but his efforts were in vain. Realising it was only a matter of time before the Allies achieved a final victory, the Roumanians reneged on the Treaty of Bucharest and declared that unless the Germans left their country, they would take up arms again. On November 9th, to Queen Marie's delight, King Ferdinand ordered his troops to remobilise.

For Kaiser Wilhelm the situation was hopeless. News had already reached his brother, Henry, Admiral of the Fleet, that his sailors had mutinied. On the 8th November revolution broke out in Munich and on the 9th the regiments in Berlin marched beneath a Bolshevist flag. In an almost identical replay of events in Russia, the Kaiser's trusted cousin, Max of Baden, urged him to abdicate in favour of his twelve-year-old grandson but, mindful perhaps of the fate of Cousin Nicky, Willy vehemently refused. The following day, his generals announced that they were no longer prepared to defend him and warned that unless he left the country, Civil War would erupt. Realising that he had no alternative but to flee, he boarded a train bound for Holland where Alice of Albany's cousin, Queen Wilhelmina, offered him a safe home at Doorn, where he would remain in modest comfort to the end of his life.

'What retribution to the man who started this awful war,' Queen Mary wrote, but in Roumania,

---

* Emperor Franz Joseph had died in 1916 and was succeeded by his great-nephew, Karl.

Missy was less ecstatic about her cousin's demise and recorded that she was distressed on hearing of his abdication.

Ironically, Willy's first words on reaching his Dutch haven were, "And now for a lovely cup of English tea."

For those he had left behind, the situation was far less civilised. As revolutionaries swept into Kiel, Irène and Henry tied red flags to their car as they fled from the city amid a shower of bullets. They eventually reached the safety of Hemmelmarck in Northern Germany where they settled into relative obscurity. Irène's brother, Ernie, meanwhile, displayed even greater courage. Refusing to flee, he calmly met the revolutionary soldiers who marched into the New Palace at Darmstadt, and voluntarily agreed to hand over his rights as Grand Duke. Though stripped of his titles and privileges he was permitted to remain in his Hessian home.

Across the border in Hesse-Kassel, Mossy's husband, Fischy, was likewise stripped of his authority but permitted to retain his land. Within a month all the minor ancient dukedoms and principalities were swept away. Charlotte's husband, Duke Bernhard of Saxe-Meiningen and her son-in-law, Heinrich, abdicated on 10th November. Alice of Albany's brother, Duke Charles of Coburg; Marie Louise's former husband, Aribert of Anhalt, and the Prince of Schaumburg-Lippe – all were ousted. In the aftermath of the First World War, the peaceful monarchical Germany, which Prince Albert had once envisaged, vanished forever.

In Britain, the Armistice of 11th November 1918 was met with a frenzy of rejoicing surpassing the revelries that had greeted the outbreak of war. As King George stood on the balcony of Buckingham Palace, his cousin, Marie Louise, mingled incognito with the crowds at the gates and joined in the cheering. For Victoria Battenberg, the only one of her siblings to witness the celebrations, victory must have had a hollow ring. Grieving for two of her sisters, her brother-in-law, her nephew and four nieces, and worrying about the ultimate fate of her brother and sister in Germany, she might well have shared the sentiments expressed by her mother half a century before, at the end of the Austro-Prussian War:

> "We must devote all our energies to the reconstruction of our suffering country. I trust all governments will do the same, and think no more of war."[184]

Since the outbreak of hostilities, the Connaughts had lost their mother; the Christians, their father; Queen Ena of Spain, a brother; Moretta, a husband; and Mossy, two sons. The power and glory of the pre-war monarchies had gone forever. Yet, who better to rise like a phoenix from the ashes, than the conquered Queen who refused to admit defeat: the brilliantly flamboyant Marie of Roumania.

On the day the Armistice was announced, as celebrations echoed through the streets of Jassy, the French Minister presented the Queen of Roumania with the Croix de Guerre in recognition of her unstinting commitment to the Allied cause. Three weeks later, on 1st December a triumphant Marie, in military dress, rode with her armies into Bucharest to be greeted by the exultant crowds bearing the flags of every Allied nation. If ever a queen were created to shine, none could have done it more brilliantly than the ebullient Marie of Roumania.

Epilogue – After the Idyll

For the royalties of Europe, whether victors or vanquished, the world would never be the same again. Even those who had retained their thrones and titles would no longer enjoy the halcyon days of the pre-war world, where queens and princesses flitted across the continent with the world at their feet.

Within a year of the Armistice, Queen Victoria's eldest granddaughter, was dead. Charlotte, who had spent much of the last few months of her life confined to bed with her various porphyria-related symptoms, died on 1st October at Baden-Baden. She was buried in Thuringia, near Hesse.

For a further ten years, her younger sister, Moretta, widowed since 1916, eked out a lonely existence in Germany attempting to restore her family ties with England. In November 1927 at the age of sixty-two, she embarked on yet another disastrous love affair, marrying a young Russian officer, Alexander Zubkhov, thirty-five years her junior. Within two years, her husband, who had apparently married her only for her money, had deserted her and she was bringing court proceedings against him when she died, virtually bankrupt and disillusioned, on 13th November 1929.

For her sister, Sophie, there were a few more glorious hours. In 1920, following the death of her son, Alexander, she and Tino were invited to return from Switzerland to regain their thrones. For two years they enjoyed relative peace but in 1923, following the Greeks' defeat by the Turks, Tino was forced to abdicate for a second time. He and Sophie left the country and, within a year, Tino was dead. Sophie spent the rest of her life in exile, enjoying a fairly peaceful existence until her death in Frankfurt on 13th January 1932.

Mossy, having seen two sons die in the trenches of the First World War, remained in Germany throughout the upheavals of Hitler's rise to power. The Second World War brought further tragedy when another son, Philipp, was interned in a concentration camp, and his wife died in the infamous Buchenwald. A fourth son, Christoph, was killed in a plane crash in 1943. Mossy died on 22nd January 1954.

Following the marriage of her younger daughter, Maud, in 1923, the widowed Louise, Dowager Duchess of Fife, withdrew into the seclusion of her Scottish estates where her health rapidly deteriorated. In the autumn of 1929, she suffered a haemorrhage and was taken to London for treatment. For over a year she remained under the care of nurses at her house on Portman Square until the 4th January 1931 when she died peacefully in her sleep. Her body was buried on her Scottish estate at Mar.

The long-suffering Toria spent the remainder of her days paying dutiful visits to hospitals and nursing homes. After her mother's death in 1925, she settled into a house named Coppins in Buckinghamshire where she became increasingly absorbed in religion. There, like her elder sister, she suffered a gastric haemorrhage and died peacefully on 4th December 1935. A month later, her elder and closest sibling, King George V, was also dead.

Maud, though frequently plagued by ill-health, continued to carry out her duties in Norway between her frequent visits to her beloved Appleton Lodge. In autumn 1938, while staying at Claridge's Hotel in

London, she fell ill. Immediate surgery was recommended but, though the doctors were optimistic, she died of heart failure three days after the operation. Her coffin was placed in the chapel at Marlborough House, where she had been baptised almost seventy years earlier, before being taken back to Norway for interment.

In 1920, Victoria Battenberg, still desperately seeking news of the whereabouts of Ella's grave, chanced upon a magazine article describing the Russian Orthodox cemetery in Peking. Following various leads, she discovered that Ella's friend, the monk Seraphim, fearing the desecration of the graves in Alapaevsk, had arranged for the transfer of the Grand Dukes' coffins to China. It might have come as little surprise to Victoria to hear that, after all the upheavals, her saintly sister's body was said to have remained intact and, according to several witnesses, often exuded the fragrance of flowers. Recalling Ella's love for the Holy Land, Victoria arranged for her coffin and that of her faithful companion, Barbara, to be taken to the Orthodox Church in Jerusalem. On 15th January 1921, Seraphim oversaw the transferral of the bodies to Palestine where Victoria, her husband, Louis, and a huge crowd awaited them in Jerusalem. The following day Ella was laid to rest on the Mount of Olives in the Church of St. Mary Magdalene. She was subsequently canonised by the Russian Orthodox Church and many miracles have been reported through her intercession. In the summer of 2004, following the restoration of her convent, relics from her body were transferred to Moscow.

Nine months after attending Ella's interment in Jerusalem, Victoria attended another funeral: that of her husband, Louis. He had contracted influenza during a holiday in Scotland and died on 11th September. He was buried at Whippingham Church on the Isle of Wight. Victoria continued her charitable works and lived to see the marriage of her grandson, Philip of Greece, to the future Queen Elizabeth II. In August 1950 she suffered a heart attack and, realising that she was no longer able to care for herself, asked to be looked after by Roman Catholic nuns. Her cousin Ena arranged for two Spanish nuns to attend her until her peaceful death on 24th September.

> "When she died," wrote Marie Louise, "she left a blank that nothing could fill, and not only her family but the many who had the privilege of knowing her and enjoying her friendship, realised that henceforth the world would be poorer for the passing of this great and courageous lady."[185]

Irène outlived all of her sisters, her husband and two of her sons. Henry died shortly before the outbreak of the Second World War, and Irène, in true Hessian fashion, continued to put herself out for the rest of the family. She died in Hemmelmark on 11th November 1953.

As they had cared for their grandmother, Princesses Thora and Marie Louise of Schleswig-Holstein cared for their mother in her widowhood until her death at Schomburg House in Pall Mall London on the 9th June 1923. The sisters lived contentedly together and travelled frequently and extensively. In her later years Marie Louise published a book, 'My Memory of Six Reigns' recalling the halcyon days of European royalty. Thora died in Berkley Square, London in March

1948, and Marie Louise died in December 1956. Both were interred with their parents at Frogmore.

Two years after the Armistice, the Dowager Duchess of Coburg, who had become so inured to violence and assassinations, died peacefully in her sleep. Her death brought about a reunion of all four of her daughters in Coburg. Queen Marie was still riding high on a wave of popularity in Roumania, which contrasted sharply with her sister's rather impoverished existence in France. Ducky and Kyril, having eventually escaped from Finland, were living in Brittany. Following Nicholas' death, Kyril's assertion that he was now the rightful Tsar of Russia provoked a good deal of criticism from the rest of the family who recalled his ungentlemanly desertion of the Tsarina in her hour of need. Nor did the struggles that Kyril and Ducky had endured together succeed in creating a happy marriage. By the early 1930s, Ducky had become estranged from her husband due to a discovery she had made about him which she refused to reveal to anyone. While visiting Coburg in early March 1936, Ducky suffered a stroke and died surrounded by her husband and her sisters, Marie and Beatrice. She was buried in Coburg but sixty years later, following the collapse of communism in Russia, her coffin was taken to the Imperial burials vaults in the Peter and Paul Fortress in St. Petersburg.

By the time of Ducky's death, Marie had already nursed her husband, King Ferdinand, through his final illness until his death in 1927, and watched the monarchy slide into disarray under the rule of her wayward son, King Carol. Her popularity remained undiminished and she died at Sinaia of oesophageal varices on July 18th 1938, surrounded by flowers from well-wishers. In 1942 Sandra died peacefully in Wurttemberg, and Beatrice lived on in Spain until 1966.

In the immediate aftermath of the First World War, the gloom of London was lightened by the first public royal marriage. On 27th February 1919, the beautiful Patsy Connaught married her father's aide-de-camp, Alexander Ramsay. Initially the Duke of Connaught had opposed the match not only because he was loath to lose his daughter but also because Alexander was a commoner. In marrying him, Patsy renounced her royal titles to become simply Lady Patricia Ramsay but it was a remarkably happy marriage that lasted for over fifty years and produced one son, born in the bathroom of Clarence House ten months after the wedding. Alexander died in 1972, predeceasing Patsy by two years.

Sadly, the popular Daisy, Crown Princess of Sweden did not live long enough to ascend the throne. A year after her sister's wedding, she caught a chill and chicken pox while pregnant and died unexpectedly after giving birth to a still born baby in Stockholm on 1st May 1920. She was only thirty-eight years old.

The post war years brought a further deterioration in Queen Ena of Spain's unhappy marriage. In 1931, revolutionaries demanded an end to the monarchy and she and Alfonso were forced to flee to Paris. They remained in exile, travelling separately across the continent, as their country was ravaged by civil war. The deposed king continued to enjoy his mistresses and openly humiliated his wife, even refusing to see her on his deathbed in 1941. Ena stayed briefly in England before finally settling in Switzerland where she received frequent visits from her cousins.

"I admire Ena from the depths of my heart for the way in which she had adapted to her altered circumstances," wrote Marie Louise. "She has made her home in Lausanne, and her little chateau, Vielle Fontaine, is in every way very charming – but what a contrast to the splendours of Madrid! Yet never one word of complaint from Ena."[186]

It was in Lausanne that Ena died at the age of eighty-one in 1969.

Paradoxically, Alice of Athlone, the only daughter of Queen Victoria's sickly son, Leopold, outlived all her cousins, her husband and her sons. The princess, who had enjoyed the glories of Queen Victoria's Golden and Diamond Jubilees, was present at Queen Elizabeth II's Silver Jubilee celebrations in 1977 and died peacefully in Kensington Palace four years later on 3rd January 1981 at the age of ninety-seven.

Appendix I - *Thoughts on the death of Prince Albert*

At the time of his death, it was reported that Prince Albert died of typhoid, probably due to the dirty drains at Windsor, and this story was repeated for decades. There are several reasons to doubt this diagnosis and it is my belief that the prince was suffering – and had been for a long time – from some pernicious illness which, combined with his mental state, eventually led to his premature death.

It is interesting that no one else in the household was reported to be suffering from typhoid in December 1861 (yet it usually occurs in epidemics) and, more noticeable, is the fact that his family – including four-year-old Beatrice – came to him during his last illness, held his hand, kissed him and sat on his bed. Would anyone allow a four-year-old child approach a person with an infectious and potentially fatal fever?

Prince Albert's symptoms did not quite fit the typical typhoid symptoms. He certainly had a high temperature and weakness but there is no mention of the purplish rash that sometimes occurs on the chest, or any sign of delirium. To his last breath, he was speaking coherently with his daughter, Alice, and with the Queen.

Most significant of all, though, is the very long history of Prince Albert's ailments throughout his life. Queen Victoria believed him to be a hypochondriac and he seems to have had a weak constitution. When he first met Queen Victoria, he was recovering from sea-sickness and fainted while they were dancing. There are many other reports of sea-sickness and, more strikingly, serious stomach problems. One of the difficulties he faced when he first arrived in England was adjusting to late breakfasts, which he could not digest and so felt exhausted throughout the day. Quite often he fainted while suffering from stomach cramps and various gastro-enteric complaints; and if he contracted any other infection (colds, measles, 'flu' etc.) his sufferings seemed to be worse than would be expected and the illness lasted far longer than was common.

In the last year of his life, his symptoms dramatically increased: toothache (with no apparent cause – and then abscesses), hair loss, weight loss, swollen ankles, muscle and joint pain, extreme cold, exhaustion, the familiar digestive problems and even irritability to name but a few. Bearing in mind that he was only forty-one years old when these symptoms became so extreme, it suggests that there must have been some underlying cause that remained undiagnosed.

I believe that Prince Albert might have suffered from some form of malabsorption syndrome, which was not recognised and could have escalated into something even more pernicious. It was this, I think which killed him.

It is significant, too, that Prince Albert's ailments were so closely connected to his mental state. Shortly after the engagement of his daughter, Vicky, Prince Albert, a young man at the time, was struck with an acute rheumatic condition which affected his shoulder and left him confined to bed for quite some time. He is said to have contracted the fatal typhoid after hearing of the death of his cousins in Portugal who died of that disease, and while being shocked by his son, Bertie's escapade with the actress in Ireland. His final illness was certainly connected in some way to his reaction to these events.

In the end, Albert decided he was dying. He had exhausted himself completely and basically 'gave up the ghost'.

Appendix II – *Queen Victoria's Excessive Mourning*

The story of Victoria and Albert is seen as one of the great royal love stories of all time and, while it cannot be denied that the Queen adored her 'beloved angel,' there is something about the excesses of her mourning (including her refusal to be cajoled from it – she actually wrote to her daughter, Vicky, that she enjoyed thinking of her sorrow!) that gives me the impression of 'she doth protest too much',

Perhaps Queen Victoria was what is now called co-dependent. Her love, though genuine, was perhaps not in the least what might be called *real/mature* love in which the object of one's affection is seen as a person in his/her own right with his/her own needs. When Queen Victoria loved someone, she **'needed'** them and, in some ways, seemed to sap the life from them. It is interesting, though very sad, that Prince Albert, John Brown and Disraeli were all such men, and, though the Queen would do anything to defend and support them, such support seemed to spring more from a need in herself, rather than a mature, respectful acceptance and love of another individual. It might even be said that her treatment of Melbourne was the precursor for this. She so needed him that she was prepared to cast the constitution aside and override parliament, even putting the monarchy at risk in order to keep him by her.

It was not only with those to whom she formed a romantic attachment, however, that she behaved in this way. Her reluctance to allow her daughter, Beatrice, to marry, and then her insistence that Beatrice and her husband remain living with her, is a similar example. "I must have a daughter with me..." she wrote to Vicky.

Another interesting fact is that in March 1861, the death of Victoria's mother threw her into a state of utter despair to the extent that even Albert felt compelled to tell her to basically 'pull herself together'. There was a great deal of guilt involved in her sorrow, due to her disregard of her mother in the immediate years following her accession. Did she also feel a sense of guilt around Albert's death? Is that why she was so excessive in her mourning and in her need to preserve his memory?

None of this is meant as a criticism – merely as an observation. The starkness of her childhood, the cruelty of John Conroy and the early death of her father seem to have left her as a very needy person. At no time in her adult life was she without a 'prop' – whether it was Melbourne or the Munshi – and such was her dependence on these people that when they (excepting the Munshi, who outlived her) died she truly felt as though a part of her own soul/being had been wrenched from her.

Appendix III - *Queen Victoria & Alfred, Lord Tennyson*

Queen Victoria's friendship with Alfred, Lord Tennyson is very fascinating. Being a neighbour on the Isle of Wight, Tennyson was sometimes invited from his home, Farringford (now The Farringford Hotel) to Osborne House, where Queen Victoria, who enjoyed his work, liked to spend time in his company, though, as she wrote to her daughter, Vicky, she found him rather dark and gloomy at times and described him as looking 'very old'.

The role of Poet Laureate cannot have been more difficult for any other poet than it was for Tennyson. With so large a family and numerous weddings and funerals, the Queen frequently asked him for a new poem to mark the occasion. Consequently, some of Tennyson's dullest and most trite poems are dedicated to various members of the royal family and nowadays sound a little like doggerel.

The Queen undoubtedly asked him to write these things and had such faith in him because she was so impressed and comforted by his 'In Memoriam' for beloved Albert. *"Next to the Bible, In Memoriam is my comfort..."* she wrote, a year after Albert's death. At the same time, the Queen told her daughter, Vicky, that she found some of his work difficult to understand and Vicky – that brilliant mind! – replied that she couldn't make sense of it either!

Queen Victoria, however, not only asked him to supply suitable poems, she also asked him if he could find a way to remove Gladstone from office – a request to which Tennyson politely and tactfully replied that it was beyond his capabilities!

Appendix IV – *Queen Victoria's Favourite Authors*

Alongside being a prolific letter-writer, Queen Victoria was an avid reader who greatly enjoyed poetry and contemporary novels, particularly those about the lives of ordinary people. Among her favourite authors were Dinah Craik, whose novel **John Halifax. Gentleman** was probably her most successful work (and, incidentally, made into a BBC television series in the 1970s).

Mrs. Oliphant was another of the Queen favourite authors and, with her love of all things Scottish, she greatly enjoyed **Merkland** which she described as 'An old – but excellent Scotch' novel.' In 1868 the Queen met Mrs Oliphant whom she considered, "very pleasant and clever looking.'

Naturally, her friendship with the Prime Minister, Disraeli, led her to greatly appreciate his novels, too, and, when her own **Leaves from a Highland Journal** was published, she was greatly flattered when he spoke to her as a fellow-writer, "We authors, ma'am..."

Marie Correlli - a writer of popular novels – also appealed to the Queen, as did Wilkie Collins, Dickens and George Eliot, regardless of the scandal of the latter's private life. Harriet Beecher-Stowe's biography of Byron, however, Queen Victoria considered shocking since it included information about the poet's incestuous relationship with his sister.

> *"That Byron scandal is too shameful; I have not read it as I have a particular horror of scandal and gossip, and it is quite untrue. Mrs Stowe has behaved shamefully."*

Appendix V – *The Murder of Archduke Franz Ferdinand*

Any list of the causes of the First World War invariably includes the assassination of Archduke Franz Ferdinand, heir to the Austro-Hungarian Empire. While researching my trilogy of novels – *Shattered Crowns* – following the lives of the royalties from 1913 to the Treaty of Versailles, however, it became increasingly apparent that, rather than being an unfortunate event which sparked the war, the Archduke's murder was probably deliberately staged in order to provoke the conflict, and ultimately to destroy the three most powerful autocracies in Europe: Russia, Germany and Austria-Hungary.

Apart from the effect of his assassination, Archduke Franz Ferdinand appears largely as a footnote in history but, looking more deeply into his life, several interesting facts come to light. While his short temper and morganatic marriage to a lady-in-waiting are often cited as reasons why he appeared so unpopular in Vienna, it is clear that his forward-looking views were the real reason why he was hated and feared by the most powerful ministers. At the time, Austria-Hungary comprised many different ethnic groups, several of which resented being ruled from Vienna. Unlike many of his contemporaries in the Austrian Court, Franz Ferdinand was well-travelled and had taken the opportunity to study alternative forms of government. It was his intention, on becoming Emperor, to give greater autonomy to each of the different groups and, while maintaining the royal traditions, to create a sort of Federal Austria-Hungary similar to that of the United States, but with an emperor rather than a president. He was also eager to maintain peace in Europe by forming stronger ties with Russia and, only a week before his murder, he was paid an informal visit by Kaiser Wilhelm who agreed to this plan, which was totally at odds with the views of many senior ministers – and bankers and industrialists – who were desperately seeking an excuse to invade Serbia, which would almost inevitably lead to war with Russia.

It was also widely known that Franz Ferdinand had already drawn up lists of ministers who would replace the present incumbents and he had stated that he would refuse to be crowned King of Hungary until a fair system of suffrage was implemented.

Naturally, the possibility of his becoming Emperor gave rise to a good deal of anxiety among the ministers and that anxiety was surely heightened in the winter of 1913-1914 when his aged Great Uncle Emperor Franz Josef suffered a serious and potentially fatal bout of bronchitis. It was during this time that the Archduke received an invitation to review the troops in Sarajevo, Bosnia (a territory annexed by Austria in 1908) the following June, and to add an extra incentive, the invitation was extended to his wife who, until then, had been frequently humiliated and snubbed due to her lowly origins. This was the Archduke's first opportunity to attend an official public engagement with his beloved Sophie and by coincidence or design it was set to take place on their 14th wedding anniversary. The date – June 28th – also coincided with a Serbian National Holiday so the arrival of the heir to the Austrian throne would almost certainly arouse antipathy among the Serbs. In the days leading up to the visit, Franz Ferdinand stated many times that he suspected that he was about to be murdered, probably by Freemasons. Nonetheless, he and Sophie travelled to Sarajevo and received a warm welcome from the crowds until an unsuccessful assassination attempt disrupted the planned visit. Franz Ferdinand and Sophie decided to visit the wounded in hospital before leaving the city, but, strangely considering the tension in the city and the possibility of further attacks, they were again driven in an open-car with no armed escort or military presence, allowing Gavrilo Princip to step out from the edge of the road and fire point-blank at his victims.

The crime was said to be the work of the 'Black Hand' – a Serbian terrorist group. I have yet to discover any other successful terrorist activities carried out by this group. Moreover, it was said to comprise senior military and political figures. Why then would they employ a tubercular boy, who had never fired a pistol before, for so important a task? History is filled with 'patsies' and I strongly suspect that Gavrilo Princip was one of them. With the death of the Archduke, however, a much larger plan could be set in motion.

The discontent, which Franz Ferdinand's and the Kaiser's plans would have prevented, was exacerbated by the horrors of the war. Within a few years, the three major autocracies were destroyed and access to the Russian oilfields, the 'grain basket' of the Ukraine, the thriving German chemical industry and the economies of Germany, Russia and Austria-Hungary was available to foreign industrialists and bankers.

Recommended Reading:

Alexander Mikhailovich, *Always A Grand Duke* (Farrar & Reinhart 1933)

Alice, Countess of Athlone *For my Grandchildren* (Evans 1979)

Alice, Grand Duchess of Hesse, Biographical Sketch and Letters (John Murray 1884)

Aronson, Theo *Crowns in Conflict* (Salem House 1986)

Aronson, Theo *The King In Love* (Guild in association with John Murray 1988)

Bennett Daphne *Queen Victoria's Children* (Victor Gollancz 1980)

Buxhoeveden, Baroness Sophie *The Life & Tragedy of Alexandra Feodorovna* (Longmans 1928)

Croft, Christina *Most Beautiful Princess* (Hilliard & Croft 2008)

Croft, Christina *Shattered Crowns: The Scapegoats* (CreateSpace 2011)

Croft, Christina *Shattered Crowns: The Sacrifice* (CreateSpace 2012)

Croft, Christina *Shattered Crowns: The Betrayal* (CreateSpace 2012)

Dehn, Lili *The Real Tsaritsa* (1922)

Duff, David *Victoria's Travels* (Frederick Muller 1970)

Fulford, Roger (Editor) *Beloved Mama* (Evans 1981)

Fulford, Roger (Editor) *Your Dear Letter* (Evans 1971)

Longford, Elizabeth *Victoria R.I.* Pan 1966

Longford, Elizabeth *Louisa, Lady in Waiting* (Jonathan Cape 1979)

Maria Pavlovna, Grand Duchess *Things I Remember* (Cassell 1930)

Marie, Queen of Roumania *The Story of My Life* (Cassell 1935)

Marie Louise, Princess – *My Memories of Six Reigns* (Evans Brothers 1956)

Mallet, Victor *Life With Queen Victoria – Marie Mallet's letters from court 1887-1901* (John Murray 1968)

Massie, Robert K. *Nicholas & Alexandra* (Victor Gollancz 1968)

Matson, John *Dear Osborne* (Hamish Hamilton 1981)

Maylunas, Andrei & Mironenko, Sergei *A Lifelong Passion* (Doubleday 1997)

Nelson, Michael *Queen Victoria & the Discovery of the Riviera* (Tauris Parke 2001)

Packard, Jerrold *Victoria's Daughters* (Sutton 1998)

Pakula, Hannah *An Uncommon Woman* Weidenfeld & Nicolson 1985

Paléologue, Maurice *An Ambassadors Memoirs* (Hutchinson 1923)

Ponsonby, Frederick (editor) - *The Letters of the Empress Frederick* (Macmillan 1928)

Ponsonby, Sir Frederick *Recollections of Three Reigns* (Eyre & Spottiswood 1961)

Pope Hennessy, James *Queen Mary* (George Allen & Unwin 1959)

Pope Hennessy (Editor) *Queen Victoria at Windsor & Balmoral* (Allen & Unwin 1959)

Ramm Agatha *Beloved & Darling Child* (Sutton 1990)

Reid Michaela *Ask Sir James* (Hodder & Stoughton 1987)

Rohl, John C.G., Warren, Martin, & Hunt, David *Purple Secret* (Bantam 1998)

St. John-Neville, Barry *Life at the Court of Queen Victoria* (Salem House 1985)

Topham Alice *A Distant Thunder* (New Chapter Press 1992)

Tyler-Whittle, Michael Sydney *The Last Kaiser: A biography of Wilhelm II, German Emperor & King of Prussia* (Times Books 1977)

Vyrubova, Anna *Memories of the Russian Court* (Macmillan 1923)

Index of People

Adolph of Schaumburg-Lippe   163-167, 345
Adolph of Sweden   275
Albert Edward, King Edward VII (Bertie) 47, 53-60, 89, 126, 129, 131, 177, 179, 205-206, 234, 267-273, 289, 292, 323-325, 394
Albert of Schleswig-Holstein   185, 265, 340-341
Albert Victor, Duke of Clarence (Eddy)   57, 169-173
Albert, King of the Belgians   342
Albert, Prince Consort   9, 52, 54, 55, 63, 170, 299, 301, 383, 393-395, 397 *et passim*
Alexander II, Tsar of Russia   76, 82-83, 125, 188
Alexander III, Tsar of Russia   127, 188, 227-228
Alexander Mikhailovich of Russia   161, 188-189
Alexander of Battenberg (Drino)   138, 360
Alexander of Battenberg (Sandro)   125, 127, 145, 146, 151, 154, 161
Alexander of Denmark/Olaf of Norway   181, 289
Alexander of Greece 160, 386
Alexander of Hesse   125
Alexander of Teck (Algie)   273-274, 332, 360
Alexandra of Edinburgh (Sandra)   80-82, 184, 185, 218, 340, 343, 349, 391
Alexandra of Hohenlohe-Langenburg   218
Alexandra, Duchess of Fife   178, 312-314
Alexandra, Queen of Great Britain   55-62, 66, 72-73, 74, 129, 157, 172, 176-184, 205-206, 271, 273, 323-324
Alexei, Tsarevich of Russia   305-310, 355-356, 361, 369-371, 375-377
Alfonso of Bourbon-Lyons 297-298
Alfonso of Spain, (Prince of the Astorias) 309-310
Alfonso XVIII, King of Spain   274, 290-295, 297-298, 325, 391
Alfred of Edinburgh (Young Affie)   78, 255-256
Alfred of Hohenlohe-Langenburg 218
Alfred, Duke of Edinburgh (Affie) 47, 74-79, 125, 126, 183, 216
Alice of Albany   106-110, 142, 180, 256-258, 265, 268, 273-275, 332, 340, 342, 360, 382, 383, 392
Alice of Battenberg   133, 134, 195, 328

Alice, Grand Duchess of Hesse   15-33, 35, 35, 37-51, 58-60, 63-64, 67, 70, 72, 76, 83, 84, 86-93, 95, 97, 99, 101, 102, 106, 125, 130, 133, 189, 190, 204, 214, 231, 235, 302, 305, 311, 393 *et passim*

Alix of Hesse (Tsarina Alexandra Feodorovna)   43-45, 72, 85, 91-92, 94, 138, 139, 140, 142, 170-172, 213, 219-229, 239-249, 251, 262, 264, 267, 276-277, 281, 282, 286, 287, 302-309, 317-321, 325, 332-334, 338-339, 343-344, 346-347, 350-357, 361-362, 368-371, 375-377, 379, 382

Alonzo of Bourbon-Lyons   297-298

Alvaro of Bourbon-Lyons   297-298

Anastasia Nikolaevna of Russia   245, 369-371, 374-377

Aribert of Anhalt   199-204, 383

Arthur of Connaught   314

Arthur, Duke of Connaught   68, 97-101, 216, 291, 294, 332, 360

Astor, Waldorf   211

Ataulfo of Bourbon-Lyons   298

Augusta Victoria, German Empress (Dona)   118-120, 137, 158, 202, 233, 260

Augusta, Queen of Prussia/German Empress   26, 33, 34, 95

Beatrice of Edinburgh (Baby Bee)   80-83, 184, 218, 286, 295-298, 304, 391

Beatrice, Princess of Battenberg   51, 53, 58, 92-93, 129, 135-138, 142, 162, 252-255, 263, 267, 291, 294, 305, 332, 393, 396

Beatriz of Spain   310

Beecher-Stowe, Harriet   398

Bernhard of Saxe-Meiningen   114-116, 122, 383

Bertil of Sweden   275

Bismarck, Otto von   33, 34, 38-40, 43, 129, 146, 192, 325

Boris Vladimirovich of Russia   210

Botkin, Dr Eugene   375-376

Boyd-Carpenter, Bishop   269

Brooke, Daisy   104

Brown, John   30, 46-47, 395

Buchanan, Sir George   361, 362

Buxheoeveden, Baroness Sophie   24, 246, 303, 304

Byron, George, Lord   398

Carl Johann of Sweden   275, 365

Carl of Denmark (Haakon, King of Norway)   180-181, 288-290, 325

Carol I, King of Roumania   206-207, 209, 211, 330, 340

Carol II, King of Roumania 209, 211, 212, 333, 390
Carroll, Lewis 108-109
Charles Edward of Albany (Duke of Coburg) 107-108, 257-258, 274, 340, 383
Charlotte of Prussia 28-30, 33, 43, 85, 113-123, 130, 139, 142, 150, 206, 207, 263, 271-272, 300-302, 332, 339, 343, 383, 386
Chotek, Sophie 336, 400-401
Christian of Schleswig-Holstein 53, 65-70, 89, 360
Christian Victor of Schleswig-Holstein (Christle) 68, 185, 254, 265
Christian, Crown Prince of Denmark 55
Christoph of Hesse-Kassel 175, 387
Churchill, Lady Jane 266
Collins, Wilkie 398
Conroy, John 396
Constantine, King of Greece (Tino) 157-161, 232, 235, 328-329, 347-348, 363, 386
Correlli, Maria 398
Craik, Dinah 397-398

Davidson, Dr Randall Thomas 266
Dehn, Lili 241, 246
Demidova, Anna Stepanova 375-376
Dickens, Charles 398
Disraeli, Benjamin 395, 398
Dmitri Pavlovich of Russia 354

Eleonore of Lich, Grand Duchess of Hesse (Onor) 276-277
Eliot, George 398
Elizabeth II, Queen of Great Britain 389
Elizabeth of Hesse-Darmstadt 218, 276
Elizabeth of Hesse-Darmstadt (Ella) 16, 19-24, 31, 42, 85, 87, 89, 91, 94-96, 116, 131, 135, 139, 142, 170, 187-197, 216, 221-226, 235-239, 246, 251, 264, 276, 281, 284-286, 302, 308, 314-320, 335, 338, 344, 346-347, 352-354, 357-358, 362-363, 371-373, 377-381, 388
Elizabeth of Hungary (Saint) 235-236
Elizabeth of Roumania 211, 212
Elizabeth, Queen of Roumania 207-208, 210, 277
Ermakov, Pyotr 375, 377
Ernest of Hohenlohe-Langenburg 185, 218
Ernst Ludwig of Hesse-Darmstadt 23, 44, 88, 213-219, 222, 250, 274-275, 337, 338, 346, 378, 382
Esher, 2nd Viscount (Reginald Baliol Brett) 270

Feodora of Saxe-Meiningen 121-122, 130, 300
Ferdinand of Hohenzollern-Sigmaringen/Roumania (Nando)
183, 199, 206-212, 216, 349, 364, 366-367, 382, 390
Ferdinand, 'Tsar' of Bulgaria 327, 328, 330, 331, 348, 381
Francis of Teck 179
Franz Ferdinand of Austria 335-336, 398-401
Franz Josef of Battenberg 125
Franz Josef, Emperor of Austria-Hungary 336, 400
Frederica of Hanover 104
Frederick Crown Prince of Prussia/German Emperor 16, 27,
31, 32, 33, 35, 39, 42, 43, 119, 128-129, 146-152, 269
Frederick Harold of Schleswig-Holstein 69
Frederick of Hesse-Darmstadt (Frittie) 41, 44-45, 215, 305
Frederick of Hesse-Kassel (Fischy) 173-175, 262, 360-361,
383
Frederick VIII, King of Denmark 288, 325
Friedrich of Hesse-Kassel 174, 345

Gapon, Father 283
George Donatus of Hesse-Darmstadt 277
George I, King of the Hellenes 157, 232, 323, 325, 328-329
George III, King of Great Britain 300
George of Greece 159
George V, King of Great Britain 57, 81, 169, 172, 182-184,
205-206, 292, 306, 325, 332, 338, 346, 359-362, 364, 366, 379,
384, 387
Gilliard, Pierre 308
Gladstone, William 396
Gonzalo of Spain 310
Gottfried of Hohenlohe-Langenburg 218
Gustav of Sweden 275
Gustav, Crown Prince of Sweden 274-275

Haakon, King of Norway *See Carl of Denmark*
Haig, Field Marshal Douglas 381
Haucke, Julia 125
Helen of Greece 160
Helen, Duchess of Albany 105-109, 256-258
Helena Victoria of Schleswig-Holstein (Lenchen) 58, 63-70,
100, 172, 198-199, 241, 267, 360, 389
Hélène of Orleans 171-172
Henry of Battenberg (Liko) 125, 136-138, 154, 252-255

Henry of Prussia (Son of Frederick III) 28, 30, 33, 43, 94, 137, 146, 150, 151, 260-261, 271, 325-326, 332, 362, 382, 383, 388
Henry of Prussia (Son of Henry) 262, 305
Hill, Octavia 19

Ileana of Roumania 211
Irene of Greece 160
Irène of Hesse-Darmstadt 20-24, 27, 85, 94, 137, 139, 142, 146, 151, 260-263, 305, 308, 332, 339, 379, 381, 383, 388
Irma of Hohenlohe-Langenburg 218
Isabella, Queen of Spain 38

Jaime of Spain 310
Johnson, Brian 373
Juan of Spain 310

Kalyaev, Ivan 286-287
Kapiolani, Queen of Hawaii 141
Karim, Abdul 216, 396
Karl, Emperor of Austria-Hungary 382
Katherine of Greece 160
Keppel, Alice 323, 324
Kerensky, Alexander 361, 362
Kolchak, Admiral Alexander 380
Konstantin Konstantinovich of Russia 282, 345, 378
Kyril Vladimirovich of Russia 215, 219, 275, 277-278, 296, 356, 365, 390

Laking, Sir Francis 269
Langtry, Lillie 126
Lenin, Vladimir 287, 366, 369, 371, 374
Leopold of Hohenzollern-Sigmaringen 38-39
Leopold, Duke of Albany 44, 47, 53, 89, 93, 101-107, 305
Lind, Jenny 70
Lorne, John Marquis of 53
Louis IV, Grand Duke of Hesse 17, 20, 25, 39, 42, 44, 85-86, 88-89, 92-93, 131-132, 135, 213, 237
Louis of Battenberg 125-127, 131-134, 137, 187, 192, 345-346, 360, 388
Louise of Wales 58, 60-62, 129, 162, 172, 176-178, 184, 273, 313-314, 387
Louise, Duchess of Arygll 53, 64, 194, 267
Louise, Duchess of Connaught 98-101, 108, 291, 360

Ludwig of Hesse-Darmstadt   277

Macduff, Alexander, Earl of Fife   177-178, 312-313
Mackenzie, Dr Morell   147-150, 152
Mallett, Marie   166
Margaret of Connaught (Daisy)   100-101, 142, 184, 216, 267, 274-275, 314, 341, 365, 391
Margaret of Prussia (Mossy)   42, 147, 153, 168-169, 173-175, 262-264, 268-269, 339, 345, 360-361, 383, 387
Maria Cristina of Spain   310
Maria Nikolaevna of Russia   245, 369-371, 375-377
Marie Alexandrovna, Empress of Russia   24, 82
Marie Feodorovna, Empress of Russia   221, 240-241, 296, 306
Marie Louise of Schleswig-Holstein   9, 69-73, 164-165, 178, 182, 198-204, 231, 252, 265, 267, 301, 332, 336-337, 340-343, 360, 379-381, 384, 389-390, 392
Marie Melita of Hohenlohe-Langenburg   218
Marie of Edinburgh (Missy)   79-83, 117, 183, 188, 205-212, 216, 251, 267-268, 303-304, 330-334, 339-340, 348-349, 363-367, 382-385, 390-391
Marie of Hesse-Darmstadt (May)   46, 85, 87
Marie, Duchess of Edinburgh & Coburg   53, 76-83, 103, 161, 206-207, 209, 210, 215, 255-256, 266-267, 286, 294, 296, 340, 349, 390
Mary of Teck, Queen of Great Britain (May)   172, 184, 268, 338, 382
Maud of Fife   178, 312-313, 387
Maud of Wales   60-62, 129, 178-182, 184, 214, 267, 271, 288-290, 302, 332, 341, 342, 387-388
Maurice of Battenberg   143, 345
Maurice of Teck   274, 311
Maximilian of Baden (Max)   171, 173, 180, 382
Maximilian of Hesse-Kassel (Max)   174, 175, 345
May of Teck (daughter of Alice of Athlone)   274
McGonagall, William   107
Melbourne, William Lamb, Lord   395-396
Mikhail Alexandrovich of Russia (Misha)   296-297, 325, 356, 373
Mircea of Roumania   211, 364
Mirsky, Prince of Russia   283
Mordaunt, Harriet   58-59
Morral, Matteo   293

Napoleon III, Emperor of France   35

Nicholas II, Tsar of Russia 157, 173, 216, 219, 221-229, 242-248, 265, 276-280, 282-284, 305, 306, 307, 334, 337-8, 350-357, 361-362, 364-365, 368-371, 375-377, 379
Nicolas of Roumania 211
Nightingale, Florence 15, 19, 40, 75
Nikolai Nikolaevich of Russia 350

Oksar, King of Sweden 275, 288
Olga Nikolaevna of Russia 244-245, 332-333, 369-371, 375-377
Olga, Queen of the Hellenes 232
Oliphant, Mrs 398
Olsufieff, Countess 244, 316

Paléologue, Maurice 26, 188, 237, 320, 338, 352
Paley, Prince Vladimir 371
Patricia of Connaught (Patsy) 100-101, 184, 216, 267, 274, 290-291, 314, 342, 391
Paul of Greece 160
Pavel Alexandrovich of Russia 129, 356, 371
Philip, Duke of Edinburgh 389
Philipp of Hesse-Kassel 174, 387
Ponsonby, Frederick 156
Princip, Gavrilo 336, 401
Pyotr Mikhailovich of Russia 161

Ramsay, Alexander 390
Rasputin, Grigori 243, 318-321, 334, 346, 350-354
Richard of Hesse-Kassel 175
Rosebery, Earl of (Archibald Primrose) 181
Rupert of Teck 274, 311

Serge Alexandrovich of Russia 129, 131, 139, 187-196, 216, 236-239, 284-285, 314
Sigismund of Prussia 262, 305
Sigismund of Prussia 31-32
Sigvard of Sweden 275
Sophie of Prussia 38-39, 42, 147, 153, 156-161, 163, 165, 182, 224, 232-235, 251, 264, 268, 302, 303, 327-329, 332, 339, 347-348, 363, 386-387
Stirbey, Prince Barbo 211
Strauss, David 25-26

Tatiana Nikolaevna of Russia 245, 369-371, 375-377

Tennyson, Alfred 99, 396
Topham, Alice 175
Treves, Sir Frederick 271

Vachot, Philippe 247-249
Vavarescu Hélène 207-208
Venizelos, Eleftherios 348, 363
Victoria Eugenie of Battenberg (Ena) 138, 142-144, 184, 255, 291-295, 309-310, 341, 342, 345, 379, 388, 391-392
Victoria Helena of Schleswig-Holstein (Thora) 69-73, 172, 178, 182-186, 219, 265-266, 340-342, 360, 389-390
Victoria Melita of Edinburgh (Ducky) 80-83, 117, 184, 214-219, 251, 267, 275-278, 296, 297, 332, 340, 343, 352-353, 365, 390
Victoria Moretta of Prussia 31, 34, 35, 128-130, 136, 145-147, 151, 153-154, 156, 161-167, 192, 263, 345, 386
Victoria of Hesse-Darmstadt 16, 19-24, 42, 85, 87, 91, 93-94, 96, 126-127, 130-134, 137, 139, 187, 192, 222, 225, 226, 266, 271, 276, 286, 306, 317, 320, 334-335, 339, 345-346, 360, 361, 379-381, 384, 388-389
Victoria of Wales (Toria) 7, 60-62, 129, 178-182, 184, 228, 271, 273, 304, 323-324, 332, 345, 387
Victoria Queen 7-9, 14-19, 24, 32, 37, 38, 40, 42, 45, 46-55, 58-59, 65-71, 74-80, 87, 88, 90, 93-108, 112-113, 128-129, 131-133, 139-144, 147, 151, 153-154, 157, 159-163, 170, 173, 177, 185-186, 187-191, 194-195, 202-203, 209, 213-216, 218, 219, 222, 224, 228, 231-234, 243, 250-254, 257, 264-268, 299-300, 326, 393-398 *et passim*
Victoria, Crown Princess of Prussia/German Empress 16, 24, 26-43, 47-48, 51, 54, 55, 80, 85, 89-90, 94-95, 113-121, 128, 146-153, 155-158, 160, 164-165, 167, 168, 173-174, 179, 216, 233-234, 257, 259-264, 268-269, 300-301, 326, 395, 396 *et passim*
Vyrobova, Anna 307, 334

Waldemar of Prussia (Son of Frederick III) 35, 51, 89-90
Waldemar of Prussia (Son of Henry of Prussia) 262, 305, 310-311
Waldemar of Schaumburg-Lippe 166
Weber, Marie 160
Wilhelm I, German Emperor 31, 33, 34, 38-39, 89, 118, 145, 146
Wilhelm II, German Emperor 29-30, 33, 34, 43, 85, 90, 94-95, 100, 118-121, 129, 137, 139, 141, 150, 152, 157, 173, 192,

199-200, 207, 211, 216, 225, 233-235, 251-252, 257-258, 265-268, 289, 301-302, 325, 327, 332, 337-340, 345, 348-349, 360, 362, 368-369, 382-383, 399, 401
Wilhelmina, Queen of the Netherlands   109, 274, 382
Witte, Count de   280
Wolfgang of Hesse-Kassel   174

Xenia Alexandrovna of Russia   296

Yakovleva, Barbara   372, 376-377, 387
Yanisheva, Catherine   372
Youssoupov, Felix   319, 352-354
Yurovsky, Jacob   374-377

Zubkov, Alexander   385

By the same author:

Most Beautiful Princess – A Novel Based on the Life of Grand Duchess Elizabeth of Russia

Shattered Crowns: The Scapegoats
Shattered Crowns: The Sacrifice
Shattered Crowns: The Betrayal

The Counting House

The Fields Laid Waste

Wonderful Walter

References

[1] Pope Hennessy, James *Queen Mary* (George Allen & Unwin 1959) © Estate of James Pope-Hennessy. Reprinted by permission

[2] Marie Louise, Princess *My Memories of Six Reigns* (Evans Brothers 1956)

[3] *Alice, Grand Duchess of Hesse, Biographical Sketch and Letters* (John Murray 1884)

[4] ibid

[5] ibid

[6] ibid

[7] ibid

[8] ibid

[9] ibid

[10] ibid

[11] Buxhoeveden, Baroness Sophie *The Life & Tragedy of Alexandra Feodorovna* (Longmans 1928)

[12] ibid

[13] Paléologue, Maurice *An Ambassadors Memoirs* (Hutchinson 1923)

[14] Fulford, Roger (editor) *Your Dear Letter: Private Correspondence of Queen Victoria and the Crown Princess of Prussia, 1865-71* (Evans Bros. 1971)

[15] *Alice, Grand Duchess of Hesse, Biographical Sketch and Letters* (John Murray 1884)

[16] Ponsonby, Frederick (editor) - *The Letters of the Empress Frederick* (Macmillan 1928)

[17] ibid

[18] Marie Louise, Princess *My Memories of Six Reigns* (Evans Brothers 1956)

[19] Ponsonby, Frederick (editor) - *The Letters of the Empress Frederick* (Macmillan 1928)

[20] *Alice, Grand Duchess of Hesse, Biographical Sketch and Letters* (John Murray 1884)

[21] ibid

[22] ibid

[23] ibid

[24] ibid

[25] Fulford, Roger (editor) *Your Dear Letter: Private*

Correspondence of Queen Victoria and the Crown Princess of Prussia, 1865-71 (Evans Bros. 1971)

[26]*Alice, Grand Duchess of Hesse, Biographical Sketch and Letters* (John Murray 1884)

[27] Buxhoeveden, Baroness Sophie *The Life & Tragedy of Alexandra Feodorovna* (Longmans 1928)

[28] *Alice, Grand Duchess of Hesse, Biographical Sketch and Letters* (John Murray 1884)

[29] Marie of Roumania *At Grandmama's Court* (McCall's Magazine 1926) Reprinted by courtesy of www.tkinter.org

[30] Marie Louise, Princess *My Memories of Six Reigns* (Evans Brothers 1956)

[31] *Alice, Grand Duchess of Hesse, Biographical Sketch and Letters* (John Murray 1884)

[32] Fulford, Roger (editor) *Your Dear Letter: Private Correspondence of Queen Victoria and the Crown Princess of Prussia, 1865-71* (Evans Bros. 1971)

[33] Marie of Roumania *The Story of My Life* (Saturday Evening Post 1933) –) Reprinted by courtesy of www.tkinter.org

[34] Bennett Daphne *Queen Victoria's Children* (Victor Gollancz 1980)

[35] Marie Louise, Princess *My Memories of Six Reigns* (Evans Brothers 1956)

[36] *Alice, Grand Duchess of Hesse, Biographical Sketch and Letters* (John Murray 1884)

[37] Reid Michaela *Ask Sir James* (Hodder & Stoughton 1987) ©Michaela Reid. Reprinted by permission.

[38] Marie Louise, Princess *My Memories of Six Reigns* (Evans Brothers 1956)

[39] ibid

[40] ibid

[41] ibid

[42] Fulford, Roger (editor) *Your Dear Letter: Private Correspondence of Queen Victoria and the Crown Princess of Prussia, 1865-71* (Evans Bros. 1971)

[43] *Alice, Grand Duchess of Hesse, Biographical Sketch and Letters* (John Murray 1884)

[44] Marie of Roumania *The Story of My Life* (Saturday Evening Post 1933) –) Reprinted by courtesy of www.tkinter.org

[45] *Ladies Treasury* 2 March 1884

[46] Marie of Roumania *The Story of My Life* (Saturday Evening Post 1933) Reprinted by courtesy of www.tkinter.org

[47] Pope Hennessy, James *Queen Mary* (George Allen & Unwin

1959) © Estate of James Pope-Hennessy. Reprinted by permission.

[48] *Alice, Grand Duchess of Hesse, Biographical Sketch and Letters* (John Murray 1884)

[49] ibid

[50] Wilhelm II, Kaiser *My Early Life* (George H. Doran & Company 1926)

[51] *Alice, Grand Duchess of Hesse, Biographical Sketch and GLetters* (John Murray 1884)

[52] ibid

[53] ibid

[54] ibid

[55] Fulford, Roger (editor) *Beloved Mama* (Evans 1981)

[56] Ponsonby, Frederick (editor) - *The Letters of the Empress Frederick* (Macmillan 1928)

[57] Wilhelm II, Kaiser *My Early Life* (George H. Doran & Company 1926)

[58] Buxhoeveden, Baroness Sophie *The Life & Tragedy of Alexandra Feodorovna* (Longmans 1928)

[59] Fulford, Roger (editor) *Dearest Child: Letters between Queen Victoria & the Princess Royal 1858-1961* (Evans Brothers 1964)

[60] Fulford, Roger (editor) *Your Dear Letter: Private Correspondence of Queen Victoria and the Crown Princess of Prussia, 1865-71* (Evans Bros. 1971)

[61] Tennyson, Alfred *Dedicatory Poem to the Princess Alice* (1879)

[62] Ponsonby, Sir Frederick *Recollections of Three Reigns* (Eyre & Spottiswood 1961)

[63] Nelson, Michael *Queen Victoria & the Discovery of the Riviera* (Tauris Parke 2001).

[64] McGonagall, William *The Death of Prince Leopold* (1884)

[65] Carroll, Lewis. ALS 12 June 1889 (unpublished). Reprinted by permission http://www.roydavids.com/details.asp?item=338.

[66] Wakeling, Edward, ed. *Lewis Carroll's Diaries: The Private Journals of Chales Lutwidge Dodgson (Lewis Carroll)*, Volume 8 (London: The Lewis Carroll Society, 2004): 596. Reprinted by permission.

[67] *The Letters of the Empress Frederick*

[68] Fulford, Roger (editor) *Beloved Mama* (Evans 1981)

[69] Marie of Roumania *The Story of My Life* (Saturday Evening Post 1934) Reprinted by courtesy of www.tkinter.org

[70] ibid

[71] Ponsonby, Frederick (editor) *The Letters of the Empress Frederick* (Macmillan 1928)

[72] Pakula, Hannah *An Uncommon Woman* (Weidenfeld & Nicolson 1985)

[73] Rohl, John C.G., Warren, Martin, & Hunt, David *Purple Secret* (Bantam 1998)

[74] *Alice, Grand Duchess of Hesse, Biographical Sketch and Letters* (John Murray 1884)

[75] Fulford, Roger (editor) *Beloved Mama* (Evans 1981)

[76] Buxhoeveden, Baroness Sophie *The Life & Tragedy of Alexandra Feodorovna* (Longmans 1928)

[77] Reid, Michaela *Ask Sir James* (Hodder & Stoughton 1987) ©Michaela Reid. Reprinted by permission

[78] Tennyson, Alfred *On the Jubilee of Queen Victoria* (1889)

[79] Pope-Hennessey, James (Editor) *Queen Victoria at Balmoral & Windsor: Letters from her Granddaughter, Princess Victoria of Prussia, June 1889* (George Allen & Unwin 1959) © Estate of James Pope-Hennessy. Reprinted by permission

[80] Reid, Michaela *Ask Sir James* (Hodder & Stoughton 1987) ©Michaela Reid. Reprinted by permission

[81] Mackenzie, Morell Sir *The Fatal Illness of Frederick the Nobel* (Low, Marston, Searle & Rimmington 1888)

[82] ibid

[83] ibid

[84] Ponsonby, Frederick (editor) *The Letters of the Empress Frederick* (Macmillan 1928)

[85] Mackenzie, Morell Sir *The Fatal Illness of Frederick the Nobel* (Low, Marston, Searle & Rimmington 1888)

[86] Ponsonby, Sir Frederick *Recollections of Three Reigns* (Eyre & Spottiswood 1961)

[87] Ponsonby, Frederick (editor) *The Letters of the Empress Frederick* (Macmillan 1928)

[88] Pope-Hennessey, James (Editor) *Queen Victoria at Balmoral & Windsor: Letters from her Granddaughter, Princess Victoria of Prussia, June 1889* (George Allen & Unwin 1959) © Estate of James Pope-Hennessy. Reprinted by permission

[89] Leslie, Ada E. *Letters of a Victorian Lady 1883-1894 (http://www.barnardf.demon.co.uk/index.htm#Index)* © Francis Barnard. Reprinted by permission.

[90] Marie Louise, Princess *My Memories of Six Reigns* (Evans Brothers 1956)

[91] Mallet, Victor *Life With Queen Victoria – Marie Mallet's*

letters from court 1887-1901 (John Murray 1968)
[92] ibid
[93] Topham Alice *A Distant Thunder* (New Chapter Press 1992)
© Wendy Reid Crisp. Reprinted with permission
[94] Marie Louise, Princess *My Memories of Six Reigns* (Evans Brothers 1956)

[95] Pope Hennessy, James *Queen Mary* (George Allen & Unwin 1959) © Estate of James Pope-Hennessy. Reprinted by permission
[96] Paléologue, Maurice *An Ambassadors Memoirs* (Hutchinson 1923)
[97] Mikhailovich, Alexander *Always A Grand Duke* (Farrar & Reinhart 1933)
[98] Princess Elizabeth of Hesse, letter to Queen Victoria 1883 (source unknown)
[99] Olsoufieff, Countess Alexandra *H.I.H. The Grand Duchess Elisabeth Feodorovna of Russia* (John Murray 1923)
[100] Marie Louise, Princess *My Memories of Six Reigns* (Evans Brothers 1956)
[101] ibid
[102] ibid
[103] ibid

[104] Pope Hennessy, James *Queen Mary* (George Allen & Unwin 1959) © Estate of James Pope-Hennessy.
[105] Marie of Roumania *The Story of My Life* (Saturday Evening Post 1934) Reprinted by courtesy of www.tkinter.org
[106] Buxhoeveden, Baroness Sophie *The Life & Tragedy of Alexandra Feodorovna* (Longmans 1928)
[107] Vyrubova, Anna *Memories of the Russian Court* (Macmillan 1923)
[108] Hibbert, Christopher *Queen Victoria: A Personal History* (HarperCollins 2000)
[109] Harrogate Advertiser *The Royal Visitors at Harrogate* (June 16th 1894)
[110] Buxhoeveden, Baroness Sophie *The Life & Tragedy of Alexandra Feodorovna* (Longmans 1928)
[111] Marie Louise, Princess *My Memories of Six Reigns* (Evans Brothers 1956)
[112] *Alice, Grand Duchess of Hesse, Biographical Sketch and Letters* (John Murray 1884)

[113] Grand Duchess Elizabeth to Tsar Nicholas. Source unknown
[114] Paléologue, Maurice *An Ambassadors Memoirs* (Hutchinson 1923)
[115] Nicholas, Prince of Greece *My Fifty Years* (Hutchinson 1926)
[116] Olsoufieff, Countess Alexandra *H.I.H. The Grand Duchess Elisabeth Feodorovna of Russia* (John Murray 1923)
[117] Dehn, Lili *The Real Tsaritsa* (1922)
[118] Vyrubova, Anna *Memories of the Russian Court* (Macmillan 1923)
[119] ibid
[120] Dehn, Lili *The Real Tsaritsa* (1922)
[121] Olsoufieff, Countess Alexandra *H.I.H. The Grand Duchess Elisabeth Feodorovna of Russia* (John Murray 1923)
[122] Buxhoeveden, Baroness Sophie *The Life & Tragedy of Alexandra Feodorovna* (Longmans 1928)
[123] Dehn, Lili *The Real Tsaritsa* (1922)
[124] Marie Louise, Princess *My Memories of Six Reigns* (Evans Brothers 1956)
[125] Ramm Agatha *Beloved & Darling Child* (Sutton 1990)
[126] Ponsonby, Frederick (editor) *The Letters of the Empress Frederick* (Macmillan 1928)
[127] Vyrubova, Anna *Memories of the Russian Court* (Macmillan 1923)
[128] Ramm Agatha *Beloved & Darling Child* (Sutton 1990)
[129] Ponsonby, Frederick (editor) *The Letters of the Empress Frederick* (Macmillan 1928)
[130] Buxhoeveden, Baroness Sophie *The Life & Tragedy of Alexandra Feodorovna* (Longmans 1928)
[131] Pakula, Hannah *The Last Romantic* (Weidenfeld & Nicolson 1996)
[132] Alice, Countess of Athlone *For my Grandchildren* (Evans 1979)
[133] Pope Hennessy, James *Queen Mary* (George Allen & Unwin 1959) © Estate of James Pope-Hennessy. Reprinted by permission
[134] Ponsonby, Sir Frederick *Recollections of Three Reigns* (Eyre & Spottiswood 1961)
[135] Pope Hennessy, James *Queen Mary* (George Allen & Unwin 1959) © Estate of James Pope-Hennessy Reprinted by permission
[136] Marie Louise, Princess *My Memories of Six Reigns* (Evans Brothers 1956)

[137] Vyrubova, Anna *Memories of the Russian Court* (Macmillan 1923)

[138] Olsufieff, Countess Alexandra *H.I.H. The Grand Duchess Elisabeth Feodorovna of Russia* (John Murray 1923)

[139] Maylunas, Andrei & Mironenko, Sergei *A Lifelong Passion* (Doubleday 1997)

[140] Olsufieff, Countess Alexandra *H.I.H. The Grand Duchess Elisabeth Feodorovna of Russia* (John Murray 1923)

[141] ibid

[142] Marie Louise, Princess *My Memories of Six Reigns* (Evans Brothers 1956)

[143] Toulmin, David (The Leopard Magazine Dec. 1976) Reprinted by permission

[144] Rohl, John C.G., Warren, Martin, & Hunt, David *Purple Secret* (Bantam 1998)

[145] ibid

[146] *Alice, Grand Duchess of Hesse, Biographical Sketch and Letters* (John Murray 1884)

[147] Grand Duchess Elizabeth to Tsar Nicholas (1910) – source unknown

[148] Buxhoeveden, Baroness Sophie *The Life & Tragedy of Alexandra Feodorovna* (Longmans 1928)

[149] ibid

[150] ibid

[151] ibid

[152] ibid

[153] Gilliard, Pierre *Thirteen Years at the Russian Court* (Publisher unknown)

[154] Vyrubova, Anna *Memories of the Russian Court* (Macmillan 1923)

[155] Pope Hennessy, James *Queen Mary* (George Allen & Unwin 1959) © Estate of James Pope-Hennessy. Reprinted by permission

[156] Olsufieff, Countess Alexandra *H.I.H. The Grand Duchess Elisabeth Feodorovna of Russia* (John Murray 1923)

[157] Graham, Stephen, *The Way of Martha and the Way of Mary* (Macmillan 1915) – Reprinted by permission of: http://orthodoxengland.org.uk

[158] Olsufieff, Countess Alexandra *H.I.H. The Grand Duchess Elisabeth Feodorovna of Russia* (John Murray 1923)

[159] Grand Duchess Elizabeth to Tsar Nicholas (1910) Source unknown

[160] Buxhoeveden, Baroness Sophie *The Life & Tragedy of*

Alexandra Feodorovna (Longmans 1928)

[161] Paléologue, Maurice *An Ambassadors Memoirs* (Hutchinson 1923)

[162] Pakula, Hannah *The Last Romantic* (Weidenfeld & Nicolson 1996)

[163] Marie of Roumania, *My Life as Crown Princess* (Saturday Evening Post, June 1934) Reprinted courtesy of www.tkinter.org

[164] ibid

[165] Vyrubova, Anna *Memories of the Russian Court* (Macmillan 1923)

[166] Marie Louise, Princess *My Memories of Six Reigns* (Evans Brothers 1956)

[167] Paléologue, Maurice *An Ambassadors Memoirs* (Hutchinson 1923)

[168] Marie Louise, Princess *My Memories of Six Reigns* (Evans Brothers 1956)

[169] Buxhoeveden, Baroness Sophie *The Life & Tragedy of Alexandra Feodorovna* (Longmans 1928)

[170] Vyrubova, Anna *Memories of the Russian Court* (Macmillan 1923)

[171] Telberg , George Gustav *Last Days of the Romanovs* (George H Doran Co. 1920)

[172] Olsufieff, Countess Alexandra *H.I.H. The Grand Duchess Elisabeth Feodorovna of Russia* (John Murray 1923)

[173] Grand Duchess Elizabeth to Tsar Nicholas 1915 (Source unknown)

[174] Buxhoeveden, Baroness Sophie *The Life & Tragedy of Alexandra Feodorovna* (Longmans 1928)

[175] Paléologue, Maurice *An Ambassadors Memoirs* (Hutchinson 1923)

[176] Buxhoeveden, Baroness Sophie *The Life & Tragedy of Alexandra Feodorovna* (Longmans 1928)

[177] Vyrubova, Anna *Memories of the Russian Court* (Macmillan 1923)

[178] Olsufieff, Countess Alexandra *H.I.H. The Grand Duchess Elisabeth Feodorovna of Russia* (John Murray 1923)

[179] http://history.hanover.edu/project.php Reprinted by permission

[180] ibid

[181] Davidson, Henry P. *The American Red Cross in the Great War* (Macmillan 1919)

[182] Marie Louise, Princess *My Memories of Six Reigns* (Evans

Brothers 1956)
[183] ibid
[184] *Alice, Grand Duchess of Hesse, Biographical Sketch and Letters* (John Murray 1884)
[185] Marie Louise, Princess *My Memories of Six Reigns* (Evans Brothers 1956)
[186] ibid

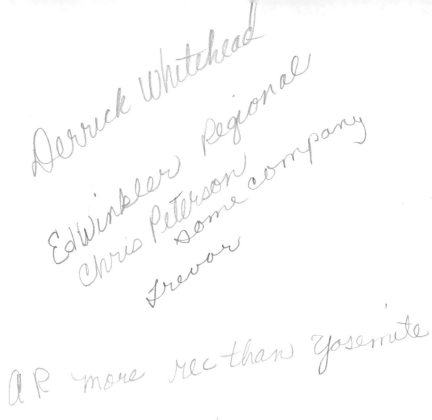

Derrick Whitehead

Ed Winkler Regional
Chris Peterson Some company
Trevor

a R more rec than yosemite

Glenn Colusa
Pump St

Made in the USA
San Bernardino, CA
09 July 2015